A Purposeful Life

Dr. Agitu Wodajo, PhD

Copyright © 2023 by Agitu Wodajo
A Purposeful Life
By Agitu Wodajo

Printed in the United States of America
ISBN 979-8-218-50729-9

All rights reserved solely by the author. The author guarantees all contents are original and do not infringe upon the legal rights of any other person or work. No part of this book may be reproduced in any form without the permission of the author. The views expressed in this book are not necessarily those of the publisher.

Unless otherwise indicated, Bible quotations are taken from the New King James Version. Copyright © 1982 by Thomas Nelson, Inc.

Table of Contents

LIST OF ILLUSTRATIONS

Acknowledgment

I am profoundly grateful to God for His countless blessings and for the privilege of serving Him. I thank Him for entrusting me with trials through which He revealed His glory, trained me, and shaped my life for His divine purpose. This book is the fruit of those experiences, and it is my prayer that it may inspire and bless readers in their own life journeys.

I thank God for the wonderful children He has blessed me with. Their achievements and steadfast Christian character make me boast in the Lord, from whom all good things come. Above all, seeing them raise their own children with the same Christian principles fills me with joy and hope that God's purpose and blessings will continue from generation to generation.

I am deeply grateful to Evangelist Mulu Ilala and Pastor Fetlework Tefera for their prayers and encouragement during my most difficult and confusing times.

I am immensely thankful to Kathleen Moore, Cheryl Bates, and Michael Moore for making our resettlement in Minnesota possible, as shared in the pages of this book.

My sincere appreciation goes to my friend in need, Ertra Namara, for standing by me when I needed support the most.

I am grateful to my sister, Tsehai, whose encouragement helped me make the life-changing decision to come to the United States with my five children—something that was not in my plan at that time.

I owe a great debt of gratitude to all the donors in Addis Ababa and Minnesota who made my calling to create positive change a reality. These include, but are not limited to, the following:

In Addis Ababa: The Swedish Development Authority (SIDA), the Netherlands Embassy, the Canadian International Development Agency (CIDA), UNICEF, the U.S. Embassy, and UNIFEM for their generous support of the Women's Self-Reliance Association (WSRA). My sincere thanks to UNDP and UNFPA for funding my study tours and training abroad, and to the Christian Relief and Development Association (CRDA) for their invaluable in-kind contributions that enabled WSRA's women to participate in income-generating training. I also thank UNIFEM for supporting the salary of the executive director who succeeded me, Rädda Barnen (Swedish Save the Children) for their funding toward the construction of the integrated women's empowerment and MCH clinic (though halted by Kebele 20 administration), and Plan International for their generous grant to build homes for families in dire housing conditions and to develop Kebele 20—efforts later redirected by the then TPLF-dominated administration.

In Minnesota: I am deeply appreciative of the Minneapolis Foundation, the Christian Sharing Fund/Catholic Charities, the McKnight Foundation, and the Patrick and Aimee Butler Family Foundation for their multi-year funding of the International Self-Reliance Agency for Women (ISAW). I extend special gratitude to the Minnesota Department of Justice's Crime Victim Services for their ongoing financial and technical support over more than a decade, which brought lasting transformation in the lives of domestic abuse victims and survivors. My heartfelt thanks go to Ms. Cindy Cook, who opened the door for our grant opportunities, and to Ms. Aida Tosca, whose invaluable guidance strengthened my skills in fiscal management and program evaluation.

Finally, I wish to thank our partner organizations—The Advocates for Human Rights, the Legal Aid Society of Minnesota, and many others—for collaborating with ISAW to provide legal assistance, housing, training, and technical support. Their partnership enabled us to maximize our impact with limited resources. I am also grateful to all those whose names may not appear here; your contributions remain deeply appreciated and forever remembered.

INTRODUCTION

A call to write a book came to me in the 1980s through two evangelists who closely observed my life as a Christian woman enduring tribulations in my marriage, career, and religious

journey in Ethiopia. Although these evangelists did not know each other, both urged me to write my story, telling me that my life reflected the gospel and could touch many lives and make a profound difference. However, for a long time, I was unable to respond to this calling—until I experienced a deeply painful and humiliating wake-up call.

The delay in responding to the call has a silver lining—It offered me the opportunity to be refined more and gain a broader experience to produce an enriched book that speaks to diverse audiences. I speak from a lived experience in all areas of life: childhood, marriage, career, family, social, religious, cultural, economic, and political. What I write now comes not from theory but from a life fully lived, tested, and transformed by God's purpose. Faith has been my compass since childhood. The love and reverence of God were instilled in me early, along with an unshakable desire to do good for others. I never had to search for my purpose—it was woven into my being.

I was born and raised in a small rural town in western Ethiopia, where cultural norms often silenced girls and denied them education. Yet God's providence intervened through my father's conversion to the Protestant faith. Shortly after accepting the faith, he purchased a property adjacent to the Swedish Mission School and church, hoping his future children would receive both academic and spiritual formation. Sadly, after my sister was born, my father took my mother and sister with him, leaving my grandmother and me to fend for ourselves. He later abandoned our family altogether. But God had already planted His purpose. Out of that hardship, my grandmother enrolled me in the Swedish Mission School a month before I turned six, ensuring that my father's original hope—to raise a child in Christian education—was fulfilled through her devotion.

At that school, I learned that true education forms both mind and morals. President Theodore Roosevelt once said, *"To educate a man in mind but not in morals is to educate a menace to society."* My teachers modeled that truth, shaping my character and conviction. Service became my first language. I began putting my gift for service into action at home. Even as a child, I found joy in caring for my parents and siblings. Every morning before leaving for school, I swept the floor, tidied the house, and brewed coffee. After school, I helped my mother and grandmother with domestic chores, fetched water from the nearby spring, and gathered firewood from the hillside.

My desire to serve others did not stop at our doorstep. I offered water to thirsty travelers passing by our home—mostly farmers walking long distances to take their produce to the market—who always thanked me with a smile of relief. I also welcomed strangers who stayed the night, washing their feet and preparing their sleeping mats. I did all this with a cheerful heart, for I believed that doing good for others was the special gift my Creator had given me. Before I realized it, I was already laying the foundation for taking my service to the next level—after my father abandoned our family and stopped providing for us financially. As the oldest child, I felt a deep responsibility to support my family.

My younger sister, Tsehai Wodajo, and I used to walk nearly three miles to downtown Nedjo to buy groceries, which we resold at a small profit. Because of the commendation I received from my Swedish teacher, I was recognized as the best student in handicrafts when I was only eleven years old. This skill became a lifeline—it helped me pay my modest tuition at the Swedish Mission School and contribute to our family's needs. I made embroidered handkerchiefs and pillowcases and sold them to my teachers. During high school, I spent my lunch breaks creating embroidered pieces to sell to students, using the earnings to buy clothes and shoes for my siblings. My early entrepreneurship was more than survival; it became training for a purpose I could not yet see—an experience that would one day equip me to empower other women both at home and abroad.

After earning an associate degree in community nursing from a public health college in northern Ethiopia at the age of nineteen, I joined Western missionaries in service as a nurse. Around that time, I married and began the second chapter of my journey—a chapter that brought the refinement I needed to define my goals and pursue them with clarity. To truly understand and meet the needs of others, I had to experience life's extremes—its pain, perseverance, and promise—through childhood, marriage, and career.

My father's abandonment when I was four, the horrific assault I endured from my school's director at ten, and the eighty-five kilometers I traveled by muleback and on foot to attend high school all shaped me. Even after finishing school, hardship continued. I escaped two kidnapping attempts and endured an abusive marriage while confronting sexual harassment and persecution in my career.

It was only by unyielding faith, optimism, and compassion that I emerged from these trials. God granted me courage to turn suffering into strength, to find treasures in tribulation. Yet the spirituality that shaped my life was not passive—it was a continual struggle between my soul, which included my mind and intellect, and my spirit, my *pneuma*, my divine consciousness that connects with God. When my soul and spirit worked in harmony, I witnessed divine intervention and miracles.

Jesus' words in Matthew 10:16—"Behold, I send you out as sheep in the midst of wolves. Therefore, be wise as serpents and harmless as doves"—proved prophetic. My life among the "wolves" tested my dove-like nature, leaving me vulnerable, yet God used those very experiences to strengthen me for the mission He entrusted to me. My faith and self-confidence grew until I possessed a boldness to take risks and follow the path of purpose laid before me.

My story became a bridge between the developing and developed worlds, highlighting our shared responsibility to make the world a better place. In Addis Ababa, I founded the Women's Self-Reliance Association (WSRA)—the first women's non-governmental organization of its kind in Ethiopia—to empower impoverished and displaced women to become self-sufficient. These women, uprooted by the 1973 famine, had lost their livelihoods. WSRA offered training in marketable skills such as leatherwork, sewing, food processing, and basic management. The women soon learned that handouts create dependency, while a "hands-up" approach builds independence. With equipment and start-up funds, we organized them into cooperatives, helping them start small businesses of their own. Economic independence became the key to empowerment—because when women are not self-reliant, they can never truly be free.

WSRA's success soon made it a national model and opened doors for international collaboration. I was sponsored by UNFPA and UNDP for study tours, trainings, and international conferences that took me across Europe, West Africa, and Central America. My study tour in Niamey, Niger, was instrumental in inspiring the establishment of Ethiopia's first Ministry of Women's Affairs.

In August 1994, I moved to Minnesota with my five children. Determined to take my service to a higher level, I enrolled at Metropolitan State University to study human services shortly after our resettlement in South Minneapolis. As part of my internship, I founded another nonprofit organization—International Self-Reliance Agency for Women, Inc. (ISAW)—to help immigrant women from many countries achieve the same transformation that WSRA had fostered in Ethiopia. ISAW provided culturally appropriate services that built self-reliance and advocated for policy changes to remove barriers to economic independence.

Though the challenges facing Ethiopian women differed from those confronting immigrant women in America, the outcome was the same: without self-reliance, women remain subject to external power structures. Immigrant women pursuing their dreams in the U.S. still encountered barriers—lack of childcare, isolation, and restrictive licensing policies.

I am grateful that my advocacy contributed to two major policy changes in Minnesota:

1. The 2004 bill exempting foreign-trained nurses from the CGFNS certification requirement, allowing them to take the NCLEX-RN exam after meeting state criteria.
2. The 2006 rule by the Minnesota Board of Barber and Cosmetologist Examiners exempting hair braiders from state licensing requirements.

In 2003, the International Self-reliance Agency for Women, Inc. (ISAW) received special consultative status with the United Nations Economic and Social Council (ECOSOC), a recognition that built upon my earlier work with the Women's Self-reliance Association (WSRA) in Ethiopia.

During those years, I was stretched thin between work, school, and raising five children as a single mother. Moving from a desirable neighborhood in Addis Ababa to a modest home in an undesirable neighborhood in South Minneapolis was difficult—but not enough to stop me. Working with these women felt like expanding my own family, and witnessing their transformation gave me profound joy. I never counted the hours or the hardships; I counted character—whether I was building it in others and living to please God.

The United States was different in many ways, as later chapters in my memoir reveal. Unlike my native country, America offered encouragement and recognition for my commitment to serving others—even while I was still a non-immigrant student. An anonymous donor sponsored my study tour to China and Hong Kong through a program titled *Case Studies in International Business/Asia 1*. In addition to raising five accomplished children and becoming a homeowner, I was empowered through awards, honors, a Bush Leadership Fellowship for my master's degree, and a tuition scholarship from Christian Leadership University toward my Ph.D.

The success that my children and I have achieved in America proves that anyone can accomplish whatever they set their mind to in this land of opportunity. When I speak of "opportunity," I do not mean a handout that creates dependency, but a "use it or lose it" hands-up venture made possible by those Americans who extend a hand to help others rise. They do so by helping others activate and develop whatever they bring to the table and thus facilitate their success. This is what makes America different. This is why it is a country of innovation.

When we came to America, my oldest child was seventeen and my youngest seven. Today, they serve their adoptive country, giving back to their communities as middle-class Americans. And here I am in Atlanta, Georgia, embarking on the final phase of my life's journey with renewed energy. God, who used elders like Moses and Joshua, has given me a new assignment in my retirement years—to serve Him through a new nonprofit and through writing books. And I am still as strong as when I began this journey, echoing Caleb's words to Joshua: "As yet I am as strong this day as on the day that Moses sent me; just as my strength was then, so now is my strength for war, both for going out and for coming in." Even now, my hair shows only a touch of gray—a testament to God's faithfulness through the seasons of my life.

PRELUDE
THE TAKEAWAYS —
IT WAS ALL PURPOSE-DRIVEN

This prelude offers a brief summary of each chapter, highlighting the key takeaways from the   book. I begin this first chapter by giving thanks to God for His abundant grace, protection, and guidance—the divine forces that sustained me through trials by fire and equipped me with the endurance to overcome what once felt unbearable. In time, I came to recognize that every hardship had purpose.

Ephesians 6:12 says, *"For we do not wrestle against flesh and blood, but against principalities, against powers, against the rulers of the darkness of this age, against spiritual hosts of wickedness in the heavenly places."* Yet the devil often uses flesh and blood against us. At times, I came to realize that the closest person the devil could use against me was me—myself. The good news is that whatever the devil uses against us ultimately serves God's purpose in shaping us. As Scripture says, *"And we know that all things work together for good to those who love God, to those who are called according to His purpose"* (Romans 8:28). After I understood the fruit of those tribulations, my prayer for my husband became: *"God, please bless the hammer You used to shape me."*

The storms of my life did not destroy me; they refined me. Like silver purified in fire, I was shaped into the vessel God intended me to be—one who lives as a testimony of His faithfulness and serves others through that experience. As Proverbs 25:4 reminds us, "Take away the dross from the silver, and there comes out a vessel for the smith." President Abraham Lincoln once said, "We can complain because rose bushes have thorns or rejoice because thorn bushes have roses." That simple truth captures the heart of my journey: learning to see God's purpose in every thorn and blessing in every scar.

The following verses have been my greatest comfort and affirmation through life's refining fires:

> "And I will bring the third part through the fire, and will refine them as silver is refined, and will try them as gold is tried." — Zechariah 13:9

> "Many will be purged, purified and refined, but the wicked will act wickedly; and none of the wicked will understand, but those who have insight will understand." — Daniel 12:10

> "But He knows the way that I take; When He has tested me, I shall come forth as gold." — Job 23:10

> "Behold, I have refined you, but not as silver; I have tested you in the furnace of affliction." — Isaiah 48:10

> "He will sit as a refiner and a purifier of silver; He will purify the sons of Levi and purge them as gold and silver, that they may offer to the Lord an offering in righteousness." — Malachi 3:3

Through these words, I came to understand that nothing in life is wasted when it is surrendered to God's purpose. Every season—joy and sorrow, triumph and pain—was divinely orchestrated to mold me into who I was called to be. Now, I invite you to journey with me through the chapters of *A Purposeful Life* and discover the purpose God revealed in each stage of my story:

Chapter 1. My Humble Beginning

My early life was the fertile ground where the foundation of my faith and character was laid. Growing up in a Christian home shaped the way I viewed myself, others, and the world around me. The values I absorbed in those formative years—love, compassion, respect, courage, endurance, and hard work—became the compass that has guided me through every season of life.

From an early age, I learned to seek solutions instead of becoming bitter, to find hope where others saw despair, and to rise above circumstances with gratitude and faith. No hardship has ever been too great for me. Facing the risk of attack from a landlord while collecting firewood from the forest and carrying it on my back, fetching water from the river for our household needs, walking eighty-five kilometers to attend high school, and moving from house to house—living with strangers while completing my high education—never made me bitter. Instead, I met each challenge with joy and gratitude.

The moral and spiritual grounding of my upbringing did more than teach me right from wrong; it gave me the strength to walk in purpose. Through my Christian upbringing, I came to understand that every challenge is an opportunity for growth and that love and humility are the truest marks of strength.

Chapter 2. Life Changes for the Better

This chapter reveals how "better" often unfolds in our lives in unexpected, stretching, and sometimes perilous ways—and how God walks through it all with us. However it arrives, "better" comes with purpose: to equip us to do good for others.

The miraculous door to a college education not only opened a better future for me, but also gave me the skills and courage to help build a better future for countless women and children. God continued opening one door after another—opportunities far beyond what my age, status, or background should have allowed—all for a purpose.

A nursing career that placed me in a Western-style home in a rural village became a platform for reform: confronting long-standing malpractice, creating life-saving referral and accompaniment systems for complicated deliveries, and launching mobile MCH clinics in underserved communities. In every moment—whether perched on a dark hotel windowsill, working in a remote jungle clinic, riding muleback through isolated villages, or serving in busy town settings—God's protection surrounded me like an unseen shield. He preserved me from danger, delivered me from predators, and guided me safely through every transition.

These years taught me that God shapes destiny through both hardship and honor. He planted courage where fear tried to take root, strengthened my voice where silence was expected, and allowed me to become part of His work in making life better for those in need. From student to nurse, from remote worker to reformer, His protection was the thread that held my story together.

When God defines a "better life," it is not merely comfort—it is calling. It is the courage to stand where others fall silent, the compassion to serve where conditions are harsh, and the wisdom to act decisively when lives depend on it. A life guided by His hand becomes a testimony—not only of survival, but of purpose, impact, and grace.

Chapter 3. Entering New Chapters of Life

Life's turning points often arrive without warning, shaking the foundations we once thought were secure. The fall of a long-standing monarchy, the rise of a new regime, the challenges of education, work, and marriage—all seemed to thrust me into storms I neither invited nor understood. I entered the world of marriage in much the same way, and in hindsight, I realize I made a choice that went against the quiet voice within me, ignoring what my heart was trying to say. Yet even behind the confusion and my mistakes, God's invisible hand was guiding and shaping every turn according to His divine plan.

Through each upheaval I learned that transitions are not the loss of stability but the classroom of faith. I came to understand that God sometimes allows the ground to tremble so that we may stand on firmer spiritual soil. My journey from one political era to another, from singleness to marriage, from village clinics to city hospitals, was not merely a change in circumstance—it was a process of refinement. Every door that closed, every disappointment that stung, and every unexpected blessing that followed reminded me that God's plan continues even when my heart trembles. In the end, the "new chapters" of my life were not of my choosing, but of His orchestration—and each one became a testimony of His sovereignty and grace.

Chapter 4. Sweet and Sour

This season of my life was a beautiful mixture of joy and trial—sweet in the new blessings of family, motherhood, and career, yet touched with the sourness of challenge and uncertainty. Moving to Addis Ababa, beginning a new job, and adjusting to life under a government that opposed Christianity tested every part of my faith. Yet, through each difficulty, I witnessed the mighty hand of God in ways I could never deny.

God's provision met me before I even knew I had a need. A fully furnished home, prepared and waiting; a custom-made baby bed generously given by the American mission guesthouse manager; a job that opened against all odds; a stroller, a baby walker, and even a car seat—rare in the city—all stood as reminders that His favor goes before those who trust Him. Even under a system that rejected Him, I witnessed how He opened doors no human could close.

There were also moments when His power was revealed through divine healing—times when physical strength and inner peace returned not by medicine, but through prayer. In those quiet moments, I understood that the same God who guided my steps was also restoring my spirit. Through this season, I learned that faith is not only for survival but for testimony. God's goodness is not diminished by hardship; it is magnified through it. The sweetness of His presence outweighed the bitterness of circumstance, and every provision and healing became a declaration that He was with me. When we walk by faith, God turns every sour moment into a testimony of His power. His provision meets our need before we ask, His healing restores what life tries to break, and His presence turns ordinary days into sacred reminders of His unfailing care.

Chapter 5. A Refining Journey

This chapter was a furnace of affliction that proved the depth of my faith. I walked through betrayal, humiliation, spiritual confusion, false accusation, and physical peril—but I also witnessed the unquenchable presence of God. The same voice that once warned and protected me began to teach me how to hear, trust, and obey. The betrayals in my home and the injustices in my workplace became the crucible through which God purified my heart and reshaped my understanding of love, endurance, and forgiveness.

In the wilderness of Bale Gadula, where isolation surrounded me, I discovered communion with God through prayer, fasting, and His Word. In danger, He preserved my life; in confusion, He gave me revelation; in hatred, He taught me forgiveness. The hands that pushed me down became the instruments through which He lifted me higher. Each trial refined me—not to break me, but to release the gold of unwavering faith and unshakable purpose.

Fire doesn't destroy faith—it purifies it. God allows refining seasons so that we can emerge with hearts that know His voice, love beyond betrayal, and stand unshaken in our purpose. The furnace you endure becomes the altar where your faith matures and your destiny is forged.

Chapter 6. Endurance Rewards

This chapter revealed that endurance is not passive waiting—it is obedient perseverance guided by faith. Through betrayal, false accusations, and the sting of injustice, you chose not to retaliate but to trust the higher court of heaven. Each trial—whether from deceitful lawyers, corrupt judges, or those who plotted evil—became a stage for God's power to be displayed. He raised up unlikely defenders, overturned unjust rulings, and transformed opposition into open doors of favor. Even when death brushed close through poison, His hand preserved me, because His purpose for my life was not yet complete.

I was misled by the pastor's mediation, and because I was not yet spiritually mature, I chose endurance. Yet God, in His mercy, redeemed that choice. The greatest reward of my endurance was not the court victory or the compensation—it was the two precious children God gave me from an unendurable marriage, when I chose obedience over bitterness despite deep misunderstandings. They became living proof that grace gives birth to new life after suffering—gifts born of surrender and endurance. Where others might have seen only loss, God saw faith, and He repaid it with life, legacy, and a joy that outlives pain. When endurance is coupled with obedience, it releases blessings no human hand can hinder. Through faith, patience, and unwavering trust, God turns injustice into testimony, pain into purpose, and obedience into generational reward.

Menase (Age 1) and Bethel (Age 2)

Chapter 7. Heeding the Call While Going Through Fire

This chapter demonstrates that divine calling is rarely smooth or simple—it is refined through trials, misunderstandings, and perseverance. Responding to God's call to serve displaced women, I learned that genuine service to God is not limited to pulpits or church work; it is meeting human suffering with compassionate action. The dream that led me to discover the poorest families in my own neighborhood revealed that obedience to God's voice transforms ordinary lives into miracles of hope.

The establishment of the Women's Self-Reliance Association (WSRA) was more than a project; it stood as a testimony that empowerment rooted in faith and dignity can break the chains of poverty. Through fasting, prayer, and unwavering trust, I witnessed God's divine provision—from miraculous supply in times of scarcity to international recognition from the United Nations. Each miracle affirmed that God equips those He calls.

Yet, the fire that followed—betrayal, injustice, and domestic violence— tested my soul as deeply as any external hardship. These experiences taught me that inner strength is forged not in comfort but in conflict. Even when falsely accused, I learned to forgive, for true leadership requires mercy as much as courage. The suffering I endured at home and in public life became part of a greater preparation for future ministry—proof that God can turn ashes into beauty when one chooses to stand firm in truth.

Above all, this chapter reminds readers that every calling has a cost, but obedience brings eternal fruit. Service inspired by love outlasts opposition, and forgiveness liberates both the wounded and the wrongdoer. When God calls you through the fire, He also walks beside you in it—and what emerges is not what burns, but what endures.

Chapter 8. Delayed but Divinely Timed: God's Answer

This chapter reveals how divine promises may seem delayed but are never denied. The fulfillment of God's word about the end of my marriage and my new beginning in America came exactly ten years after He first spoke it. Every detail—from the unexpected visas for all my children to the flight first routed through Nairobi, just as I had dreamed years earlier—proved that God's plans unfold with precision, not coincidence. His timing is perfect even when it feels inconvenient.

What began as a trip for my sister's wedding became the turning point of my destiny—shifting me from the path I had planned to the one God had intended all along. I arrived in America not as a seeker of comfort but as a vessel prepared through years of trials to serve a new mission. In Minneapolis, I was met by angels in human form—Kathleen, Cheryl, Jerry, and many others—whose generosity embodied God's faithfulness. Through them, I learned not only to give but also to receive, understanding that humility allows others the joy of serving too.

The harsh winter, cultural shock, and financial struggles could have discouraged me, but each challenge confirmed that this new land was fertile ground for the same calling that began in Ethiopia. When God led me to help an abused immigrant woman through the newly enacted Violence Against Women Act, I realized that my purpose had crossed continents with me. The skills I gained through the WSRA became the foundation for the International Self-Reliance Agency for Women, Inc. (ISAW)—a new seed of empowerment planted in American soil.

This chapter teaches that faith is not passive waiting; it is moving forward in obedience even when the destination is uncertain. Every divine delay conceals preparation; every closed door redirects us to a higher assignment. God turns displacement into mission, strangers into helpers, and hardship into opportunity. The long-awaited answer was not merely a new beginning for me—it was the birth of a new movement for immigrant women to rise with dignity, purpose, and faith.

Chapter 9. My Second Humble Beginning

This chapter testifies that true success is not built on comfort, but on courage, faith, and perseverance. The journey from a respected life in Ethiopia to humble living in South Minneapolis was not a fall from grace—it was a divine repositioning. God used that season of scarcity to strip away pride, deepen gratitude, and rebuild our lives on stronger spiritual and moral foundations.

I learned that the same God who provides in abundance also sustains in lack. When bread from a community pantry replaced the luxuries we once knew, humility became my teacher. The words of my daughter, "Now it is our turn to be poor," reminded me that life's seasons shift, but God's faithfulness does not. Even in our most modest beginnings, His purpose was unfolding: teaching my children responsibility, discipline, and the dignity of labor. Within months, they were thriving—earning incomes, excelling in school, and discovering talents that opened new doors.

God also surrounded us with His earthly angels—Kathleen and her son Michael—who became family. Through their love, I learned again that generosity has no borders and that divine relationships are often the bridge to new blessings. Every kindness we received reaffirmed that no one ascends alone; God works through people to lift His children higher.

My academic journey and the miraculous provision for my trip to China revealed that obedience always attracts divine favor. When I could not afford to go, God sent an anonymous donor to pay my way. That miracle, followed by the Bush Leadership Fellowship, confirmed that faith without fear leads to unimaginable breakthroughs.

This chapter reminds us that humility is the birthplace of destiny. God often leads us through humble paths to prepare us for higher callings. From seasons of struggle to rooms of influence, from simple beginnings to leadership recognized by the United Nations, the same God who planted the vision in Ethiopia faithfully watered it in America. When we trust Him with our small beginnings, He multiplies them into testimonies that can inspire generations.

Chapter 10. Making a Difference in America Is Different

This chapter marks a turning point in my journey—from serving women one by one to shaping policies that touched thousands. It revealed to me that making a difference in America is not just possible; it is protected by freedom, justice, and opportunity. In Ethiopia, my compassion once drew persecution; in America, it drew partnership, recognition, and honor. Here, vision is not silenced—it is celebrated and supported. That is the true greatness of this nation.

Through ISAW, I witnessed firsthand how God can turn the voice of one immigrant woman into a channel of hope for many. Every door that opened—from the church basement that housed our first office to the halls of the Minnesota Legislature—was a testament that divine purpose transcends geography. What began as small acts of compassion grew into policy-change movements that redefined access, justice, and dignity for many immigrant families.

I learned that serving with integrity invites both earthly favor and heavenly validation. Letters from the White House, grants from major foundations, and testimonies from women whose lives were restored reminded me that God honors obedience with influence. When I once prayed that He would show me the problems of those He called me to serve—and make me a solution—He answered beyond measure. From helping a single mother avoid eviction to helping immigrant nurses and hair braiders overcome systemic barriers, I saw His hand guiding every reform.

This chapter also affirmed that leadership is not about power but about purpose. The courage to stand for others—to speak truth before legislators, to challenge unfair systems, to act when others remain silent—is what turns calling into legacy. I came to understand that true advocacy is not born out of anger but out of love—love for justice, for human dignity, and for the God who equips the willing.

The America I came to know through these experiences is not perfect, but it is a land that allows purpose to breathe. Here, faith meets freedom, and humble beginnings can lead to national impact. From an immigrant mother in Minneapolis to a policy advocate influencing state law, I witnessed the miracle of what happens when divine calling aligns with a nation's promise of liberty.

Chapter 11. Raising Successful Children as a Single Mom

This chapter celebrates the faithfulness of God who stood as the Father in our home and the unseen co-parent in every decision I made. What the world calls "single motherhood," I came to understand as a divine partnership—a sacred journey guided by wisdom, prayer, and grace. I was never alone; God's hand was present in every trial, shaping my children's lives through love, discipline, and unwavering faith.

I learned that raising children well is not about having wealth or comfort but about building character anchored in God's truth. My role was to plant the seed of righteousness, nurture it with prayer, and trust God to bring the harvest. Even when the road was steep—through poverty, cultural transition, and teenage challenges—His Word remained my compass. Proverbs 22:6 and Matthew 6:33 were not mere verses to me; they were living promises that kept my family grounded and growing.

Humor often became my tool for correction while fasting and prayer—along with gatekeeping—became my weapons of protection. God gave me discernment to intervene at the right time—whether by transferring a child to a new school, hiding a car during a snowstorm, defending them when they got into trouble, or staying up through the night interceding in prayer. I saw firsthand that a mother's firmness guided by faith is far more powerful than fear or anger. When my son turned his life around at the altar, when each of my daughters excelled with distinction, and when my youngest matured into a man of integrity—those were not merely moments of success; they were miracles of grace.

The success of my children taught me that obedience to God is the highest form of parenting. My task was not to make them perfect but to equip them with the moral strength to choose right when no one was watching. Their achievements—in education, career, and character—are not my glory, but God's. He turned our humble beginnings into a generational blessing.

Above all, this chapter reminds me that love, discipline, godliness, and prayer can raise nations within households. When faith governs the family, even absence turns into divine presence, and pain becomes preparation for purpose. I did not raise my children alone—God did it through me, and for that, I give Him all the glory.

A Late Detour, a Loving Redirect

In the end, I realized that my spiritual life had deteriorated to the point where I abandoned what I was called to do and settled for a wrong career. Because I no longer made time to listen to God as I once had, I lost focus and pursued what seemed right in my own eyes. Forgetting the tribulations and hardships I had faced with the WSRA in Ethiopia before moving to the United States in 1994, I returned to Ethiopia in 2007 with an adoption agency—and put myself through Gehenna.

When Mrs. Mitike George, the late director at the Ministry of Women, Children, and Youth Affairs (MOWCYA) and former WSRA representative in Addis Ababa, visited Minneapolis in 2006, she urged me to start an adoption service from Ethiopia. Stressing the great need, she said there were over four million orphans and countless abandoned children in the country. Without taking time to seek divine counsel, I accepted her idea right away. Before I realized it, I had begun placing my trust in human authority. Unaware of the unwinnable threats to the agency's existence, our board president and I met with the late President Girma Wolde-Giorgis in 2009 to introduce our development project.

Meeting Ethiopia's late president Girma Wolde-Giorgis in his office

The tragedy was that I lingered in my poor decision, convincing myself that perseverance was faith and boasting that I was not a quitter—still thinking that the devil was attacking me for serving God. Yet God, who knows our weaknesses, had to close that wrong door to stop me from settling for less than what I was predestined for.

Sadly, I failed to recognize it as a final warning exposing my blind spot. Instead, I grew bitter, believing that God had let me down and failed to show me justice. But by His grace, I finally understood that the many challenges and deep trauma I endured through the adoption agency I took on without God's guidance were the very jolts I needed to embrace the assignment the Lord had given me long ago—to write books and to serve Him through His institutions and among His people.

Indeed, Pastor Joel Osteen's timely sermon *"The Power of Letting Go"* deeply impacted me. These particular words transformed my life: "If you will let it go and move forward, you're going to come into something awesome God is about to do—not ordinary like you had planned, but extraordinary like God has planned. Now, let it go and step into the new beginning God has in store." He even said, "You will write an exceptional book." The same voice that had instructed me in the 1980s to take one step forward was again reminding me that I would not be left behind or remain playing small.

After all was said and done, the trauma I faced with the adoption agency opened my eyes to reclaim the call I had received in the 1980s—to write my story. That calling became my first book, *The Secret to Finishing Well: A Quest for Authentic Leadership*. My goal was to promote good governance in Ethiopia using the painful evidence of my own experience. The book documents what I endured with the Women's Self-Reliance Association and the adoption ordeals.

The Secret to Finishing Well explores forms and effects of leadership, from God's original system of government to Ethiopia's monocratic, communist, and democratic regimes, and relates them to the U.S. constitutional system. Drawing from my years of study, work, and life in both Ethiopia and the United States—along with biblical evidence, research, global travel, and historical context—the book emphasizes how the past shapes the present and the future.

After *The Secret to Finishing Well* was published in 2014, I asked Ambassador Girma Birru, then Ethiopian ambassador to the U.S., to read it. I did so cautiously, fearing retaliation since the book exposes, with evidence in its appendix, the absence of good governance in Ethiopia. To my surprise, the ambassador warmly applauded my work when we met in his office in September 2014. He encouraged me to send the book to former Prime Minister Hailemariam Desalegn and his deputy, assuring me that he would personally call them and tell them to read it. I believe *The Secret to Finishing Well* made a meaningful contribution to the changes now unfolding in Ethiopia.

The book's inauguration in Addis Ababa on April 18, 2015, drew coverage from all eight local media outlets and attendance from government officials, the Ethiopian Writers Association, women's and Oromo writers' associations, Addis Ababa University, and UN representatives. A history professor from Addis Ababa University presented a review, and the Oromia president, impressed by my televised interview, requested an extended recording of my recommendations. I later appeared on a ninety-minute

Araya Seb (Who Is Who) TV program that aired repeatedly, and other international radio and press outlets followed suit.

Book Launch in Addis Ababa

H.E. Price Ras Mengesha Siyum Speaking at the event

In February 2016, former U.S. Ambassador to Ethiopia Patricia Haslach met with me and expressed interest in involving me in State Department initiatives. She also invited me to blog about my book on the U.S. Embassy's "Kimsha" site, but left Ethiopia later that year.

Ambassador Haslach's encouragement inspired me to include in the second edition of *The Secret to Finishing Well* the long-buried story of Colonel John C. Robinson, an African American aviation pioneer who helped establish the Ethiopian Air Force and Ethiopian Airlines in the 1930s and 1940s, ultimately giving his life for Ethiopia in 1954. His heroism had been forgotten until 2015, when Andrew Laurence rediscovered his grave beneath another at Gulele Cemetery in Addis Ababa. I hope future generations will honor his legacy with statues at the Air Force Academy and Bole International Airport.

I am now updating *The Secret to Finishing Well* in English, Amharic, and Afaan Oromo for a second edition. The ongoing civil war, ethnic unrest, and foreign intervention in Ethiopia have made this work even more urgent.

In the end, I set my heart to dedicating the rest of my life to serving the whole person—meeting both physical and spiritual needs. In 2016, I applied to volunteer with Our Redeemer Oromo Evangelical Church in South Minneapolis. The head pastor, Reverend Melkamu Nagari was enthusiastic, but after two weeks, he called back with the elders' decision:

"Because she divorced her husband against the Word of God, she needs to join the women's group and prove herself first."

Though I was aware of false gossip circulating about me in that church, I humbly joined the women's prayer group. But on my very first day, I was deeply wounded. After prayer, the women's group leader, Birtukan Ayana, spoke admiringly about my children and remarked, "Her children don't look like they came from Agitu." Because I liked her and naturally do not hold grudges, I tried to meet with her to discuss the remark. Sadly, she passed away before she gave me the chance. Her premature death affected me deeply, and I traveled all the way from Atlanta to attend her funeral.

For context, I had refused my church's permission to divorce in 1985 and endured that painful marriage for eighteen years until I left Ethiopia. Under Ethiopia's Family Law Proclamation No. 213/92, Article 53(1), marriage requires cohabitation; after two years of separation, a marriage becomes legally invalid. Nevertheless, I continued to maintain my married status for more than ten years while living in the United States. Accordingly, my marital status on the citizenship I obtained in 2013 is listed as "married."

With renewed spiritual vigor, I sought God's direction once again. In 2017, the Holy Spirit led me to Eagle Christian Worship Center International in South Minneapolis. There, I met Pastor Dr. Tolosa Gudina, to whom I introduced my book. Two weeks later—after returning from an overseas trip—he called to tell me that he had started reading the book as soon as I gave it to him and couldn't put it down until he finished. He invited me to present it at his church in Atlanta. When I did, every copy sold out within minutes—an unmistakable confirmation that God's hand was guiding me in the right direction.

In April 2018, I moved to Georgia to serve as volunteer development officer for the Ethiopian Evangelical Church of Atlanta. I formed a development committee, drafted a ninety-day work plan, and began my service. Yet, when the church was not ready to implement the plan, God redirected me again. One Sunday, as I prepared for church, the Holy Spirit led me to watch Pastor Joel Osteen's sermon *"Closed Doors Can't Stop You."* Through that message, the Lord opened the door for me to pursue a doctoral degree in Christian Leadership at Christian Leadership University. Because I had already completed my dissertation and could dedicate forty-five hours a week towards course work, I finished quickly—with gratitude for the scholarship that made it possible.

Christian Leadership University revealed another calling. Through the course *"Prayers That Heal the Heart,"* God transformed my life and equipped me for a deliverance ministry I had never imagined. After much prayer and discernment, I formed a board and founded Holistic Freedom International, Inc. (HFI)—a nonprofit organization devoted to serving the whole person following the model of Jesus: proclaiming the Good News, healing the sick and brokenhearted, and delivering those bound by addiction, poverty, or generational curses. HFI partners with faith-based and community organizations to equip them with the skills and resources necessary to serve effectively and sustainably.

Letting go became the doorway to greater grace. As I released bitterness and surrendered my plans, God reopened wells I thought had dried up—restoring vision, sharpening discernment, and guiding my steps with precision. He turned trauma into testimony, closed doors into classrooms, and detours into destiny. The books, the mentors, the pulpits, the degree, and the birth of Holistic Freedom International were not accidents; they were confirmations that obedience still has a future.

If I could whisper to anyone standing before a closed door, I would say: *do not mistake divine redirection for defeat.* Make time to listen again. Lay down what you've gripped in your own strength, and pick up what

God placed in your hands from the beginning. He wastes nothing—not your tears, not your waiting, not your wandering. In His timing, what once felt like an ending becomes the path that leads you home—to purpose.

1

MY HUMBLE BEGINNING

My early life had more in common with that of a girl from the fourth century than with someone coming of age in the 1960s in the United States. Instead of watching Saturday morning cartoons while eating bowls of sugary cereal and playing after school, I fetched water from the stream closest to my parents' home in Nedjo, Ethiopia, and gathered firewood for cooking because we had no electricity. During the rainy season, our country roads turned into rivers of mud, completely impassable to automobiles.

Today, I write this from the comfort of my desk in Atlanta, Georgia, with the soft whir of my laptop fan beside me. In the distance, an impatient motorist honks her horn. How did I get from there to here? To answer that question, we must go back to my childhood and the strong Christian foundation that shaped my life.

Soon after I was born, my father accepted the Protestant Christian faith and purchased a property adjacent to the Swedish Mission School and church in Nedjo, a small town in western Ethiopia. He moved to the new location with his family—my mother, my paternal grandmother, and me, their only child at the time. God used my father to make what seemed impossible, possible: I was able to start school at the age of six. The house he bought had one spacious bedroom and one living room.

Grandmother's Tale of How it All Began

When I was a child, my grandmother, mother, siblings, and I spent our evenings sitting by the fire, telling stories, and playing riddles. I don't remember how old I was when my grandmother told us the story of my father's conversion, but one evening, as we sat in front of the fire, she began:

"We lived in a remote rural area," Grandma said, "where homes were few and far apart. We cooked with firewood, fetched water from nearby rivers and streams, and relied on mules and donkeys for transportation. She paused for a moment, the firelight dancing across her face: "My son lost his father when he was only eight. At thirteen, he developed an ulcer on his right leg that left him crippled. There were no health-care services in our area, so I took him to what people called *holy water[1] (Tsebel In Amharic)*—the only treatment we knew—but it did not work."

Leaning closer to the fire, Grandma continued. "The infection worsened, and I took him to the *qaallu*.[2]" She explained that the qaallu was believed to possess ancestral wisdom and the power to heal. "People went to the *qaallu* to ask the causes of illnesses and to seek healing. He ordered me to sacrifice a lamb under the neighborhood's sacred offering tree so my son could be healed. The next day, without telling me, my son cut that tree at its root. It took him the whole day. If anyone had seen him, he would have been killed, for the offering tree was sacred. But no one found out.

"When he finally came home after disappearing early in the morning, he said, 'Mother, come and see your god.' He recovered in a very short time without any treatment. At age twenty, shortly after he married, he

---

[1] Holy water (*tsebel* in Amharic) in Ethiopia refers to hot spring or thermal spring water, traditionally believed to cast out evil spirits and to heal illnesses.

[2] Qaalluu refers to a spiritual leader and ritual authority who serves as a mediator between the physical and spiritual realms and performs ceremonies to communicate with spirits or ancestors.

heard about salvation through Jesus Christ. Desperate to find the true God, my son learned the Amharic alphabet with the help of a friend."

Amharic was Ethiopia's official language, while our family spoke Afaan Oromo. "He went to school for just one year," Grandma went on, "long enough to learn to read the Bible, which had been his greatest desire. When he reached Exodus 20: 3–5—'You shall have no other gods before Me. You shall not make a carved image for yourself'—he stopped reading, went straight to the Swedish Mission Church (now the Ethiopian Evangelical Church Mekane Yesus), and accepted the Protestant faith. Soon after, he purchased land next to the church and school."

I can imagine my father's joy when he settled his family a mile away from the Swedish Mission Clinic. Sadly, what should have been a blessing turned out to be a disappointment. The clinic was run by Lydia Larson, a Swedish missionary assigned to the Synod's rural clinics as a registered nurse. Years later, when I was twenty and working at another Synod clinic thirty miles away—after graduating from the Public Health College in Gondar—I learned how unqualified she had been. Nearly two decades later, when I visited the folk high school, she had attended in Sweden, I discovered she had never even completed high school before being sent to Ethiopia as a "nurse." I will tell that story in greater detail in the pages to come.

When my father moved to Nedjo in the 1950s and began his life as a businessman, life was good. Our family never lacked food; our meals were rich with meat, chicken, and eggs. I was deeply attached to my father because he spent time with me and cared for me attentively. My father was a short man, about five foot six, but he possessed remarkable physical strength. His muscles were round and solid, like stones. I remember him folding his arm tightly and daring strong men to straighten it—none ever could. He was a man no one wanted to anger. He would laugh before his temper rose, and those who knew him well took that laughter as a warning and kept their distance. His oval face and warm smile comforted me, and his quick, decisive movements made him seem always in command of his world.

Betrayal, Misfortune, and Pride Ruining our Family

A few years later, my father went into business with a local moneylender—the only creditor in the area—who charged an outrageous interest rate per month. In those days, Nedjo had no banks or formal lending institutions, so people relied on men like him for loans. Together they bought mules from Nekemte, about three hundred kilometers away, expecting to sell them in Nedjo at a large profit. Confident of success, my father added an impressive new extension to our home before traveling. The addition included a living and dining room, a spacious bedroom, an upper-level storeroom, and a walkout basement for the mules, accessible through a door that opened to the backyard. I never saw another house designed like that in Ethiopia—and nor again until I came to America in 1994.

Tragically, all the mules died on their way to Nedjo, and another loss soon followed. While my father was away on business, a close friend came to our home at night and deceived my mother. He claimed he needed to hide my father's brand-new industrial sewing machine at his house so the creditor would not confiscate it. Trusting him, my mother had a carpenter break the heavy-duty lock on the cupboard where it was stored. The man took the machine and later denied having done so. That betrayal deeply damaged my parents' relationship.

When I was four years old—soon after he built the new extension—my father abandoned our family and moved to a rural village seventy-two kilometers away. He could not humble himself to face the misfortunes we were experiencing. Looking back, I understand that he still needed income to support us, but I wished he had stayed and used his many skills to provide for us differently. He was talented with his hands. I remember the dome-shaped wood mold he used to make hats for the market, which we called *fabrica*, meaning "factory" in Afaan Oromo. He also crafted a beautiful round dining table—*gabatee* in Afaan Oromo—from which we ate together every evening.

A few months after he left, my father returned and took my mother and sister with him, leaving me behind with my grandmother. It was devastating to be without my parents and my only sister, Tsehai Wodajo, who was three and a half years younger than I. When I asked my grandmother why I had been left behind, she said gently that she loved me too much to be apart from me. My father was her only son, and I was her first grandchild—the apple of her eye.

A month before my sixth birthday, my grandmother took me to the Swedish Mission School to enroll me in first grade. While we waited to see the school director, we met another grandmother and her grandson, Kifle Umata, who was about my age. When the Swedish director arrived, she invited us in for an interview.

She asked, "How old are the children?"

"They are seven," both grandmothers replied quickly, afraid that admitting our true age would lead to rejection, since the school's policy was not to accept children under seven. The director didn't believe them. She pulled down our lower lips, saw our milk teeth, and shouted, "You Christian liars! Go away!"

Our grandmothers left humiliated and went to see Reverend Jaleta Wase, a highly respected pastor. My grandmother pleaded with him: "These children were abandoned by their parents. Our homes face the main road, and we only want them in school so they won't be run over by cars."

The pastor returned with us to the school and explained our situation to the director. The director finally agreed to admit us. We became the youngest children ever enrolled there. I had to stand on a stool to reach the blackboard, while most of my classmates were much older. Despite that, I loved school. The Swedish Mission followed a *learning-by-doing* method that made every lesson exciting. Sunday school was especially enjoyable—our teachers used colorful stickers to bring Bible stories to life.

Three years later, my mother sent a messenger asking my grandmother to help her return home to Nedjo. Grandma went immediately. Before leaving, she prepared the spacious bedroom in the new extension my father had built. My mother, twenty-eight weeks pregnant, made the seventy-two-kilometer trip home on muleback. Shortly after arriving, she gave birth prematurely to my second sister. I remember her tiny body wrapped in two pairs of handwoven cotton blankets to keep her warm. I had seen babies before, but never one so small and delicate. Her unfocused eyes and little reaching hands fascinated me. No one believed she would survive, but her godmother prophesied that she would be the strongest in our family. Thanks to God and my grandmother's care, she lived—and just as her godmother said, she grew up to be the tallest and strongest among us.

I was overjoyed to have my mother and sister Tsehai back and to see our family growing again. A few months later, my father renovated our house, adding a bedroom, a kitchen at the back, and two front rooms with private doors and windows facing the street. The room on the right was used for guests, and the one on the left became a small retail shop, or kiosk. He even built a pit latrine behind the house, about a hundred feet away. In those days, bathrooms were unknown in our community, and people still used open fields.

I slept with my grandmother, while my sisters, Tsehai and Rahel, slept with my mother. Grandma always woke me up very early, which I disliked at first. It was hard to leave the sweetness of morning sleep, but she trained me to be an early riser—a habit that shaped my discipline in life.

God Taught Me Responsibility from Childhood

When I was eleven, my father demolished the extension he had added to the left side of the house when he first established himself as a businessman in the 1950s. He replaced it with a new addition that included a spacious bedroom and a living room. My mother, Tsehai, and I moved our beds there, while Grandma and Rahel stayed in the old rooms. My father came and went, visiting occasionally. Though he provided no financial support, my mother welcomed him each time, bound by a culture that gave husbands authority and left wives little say. Cultural tradition required my mother to cook for her husband, serve him his food, and wash his feet before he slept. My sister and I never allowed her to do it—we took turns instead.

I was eleven when I was blessed with my third sister, whom I named *Destaye*, meaning "my joy." Despite my young age, I helped raise her. I took her to the Maternal and Child Health (MCH) clinic every Thursday afternoon. The clinic offered checkups, health education, vitamins, and food for children—supplied by UNICEF. I attended with great enthusiasm, determined to give my baby sister the best care. I was the only young girl there; everyone else was a mother. I listened carefully to the health lessons and followed the instructions diligently at home.

Two years later, my brother was born—the last child and only son. His birth revealed a painful truth about the preference for boys in Ethiopian culture. Relatives came from far away, bringing gifts to congratulate my mother on having a male child. It was the first time I met my maternal grandmother. Though I felt sad witnessing such favoritism, it did not diminish my spirit. I remained confident because my father had raised me to value myself and to stand tall, regardless of gender.

Being abandoned by my father hurt more than any other hardship I endured. I had been deeply attached to him. I missed his warm hugs and the gentle head massages he used to give me. His presence meant more to me than any financial contribution he could have made. After leaving us, my father never provided for his family again. Our only source of income became our small home-based shop. My mother and grandmother earned a little money by selling food and homemade beverages. My sister and I helped by buying groceries such as bread, coffee beans, tea, and sugar from larger stores in downtown Nedjo—about three miles from our house—and reselling them at a profit.

We had to walk that long road daily, breathing in the dust from cars passing on the dry dirt path. During the rainy season, walking became a real struggle; the road turned to slippery mud, and we often returned home soaked and splattered. Sometimes we slipped and fell, but we would turn each tumble into a joke—saying, "I just bought a piece of land"—laughing at our misfortune to make the hardship lighter.

The marketplace in downtown Nedjo was an open square surrounded by small retail stores, bars, restaurants, and homes. Market day came every Tuesday, and it reminded me, years later, of the Minneapolis Farmers Market—except there were no tables. Rural farmers brought their produce—root vegetables, beans, grains, honey, butter, fruits, and cereals—and displayed them on rags spread across the ground. They used tin cups for measuring and selling. One grain mill stood nearby, owned by an elderly Italian man named Lombardo, and most of the surrounding retail stores belonged to Arab merchants. My sister and I bought our supplies from them and resold them for a small margin.

Nedjo is a fertile place of natural beauty. Its breathtaking landscape is covered with green vegetation—different kinds of trees and shrubs—and blessed with a very pleasant climate. The air is clean and fresh, and the area is rich with streams, rivers, and many of Ethiopia's ten thousand native bird species. Root vegetables and beans that were not found in other parts of Ethiopia grew there. Guava, blackberry, rose berry, passion fruit, and more grew wild, free for us to pick and eat. I liked passion fruit and blackberry the most. I still enjoy passion fruit very much, but not the blackberries in this country—they are not as sweet.

Nedjo is also rich in natural resources, especially gold. Some rural farmers found gold flakes and small nuggets by filtering sand from nearby streams and rivers. After heavy rains, erosion sometimes revealed hidden deposits, and lucky farmers would take home what they found. Downtown Nedjo even had goldsmiths who sifted gold powder and used it to craft twenty-four-karat rings and necklaces on the spot. Many Ethiopians in the diaspora—particularly Oromos from Wellega—still treasure such jewelry.

When I was a child, there was only one public school in downtown Nedjo. Yet many students from Nejo town and the surrounding rural areas preferred the Swedish Mission School because of its quality education. Some walked miles each way to attend, but for my siblings and me, the school was just down the road. We were never late; even when the bell rang, we could run and still arrive on time.

A Happy Home, A Loving Family

Although we were poor, my siblings and I were admired as the happiest and most disciplined children in the neighborhood. We rarely fought. My greatest struggle was adapting to the simple food poverty allowed us after the abundance we had once known. We never went hungry, but our meals became almost entirely vegetarian—beans, peas, chickpeas, lentils, kale, potatoes, and pumpkins. I often longed for meat so much that I went to bed before dinner to avoid being forced to eat.

Evenings were filled with joy nonetheless. We sang Christian hymns, played traditional games such as hide-and-seek, and entertained each other with riddles and stories. Each of us took turns posing *Ebbo*[3] (riddle) or asking a question that challenged the others to think. My favorites in Afaan Oromo were Ibbonten, a riddle that helped us identify families in our neighborhood—"Husband, wife, a female calf, and a male calf: who is this family?"—and Ibbo, which went, "Too bold and disrespectful to greet royalties," with the answer being *fly*.

I liked singing Christian songs. I joined the choir at the age of ten as a soprano. My Swedish music teacher taught me to play the flute when I was twelve, with plans to teach me the piano as well. I had to leave for high school before she could, but many years later, when I visited her in Sweden in 1991, she showed me a photograph of us together—me standing by her right hand, singing a solo while she played the piano. In the picture, I was barely the height of the piano itself. I still remember many of the hymns she taught us, along with two African American songs: "Old Black Joe" and "My Old Kentucky Home."

Christmas was—and remains—my favorite holiday. The memory of celebrating Christmas at the Swedish Mission School is still vivid. The

---

[3] Ebbo: a mystifying, misleading, or puzzling question posed as a problem to be solved

Swedish missionaries hosted a Christmas Eve party every year from 4:00 to 6:00 p.m. in the missionaries' residence compound behind the church. Afterward, everyone moved into the church for the Christmas service. We children lit candles placed on the branches of a tall balsam fir tree and recited Bible verses about light that we had memorized, such as: "The people who sat in darkness have seen a great light" (Matthew 4:16). I sang Christmas carols with the choir and never missed a single rehearsal. Christmas Day was even more thrilling. The program began at 5 a.m.—which I firmly believed was the exact hour Jesus was born—and I always woke my family to make sure we arrived on time. We didn't own a clock, but somehow, I always knew the hour.

The best time for my siblings and me to play outdoors was Tuesday—market day—when our mother was away. While my siblings played, I used that time to prepare food and coffee so everything would be ready when my mother and grandmother returned home. Once I had finished, I waited outside to watch for them. My mother's light complexion made her face glow from a distance as she walked down the road, and I would run to meet her.

My mother often told me, "You were not born to your father and me—you were sent to us from heaven." Though her words could have made me feel special, I didn't see myself that way. The desire to do good was already rooted in me. Every morning before school, I cleaned the house and brewed coffee; after school, I helped my mother and grandmother with chores, fetched water, and collected firewood. I was a busy young girl, but always happy. Sometimes I wanted to play instead of doing my tasks, but seeing my tired mother enjoy her coffee, watching her eyes rest on the pile of firewood I had brought, and receiving her approving nod made me feel warm and satisfied—as if everything would be all right.

My peaceful life changed dramatically when I was ten years old. One morning, as I entered my classroom, the school director—an Ethiopian man who had replaced the Swedish missionary director—rushed toward me, grabbed my hand, and began shouting insults. While he yelled, he stepped on my cracked bare feet, grinding them into the dirt again and again. Blood came from the cuts on my heels, and the pain was unbearable. More than the physical agony, it was the humiliation and fear that left lasting scars on my spirit.

I limped home in agony but said nothing to my mother. I did not want to add to her burdens. Later, I thought of how my father had once defended my younger sister when she was beaten by a teacher. He had noticed her tears, examined the marks on her back, and, upon learning who had hurt her, stormed into the teacher's house and beat him soundly. I could only imagine what he might have done to the director if he had been there, but I never told him what had happened.

I went home crying and told my mother everything he had done to me. She explained that he was taking revenge on her. Because she was illiterate, she had me write a complaint to the church elders on her behalf. In it, my mother stated that the school director had treated me that way because she had refused to have an affair with him. A week after my mother submitted her complaint, the school director reinstated me in the school.

During those days, the church prohibited members from taking Holy Communion for a certain number of months if they were guilty of adultery. However, the school director—an Ethiopian—was not held accountable for his sexual harassment of my mother, nor for the horrible crime he had committed against me. In a pattern that would be repeated time and time again, the church placed skin color and job rank above the biblical principles it taught. The white missionaries were highly revered in the community, and Ethiopian employees in leadership positions at the Swedish mission, like the school director, were untouchable. The only silver lining to the whole situation was that I was never barefoot again. My mother made sure I always wore beautiful shoes.

I was not the only victim of cruelty at that school. I remember a beautiful teenage student, Atsede Girma, being flogged on her bare bottom in front of the class for an offense I never learned. Corporal punishment was common, and all students were forced to watch as others were beaten. After that day, Atsede never returned. She lived with her single mother, and I often defenseless.

Unfortunately, the school director's assaults on me did not stop after I was reinstated. He conspired to make me lose a scholarship opportunity that a Swedish missionary couple had offered me by falsely telling them that I had failed the national exam. The scholarship would have allowed me to attend a private Christian high school in Debre Zeyit (Bishoftu), a school where wealthy parents sent their children. To enter high school, eighth-grade students were required to pass a national exam, earning at least a 50 percent score from the Ministry of Education and a 50 percent score on the school's final exam. To support his false calm that I had failed the national exam, he used his authority to prevent me from meeting the minimum 50 percent score on the school's final exam. One day, a classmate who worked as the director's assistant confided that the school director had deliberately lowered my grades before sending them to the Ministry of Education. But his evil attempt didn't work as I had higher score on the national exam.

A Man out of His Time

My father visited us about four times a year after he abandoned us. His first words upon entering the house were always, "Is Aga home?"—Aga being short for Agitu. He would then lift me into his lap, hold me tightly, and shower me with affection. My mother resented the favoritism, often saying, "She is your ushu," meaning "your favorite." But those few days when he was home were the happiest of my childhood.

When my father was with us, we ate well and listened to his bedtime stories—something unheard of in our culture. He sat us down and read to us, as Americans do for their children. I never understood where he learned that habit. In our society, men did not fetch water, cook, or care for children; those tasks were considered women's work. Yet my father often defied these norms. Each time he visited, he repaired our house himself and had me climb the ladder to help him, saying, "This is not only a man's job." He took me everywhere he went—even to the bars—though, of course, I was served only soft drinks.

He taught me how to sew and had planned to teach me how to swim before I left for high school—another radical idea in a society that did not allow girls such freedoms. Girls did not go to bars, and swimming was considered inappropriate. In those days, it was rare for girls even to be educated; the national illiteracy rate was around 95 percent, and to this day, it remains high.

Finding Joy in Good and Bad Memories

Because of the praise I received from my Swedish teacher, I was recognized as the best student in handicrafts when I was twelve. She even asked me to assist my classmates. That skill became a source of income for me: I embroidered handkerchiefs and pillowcases and sold them to my teachers and fellow students, using the earnings to help pay my tuition at the Swedish Mission School. I also worked a few hours each week cleaning and organizing the missionary couple's home.

Not all my memories of the Mission School were painful. I shared laughter with a close friend, one year older than I. Whenever we saw menstrual stains on older girls' uniforms, we giggled and teased, saying, "You became a bad girl!"—because in our culture, menstruation was never discussed. We had no idea what it meant. We also found amusement reading love notes the boys slipped into girls' notebooks. One began, "*Yelelit hilme yeken himeme*"—"My night dream, my day sickness."

Collecting firewood with neighborhood girls after school and on Saturdays was another adventure. It was both fun and frightening. A cruel landowner whose forest we used to gather wood always seemed to catch us. He would shout, "Leave my property before I shoot you!" and we would scatter in terror as he confiscated our bundles. It happened again and again; we had no other place to find wood.

A Rural Ethiopian Girl Carrying Firewood the Way I did.

Fifteen years later, our roles reversed. One day, that same man came to my home in Addis Ababa—a beautiful house in an affluent neighborhood—begging for food and shelter. His clothes were in rags, and his hair was crawling with lice. I could hardly believe it was the same man who had once terrified me as a child. Yet I remembered the grace God had shown me, and I welcomed him in, fed him, and gave him rest. In that moment, I realized that compassion is the highest form of victory.

With Neighborhood Children, Carrying My Brother

A Home Open to All

The people of Nedjo saw my parents' home as a social welfare center because we were the most welcoming family in the neighborhood. Visitors who came to town to tend to their sick relatives cooked meals at our house since the Swedish Mission Clinic did not provide food for inpatients. Students from distant villages often ate their packed lunches at our home. Strangers who knocked on our door after dark, saying, "I am a traveler, unable to continue my journey after sunset," were also welcomed. My parents would always respond, "Our house belongs to God," and hosted them as though they were close relatives. My mother prepared dinner, while I washed the strangers' feet and arranged their beds in the living room. I did it joyfully, and even today, I still find happiness in serving others.

Washing a stranger's feet filled me with delight. I remember two families who lived with us at different times until they found a place of their own. We ate together like one family. I still laugh when I recall the second family—each time my father visited and led evening prayers, the husband, who was always drunk, interrupted, shouting, "Wodajo, say Our Father!" He wanted to end the service quickly, as we recited the Lord's Prayer at the end. Another of my duties was offering water to thirsty passersby. Farmers traveling long distances to market often stopped for a drink, grateful for the refreshment. Though I never expected anything in return, they often brought me small gifts of food as tokens of appreciation.

My mother was a gentle and hardworking woman who ensured our needs were met. She was the same height as my father but different in appearance—light-skinned with coarse hair, while my father was dark-skinned with soft, curly hair. We children were a mix of both, our skin the color of chocolate. I inherited my father's curls.

My mother's face often looked tired and serious, lost in deep thought, but when she was happy—especially after feeding us well—her face radiated light. She and my paternal grandmother worked together in raising us. My mother adored her mother-in-law and often said she loved her even more than her own mother, who used to warn her, "You will never be a good wife to that foolish man who thinks you will."

I still remember my mother saying, "Your grandma means a lot to me. Your father could not beat me in her presence because she always defended me." In those days, the culture allowed husbands to beat their wives for whatever they deemed a wrongdoing, and Ethiopian women accepted it as normal. I even recall a classmate at the Public Health College insisting that a husband beating his wife was a sign of love—she said she would doubt her husband's affection if he never did so. She was from Gojam, in northern Ethiopia. I disagreed completely. The Bible I cherished taught otherwise:

> "Husbands, love your wives, just as Christ loved the church and gave Himself up for her." (Ephesians 5:25)

> "He who loves his wife loves himself. For no one ever hated his own body but nourishes and cherishes it, just as Christ does the church." (Ephesians 5:28–30)

Yet many men distorted scripture to justify domination. They quoted only, "Wives, submit to your husbands," leaving out Christ's command to love sacrificially.

My paternal grandmother truly filled the father's role in our household and was my greatest role model. She established clear house rules. We were taught to chew with our mouths closed, never belch in public, speak with kindness, and never clean our noses with our hands but to use a piece of cloth. We never knew bad words. She corrected even our smallest mistakes, always explaining why.

Every morning, she woke me early, saying, "Sleeping in the early morning invites distraction; sleeping in the daytime brings nakedness." Her sayings taught me diligence. She also trained me in hygiene: "Never place a lid upside down—it will collect dirt. Don't hold a lid from the inside—your hands will transfer germs." These small habits stayed with me, and years later, they proved invaluable when I trained in an operating theater. During one procedure, a surgeon yelled at my classmate for breaking sterile technique and said, "Don't you see the girl next to you?" I smiled quietly, thinking, this is not new to me—this is my upbringing.

The Rough Path to a Better Future

My father always came home a few days before the end of the school year to see our report cards. When he learned that I had failed eighth grade, he encouraged me, saying I would do well if I repeated the year. He had no idea that the school director had forged my results, because we kept the assaults secret from him. I showed my father my genuine exam papers and convinced him otherwise. He assured me he would enroll me in a public high school in Gimbi, seventy-two kilometers from Nedjo.

The journey to Gimbi was difficult because the roads were not accessible to automobiles during the rainy season, which lasted from June to September. The means of transportation between Nedjo and Gimbi was usually either a lorry truck loaded with goods or a pickup truck that could manage the muddy road. However, during the rainy season, trucks and cars often became stuck in the mud for many days, and nobody wanted to be stranded in the wilderness for more than a week. Eventually, my father had to take me to Gimbi on muleback before school began in September.

On the first day of our journey to Gimbi, I had a terrifying experience crossing a river that was flooding due to the heavy rains. My father had me wait while he crossed to the other side of the river with the mule. It was so frightening to watch him struggle to cross that muddy, roaring river, surrounded by dense forest and striking landscape. The water reached just below his shoulders. I thought he was drowning as he struggled with the mule, and I screamed loudly, "Daddy, don't die!" Thankfully, he was safe and successfully reached the other side. After tying the mule to a tree, he came back to retrieve me. He lifted me onto his shoulders, and we crossed the river together. From that day onward, I refused to travel to Gimbi on muleback, choosing to go on foot instead.

Glory to God, we arrived safely in Gimbi after two days. The next day, my father took me to Gimbi High School to submit my eighth-grade transcript. We were told to wait another week as they had not received the ninth-grade entrance results yet. After two weeks, we received the good news that I had passed and would be admitted to the school. My father then returned home, leaving me in the custody of his aunt in Gimbi. The city of Gimbi was bigger and more developed than Nedjo. The city had things that didn't exist in Nedjo, like a gravel road to Addis Ababa, electricity, and a commercial bank. But the landscape was so hilly that it was difficult to walk around. Coffee was their main cash crop. Market day in Gimbi was on Saturdays and was no different than that of Nedjo.

In Minneapolis, where I resettled in the United States, the bus promptly arrives and slows to a cautious halt before scooping up my children and carrying them on their book-bound routes with the other kids. But when I was growing up, most students were adults, and there was no such thing as a school bus. The only bus I knew was the one public transportation that was somewhat like a metrobus in America and ran between Gimbi and Addis Ababa. I started high school just a month before I turned fourteen. During my first week of high school, many students came out to see me. In those days, most high school students were adults, so they didn't believe I was a ninth-grade student. I was (and still am) short in stature, and they seemed to think I was a dwarf. But being the youngest among them didn't seem strange to me because most of my classmates in the Swe dish mission school were also adults.

Gimbi High School was nothing like the Swedish Mission School in Nedjo. The atmosphere of the public high school in Gimbi was completely different from that of the Swedish mission school. The secular lifestyle did not match my spiritual background in Nedjo, where studying the Bible was a required part of the curriculum. When boys showed romantic interest in girls, I used to think it was a cardinal sin. I understood it as breaking the commandment in Exodus 20:14: "You shall not commit adultery." Whenever male classmates hugged me, I would run to the office of Mr. Sanyal, the school director, to file a complaint. Whenever I found his office locked, I would wait at his door, crying. Without realizing it, I would always stand on one foot with the other foot against the wall. I never noticed this habit until I heard other students referring to me as "the girl who stands on one foot and cries."

My male classmates continued sitting beside me in the classroom and hugging me. Eventually, I tried sitting next to respectable students, but even that failed. Soon, I switched my seat to sit beside our classroom monitor monitor—a much older student. A few days later, while we were waiting for our teacher, —he pretended to show me something under the desk. He grabbed my hand and placed it on his private part. I screamed in horror because it was a shocking and disgusting experience. Relying on his role as class monitor, he retaliated by filing a false report claiming I had skipped four hours of class.

As a result of this, I was whipped by the sports master while the associate school director stood by and watched. Students were given two lashes for every hour of class they missed. In my case, I was supposed to receive eight lashes, but I ran away. As soon as the first lash landed on my bottom, I bolted down the stairs. I ended up rolling on the ground, screaming, while the associate director laughed. Because it was against our culture for girls and women to wear pants, I am sure they could see my underwear as I rolled on the floor. I ran to the handicraft teacher's office, which was located at the back of the high school building, and the associate director continued to laugh behind me. I begged the handicraft teacher, "Please hide me." Then I crawled under her desk. In the end, I received only one lash that day, but my problems continued in many different forms afterward.

The Qaallu and a Seed of Fellowship

On my very first morning at my father's aunt's house, I came to learn about the qaallu I had heard about in my grandma's stories. The neighbors held a traditional coffee ceremony together every morning, and my father's aunt always threw part of the bread or roasted cereal outside for the qaallu before serving it with the coffee. Each time she did this, she said "Soorradhu," asking it to accept her sacrificial offering. Later, I went around and picked up every piece she had thrown out and ate them. Because of the freedom and peace I had experienced in my Christian faith growing up, I hated that so many people there worshipped the qaallu.

When I went home to Nedjo during my first school break, I explained this to the Swedish missionaries who had helped me rent a place to start a Christian fellowship in Gimbi. I invited a Christian bank manager and my Indian science teacher to join me, and together we began a small fellowship. Later on, the church in Nedjo planted a church in Gimbi. I believe that the tiny seed God helped me plant through the fellowship I started while in high school eventually bore much fruit.

A few months after my father placed me in his aunt's custody, her house was demolished due to road construction. My father then had me move to his friend's house. One evening, the man touched me inappropriately. It was distressing and outrageous to face that from a man who was probably older than my father and was entrusted to treat me like his child. Consequently, I left his home before the break of dawn and went to stay with one of my father's relatives in a rural village named Gassi, approximately twelve miles from the high school.

This relative of my father also believed in qaallu, but I worked hard to maintain my Christian lifestyle, singing all the time and praying before I went to bed. Little did I know, I was about to witness how powerful the name of Jesus is. One Saturday, when I went with my father's relative to fetch water from a stream approximately five hundred meters away from her house, I saw a woman under attack by an evil spirit right by the stream. Another woman was standing beside her, bowing down and pleading with the demon.

She begged, "Please, my lord, enable her to walk to the gold-crowned Dela." This was the name of a qaallu. My father's relative also joined her in bowing down and begging the demon.

At that point, I asked, "Why do you guys beg the devil? It will leave her if you call the name of Jesus."

Immediately after hearing the name of Jesus, the woman under attack came to her senses and asked me, "What did you say?" I didn't say a word because I was scared. I had seen evil spirits being cast out in the church in Nedjo, yet I was afraid to respond. But that powerful name still worked. The woman filled up her waterpot and left, carrying it on her back. When I went home for Easter after this incident, I saw new believers denounce the devil in front of the congregation, and I cried bitterly for being scared to respond to that woman who was under the attack of an evil spirit.

My father's relative took good care of me, and life was good, but her house was very far from the school. The students who lived in that village—all male—had to walk for hours each way to and from school. I was the only girl who walked such a long distance, and they eventually began to bother me with their romantic interests during my commute. This situation made me decide to leave my father's relative's home. I was fifteen years old. I asked the bank manager from my small Christian fellowship if I could stay at his house.

The bank manager's wife was illiterate, but she was from a wealthy family. She even had a servant who was a teenage girl from their former enslaved household. Ethiopia had abolished slavery, and only a few slaves had stayed with their former owners. When wealthy slave owners gave away one of their daughters in marriage, they used to send along what they called a *tirma*[4]. In those days, the bank used to give their bank manager a fully furnished house. The bank manager and his family welcomed me because they wanted me to help with chores and cleaning.

At the bank manager's house, I made a rug out of some grain sacks and slept next to the servant girl on the floor. This was my first experience sleeping on the floor next to a servant (who was just a girl like me, of course), but I was so happy for the shelter that I never complained. However, the problems that I had fled followed me there too. The couple had a male relative who also lived there, and the young man began

---

[4] *Tirma:* A female slave sent as a servant alongside the slave owner's daughter when she was given in marriage, prior to the abolition of slavery in Ethiopia.

annoying me. He stayed up on watch, like a cat waiting for its prey, and every time I went to use the toilet, he followed me in the dark and hugged me even though the slave girl always escorted me for my protection.

I had a very busy life while attending high school—helping with chores at the bank manager's house and earning money at school. During my lunch breaks, I embroidered handkerchiefs and pillowcases, which I sold to students. With the money I earned, I bought clothes and shoes for my siblings. Although my father showed me a great deal of love, he did not provide financially for his family. Because of this, I took it upon myself to support our household, and I did so with joy.

Many young girls in Ethiopia have faced the same painful circumstances I experienced. For generations, Ethiopian culture relegated women to a lower social status. In those days, few girls advanced beyond secondary school. I was the only female student from a distant town at Gimbi High School. Countless young girls who worked as domestic servants were vulnerable to sexual violence from men in the household—fathers, sons, or guards. If a girl became pregnant, she was often cast out, left to face a life-altering tragedy alone. Though she bore no fault, society branded her with shame and rejection. With nowhere to go, she could neither find work nor shelter, whether pregnant or after giving birth. Many, in utter despair, saw only two desperate options: to take their own lives or to abandon their newborns—in latrines, in the streets, or in front of orphanages and hospitals.

This cycle of silence and suffering was widespread until change slowly began to take root. One of the most transformative milestones came in 1992 with the establishment of the Ministry of Women's Affairs, a result of my lobbying, undertaken in obedience to God's direction. A study visit to the Ministry of Women's Affairs and Social Promotion in Niamey, Niger, proved instrumental in the creation of Ethiopia's first Ministry of Women's Affairs, dedicated to advancing the rights of women and children. This moment marked a pivotal turning point for the nation's most vulnerable.

A Miraculous Door to a Better Future

In the United States, children are often asked what they want to be when they grow up. Their answers come easily, surrounded by possibilities. But in my childhood, choices were few. Students pursued whatever opportunity promised a paying career. Even so, I held a dream deeply rooted in faith and service. Spirituality had always guided my life, and from a young age I was determined to do "the most-good for the most people."

During high school, tenth-grade students could apply to nursing school, teachers' training college, or vocational school. Those who completed twelfth grade could then enroll in university. When the opportunity came to Gimbi high school to apply for nursing school, the four other girls in my class hid the information from me.

One day, the associate dean of the Public Health College in northern Ethiopia arrived in Gimbi with his assistant to recruit students. He explained that most applications had been rejected because they didn't follow the proper guidelines. Only female students were eligible for the community nursing program, while the sanitarian course was for male students. He distributed new application forms and collected them that day. By God's grace, that was how I had the chance to apply for the community nursing program.

A few days before the school year ended, my father arrived to take me home for summer break. I went to the school director, Mr. Sanyal, to request permission to leave early. He asked me to bring my father to his office. When we entered, he said, "Your daughter has been accepted to the Public Health College in Gondar, but I did not tell her—she is too young for college." I was fifteen years old. My father stood up with great joy. "This is beyond my expectations," he said. "I brought her here for this very reason. I'm relieved she will attend a boarding school where she will be cared for and protected."

Mr. Sanyal handed him my official acceptance letter and registration instructions. None of my classmates had been accepted—their grades were too low. Many had joined a student strike and refused to take midterm exams, which accounted for 30 percent of their final grade. Only those of us who scored fifty out of seventy on the final exam were promoted.

Schools in Ethiopia began after Ethiopia's favorite celebration Meskel in September, but my father had to accompany me to Addis Ababa before Meskel to get me registered for college. Meskel is an annual holiday in the Ethiopian Orthodox Church, which commemorates the discovery of the true cross by the roman empress Helena in the fourth century. The national Meskel falls on Meskerem 17, Ethiopian calendar (September 28), each year and is celebrated at Meskel Square, a huge gathering place in the heart of Addis Ababa, named and dedicated for the celebration. The celebration follows the same routine in all parts of the country. People prepare the Demera, a tall pyramid of branches that looks like a fire tree, in the middle of Meskel Square and decorate it with woven ornate crosses and yellow flowers before it is lit.

The festival begins with a colorful Demera procession in which many believers dressed in robes are joined by hundreds of priests and deacons from the Coptic Orthodox churches in the area who bang the drums and carry ornate crosses used in religious ceremonies. In the late afternoon, people dance around the Demera and celebrate. Before sunset, the Demera is lit. After the bonfire has died out, Coptic Orthodox believers collect the charcoal and use it to mark the shape of a cross on their forehead. Many Coptic Orthodox Christians believe that the Demera bonfire has the power to cancel sins, while others think the direction of the smoke and the way the bonfire col lapses can be used to predict the future. Meskel is a time when many return home to their respective towns and villages to celebrate Meskel, like Thanksgiving Day in America.

All college-bound students in Ethiopia were required to first register at Haile Selassie I University (now Addis Ababa University) before proceeding to their assigned colleges. My father and I traveled back to Gimbi to catch the daily bus to Addis Ababa. At the time, there was only one gravel road connecting the two cities and only one bus per day. It departed at 5:00 a.m. and arrived around 6:00 p.m.—a long, exhausting journey that now takes less than six hours on the newly asphalted highway.

In Gimbi, we met Mr. Namarra Deressa, a parliament member and one of my father's close friends and neighbors. My father had helped him win his election years earlier. Mr. Namarra offered to escort me to Addis and ensure I registered properly. Trusting his friend, my father left me in his care and returned to Nedjo. The day after our arrival in Addis Ababa, Mr. Namarra took me to meet his brother, who was the university registrar. He personally drove me to the university and completed my registration. I was instructed to take the chartered bus to Gondar the following week.

The next day, Mr. Namarra's daughter, Ertra, took me on my first tour of Addis Ababa. We boarded a taxi that dropped us at Arat Kilo, where I stood in awe for several minutes, mesmerized by sights I had never imagined—a two-story Ministry of Education, a modern hotel, a café with a "Jolly Bar" sign, and the tall trees hiding the science faculty of Addis Ababa University. From there, we walked toward Sidist Kilo, only half a mile away. The streets were alive with movement—shops, churches, cafés, and restaurants lined both sides of the asphalt road, and cars, trucks, and buses sped past us. In the middle of the Sidist Kilo roundabout stood the Yekatit 12 Monument, commemorating the thousands of Ethiopians massacred by the Italians in retaliation for the 1937 assassination attempt on Viceroy Graziani. Ethiopia remains the only African nation never colonized by foreign powers, aside from Italy's brief five-year occupation from 1935 to 1941.

From Sidist Kilo, we backtracked a block toward the intersection between Arat Kilo and Sidist Kilo, then turned right at the stoplight to continue on the road leading to Piazza. My heart pounded with fear every time I tried to cross the streets, anxious about being run over by cars. During my long walk, I took in a detailed view of Piazza, which felt like an entirely different world—boutiques displaying posed white, non-talking, non-walking human replicas—mannequins—dressed fashionably and professionally; jewelry stores; cafés; restaurants; a cinema house; and more. One of the cities I visited in Italy twenty-two years later reminded me of Piazza.

We then crossed a roundabout and turned left onto Churchill Road toward Legehar, the only station for the train that ran between Addis Ababa and Djibouti. That marked the end of my tour for the day, and I returned to my transitional home with a large collection of brand-new images stored in my natural memory disc.

The following day, Ertra took me to Markato, the largest market in Africa. You can find everything in Markato—from nearly any product imaginable to expert pickpockets. The streets were completely clogged with streams of pedestrian traffic. In fact, it was much faster to walk than to drive through Markato. Navigating the many different sections of the market, along with the pressure created by the uninterrupted flow of people, vehicles, and livestock—mostly donkeys used to transport goods—was hectic and challenging. Shoppers combed through the streets, searching for the best bargains and negotiating prices for the items they wanted.

That day marked the end of my tour of Addis Ababa—and the beginning of a new chapter in my life. Having seen the vastness of my country's capital, I felt ready for the journey ahead to Gondar, where my dream of becoming a nurse—and serving others in need—was about to begin.

2

LIFE CHANGES FOR THE BETTER

My life seemed to be changing for the better, and I was eager to embrace this new beginning. I was ready to board the chartered bus to Gondar, as instructed when I registered the previous week. The Public Health College provided a chartered bus for students from all over Ethiopia, covering our hotel and meal expenses along the route. The school also reimbursed our travel expenses during breaks for those who needed to return to Addis Ababa to catch the college bus.

On the scheduled day, Mr. Namarra and his wife, Mrs. Megertu Gemmedaa, drove me in their Volkswagen to the bus station in Addis Ababa. It was my first time traveling on a long-distance bus with other students. The trip to Gondar took two days. We spent the night in Finote Selam, a city in Gojjam, at a hotel reserved for us by the college. We departed early the next morning, stopped in Bahir Dar for breakfast, and arrived at the college campus around two o'clock in the afternoon.

During my second week on campus, the college hosted its annual Freshmen Welcome Party, which included dancing. I had always considered secular dancing sinful and had avoided it throughout high school. I initially refused to attend, but my roommates insisted I shouldn't stay alone in the dormitory and dragged me to the event. Few minutes after I sat down, a tall male student grabbed my hand and asked me to dance. I refused, but he pulled me to the dance floor anyway. I stood stiffly, my body cold and unresponsive. For him, it must have felt like dragging a dead weight around. Eventually, he gave up and left me alone.

A Scripture verse from my days at the Swedish Mission School echoed in my mind—Galatians 5:21–23, warning that those who practiced wild parties (translated as "dance" in my language) would not inherit the Kingdom of God. My devotion to the faith I had embraced as a child guided every thought and action. Even watching others dance made me feel uneasy, but I waited quietly until the event ended.

There were twenty-eight of us female students in one dormitory building. We elected a father and mother from among us, and they acted as true parental figures until graduation. They forbade us from calling them by name; instead, we addressed them as "Mother" and "Father."

Our housemother inspected our dorm every night, ensuring we were all in bed by 10:00 p.m. before turning off the lights—except in the laundry room and bathrooms. Many of my roommates studied in the laundry room late into the night, but I never joined them. Studying always made me sleepy. Reading, to me, was a sedative.

One day, my roommates advised me to study under the large tree outside that had a light shining all night. Following their advice, I took my blanket and books and went out to study. Later that night, when my roommates realized I wasn't in bed, they searched everywhere until they found me fast asleep under the tree. They scolded me, "Don't you know hyenas could eat you alive?" and escorted me back to the dormitory.

Despite my unusual study habits, I always earned high grades because I paid close attention in class and memorized my detailed lecture notes during breaks.

On my return to college after the Christmas break, I had a terrifying experience. I arrived in Addis Ababa one day late and missed the chartered bus to Gondar, so I had to travel by public transportation. By coincidence, I boarded a bus filled with members of a football (soccer) team—young men who had taken up most of the seats.

One man in the third row kindly offered me his seat and moved to the back. During our lunch stop, two of the men sitting near me paid for my meal, treating me courteously. I thought they were God-sent angels. Later, I would realize their intentions were far from pure. That night, the bus stopped in Finote Selam again. The two men booked a hotel room for me before I even reached the reservation desk. They treated me to dinner and then left, saying they had a meeting. But when I noticed that one of them had left his jacket on the bed, I became suspicious. My instincts told me something wasn't right. I quietly changed rooms, leaving his jacket behind.

At midnight, I awoke to persistent knocking on my door. Startled, I looked at my watch—it was 11:55 p.m. My heart raced as I realized who it was. From the other side of the door, the man called out softly, "Kir yelishal?" ("Would you feel uncomfortable?"), repeating the question again and again. Frozen in fear, I climbed onto the windowsill. Below was the hotel kitchen, where I heard women cooking. I resolved to jump if he forced the door open. My heart pounded violently, and soon I felt the urgent need to relieve myself. Too frightened to leave the room, I gave in to the urge while still perched on the sill. I imagined the ruin that awaited me if he broke in—rape, pregnancy, disgrace, and a destroyed future.

After what felt like hours, the knocking finally stopped. I remained on the windowsill until dawn. At 5:00 a.m., when the bus driver opened the door for early boarding, I was the first to get on. When the man entered later, he asked softly, "Where is my jacket?" I replied calmly, "It's where you left it." He stepped back to retrieve it, then returned to the bus and boarded. When we stopped in Bahir Dar for breakfast, the two men once again offered to pay for my meal. This time, I declined. By God's grace, I arrived safely at the college gate that afternoon. My "paradise," as I called it, had never felt so safe.

Academic Life in Gondar During a Golden Era

Campus life was rich and fulfilling. We were served three meals a day, each with one or two side dishes, and tea at 4:00 p.m. daily. Lamb was served every day except Wednesdays and Fridays, which were fasting days.

At Emperor Haile Selassie I's command, the college food was inspected weekly to ensure quality. Leftover portions were collected to feed the poor through the students' humanitarian program. We also received a monthly stipend and enjoyed free bus service running every ten minutes to downtown Gondar. Evangelical Christian students, including me, met daily after lunch for a fellowship we called Berhan le Hullu—meaning "Light for All."

The college trained health officers, community nurses, sanitarians, and laboratory technicians—collectively known as the health team. The instructors, both Ethiopian and American, upheld high professional and ethical standards. The head of the nursing school was an American woman, Ms. Munihan, and my midwifery instructor, Ms. Long, was another dedicated American who equipped me with the professional discipline and ethical foundation that shaped my lifelong practice. The first semester focused on theory; practical training began in January of the second semester. Our clinical practice included both curative and preventive health care—providing direct nursing care every other day and home visits once a week.

Our uniform was blue, with short nails and neatly tied hair. Perfume and nail polish were forbidden. Our clinical supervisor, Ms. Tenagne Deribe, was both strict and excellent. Once, she deducted ten points from my grade for "falling hair" after spotting a soft curl dangling down my back. The first month of practical training was hard—the patient wards had a strong odor that made me nauseous. At first, I tried to secretly block my nose, fearing Ms. Tenagne would notice. When that didn't help, I sprayed perfume on cotton balls and tucked them into my nostrils before leaving the dorm. But nothing worked.

Though I loved caring for the sick, I couldn't stand the smell and decided to quit. I packed my things, but before leaving, reality struck—what would I return to? Poverty, uncertainty, and disappointment. I took a deep breath and decided to stay. Eventually, I adjusted to the environment and fell in love with nursing. Patients' families often expressed deep gratitude. They nicknamed me "Beruke"—the blessed one. Each morning, as I approached the ward, they would say joyfully, "Beruke came!" Their words strengthened my calling.

Not all experiences were pleasant. During my microbiology lab, I discovered Schistosoma—a parasite—in a stool sample labeled "negative." Knowing the suffering it causes still haunts me. Schistosomiasis can lead to liver fibrosis and bladder cancer if untreated. I felt deep sorrow for that patient, whose diagnosis had been missed.

Another memory remains vivid: during practical training in the male ward, a patient addicted to morphine after a femur fracture became violent. As I tried to help him with a bedpan, he suddenly slapped me across the face. The shock stung more than the pain.

Home visits, however, were uplifting. Each week, two students were assigned to visit three homes, offering health education and care. The people of Gondar were warm and generous. Every household insisted we eat and drink before leaving, saying, "Upon my death, please have some milk, eat some food." Their kindness left lasting impressions of Ethiopian hospitality.

The Student Strike

A student strike broke out during the first semester of my second year. I didn't like it, and I didn't even know the reason, but I felt compelled to participate. The student union wielded a great deal of power and coordinated the demonstrations with complete freedom. Throughout the strike, we continued eating our usual high-quality meals in the cafeteria, lived on campus, and held meetings in the student hall without fear of retaliation. The protest lasted three days without interference from the government.

From my exposure to American culture and leadership, it seemed to me that Emperor Haile Selassie I, Ethiopia's last emperor, had adopted a Western-leaning leadership style—despite feudalism's contradictory role in national life. My experience of the strike suggested there was meaningful respect for human rights in his day: freedom of expression, freedom of assembly, and even freedom to bear arms. The spirit of democracy I later encountered in the United States felt present.

On the third day, the emperor sent mediators to ask what we wanted. The student union met the fourth evening and presented two demands: immediate and unconditional release of all political prisoners, and construction of health centers throughout the country. The emperor resolved the dispute peacefully. He released political prisoners at once. As for health centers, he said they could not be built overnight but would be completed over time.

Internship at Gorgora Health Center

The last semester of my third year was a six-month internship at Gorgora Training Health Center, one of four training sites. Gorgora sits on the banks of Lake Tana and is surrounded by cultural treasures: a church dating to 1334 with vivid frescoes, the ruins of a seventeenth-century palace overlooking the lake, and Emperor Susenyos's cathedral.

Lake Tana, perched in the Northwestern Ethiopian Highlands at 1,788 meters (5,866 feet), is Ethiopia's largest lake and the source of the Blue Nile. It stretches roughly fifty-two miles long and forty-one miles wide, reaching a depth of about forty-nine feet. Of its thirty-seven islands, twenty hold sixteenth- and seventeenth-century monasteries that still draw visitors. The lake teems with birds and ancient trees. The Nile flows north, skirting ten African countries. Its banks hold rich silt, and the Blue Nile contributes roughly two-thirds of the Nile's discharge to Egypt, carrying most of the sediment on its 4,750-kilometer journey to the Mediterranean.

Our internship cohort, reflecting the college's "health team" model, included one health officer, four community nurses, two sanitarians, and one laboratory technician. During the first month, we learned to ride mules before starting weekly field clinics. We worked in two shifts—Tuesdays and Thursdays—traveling on muleback. My shift was Thursday, and for me it felt like a picnic. Life at the training center differed from campus:

we even had a male cook and a janitor, much like the Ethiopian working classes who employ domestic help.

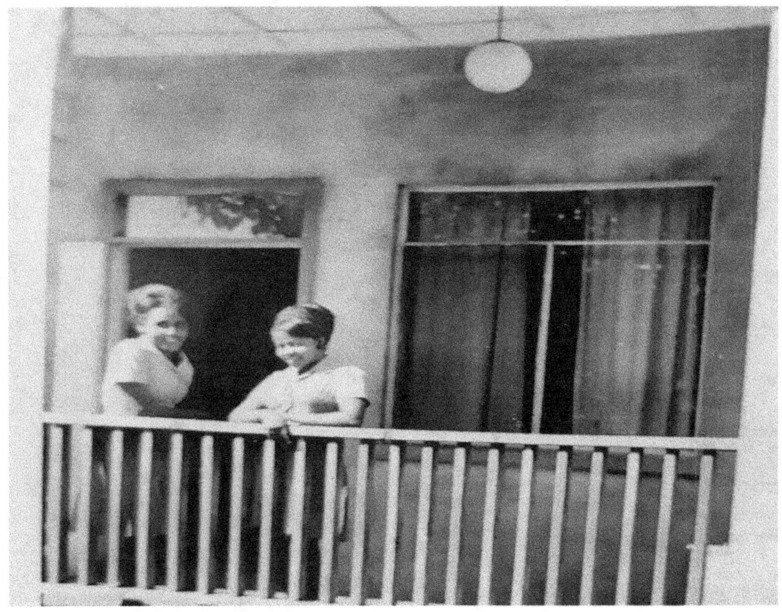

At Gorgora Training Center With my Teammate

Graduation and Assignment

I completed my internship in May. Graduation came in June—glorious in those days because Emperor Haile Selassie I himself handed out the diplomas. Champagne was served at the reception; I was offered a glass of champagne. I drank it in one gulp and asked for a cup of champagne, not knowing what it was. My classmates laughed kindly, and I learned my lesson.

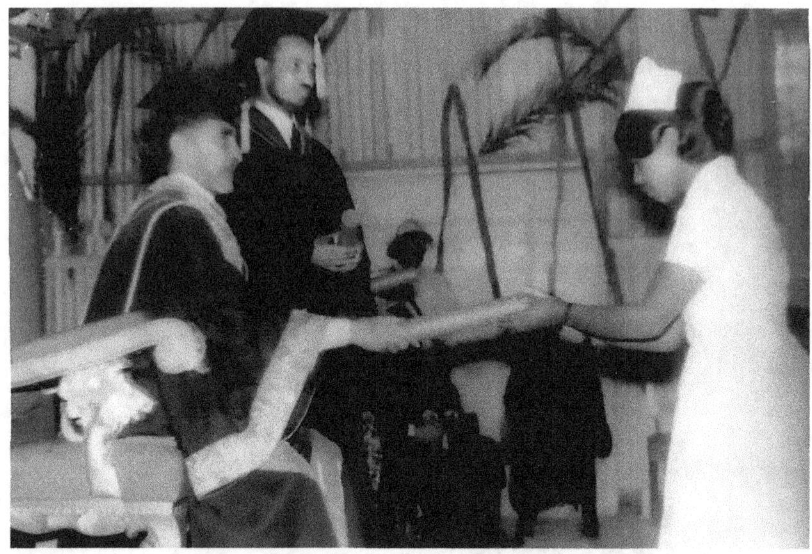

Receiving my Diploma from Emperor Halesellasie I

After graduation, the college assigned us to rural health centers across Ethiopia. I was posted to Mizan Teferi, the most remote site in the Kafa region of Southwest Ethiopia, alongside another community nurse, a health officer, a sanitarian, and a laboratory technician. To help us resettle, the college advanced three months' salary, to be repaid over six. I felt rich—meals at a restaurant cost only twenty-five cents then. The exchange rate was one Ethiopian birr to $2.07 USD until a decade after the emperor was deposed. Before reporting to duty, I went to Addis Ababa and bought clothing for my parents, grandmother, and siblings. Their pride in my diploma mattered more than the gifts. After a farewell dinner, I left for Mizan Teferi eager to fulfill my calling.

My Career Life Begins

After a week with my family, I started the four-day journey to Mizan Teferi—the hardest trip I had taken. There was a weekly helicopter from downtown Nedjo, but I had spent my money helping my parents. The only other option was finding space in an overloaded pickup truck; climbing onto a lorry was unthinkable. By then I was nineteen, already seasoned in living independently, and didn't need my father to escort me.

I found a spot in a pickup to Gimbi, spent the night at my uncle's, and caught a 5:30 a.m. bus to Addis Ababa, arriving in Markato around 6:00 p.m. I stayed the night at Mr. Namarra's home. Early the next morning, I took a taxi to the station for a bus to Jimma, the capital of Kafa and the birthplace of coffee. It was my first time booking a hotel room by myself.

On the fourth morning, I boarded a bus to Bonga. Jimma is 227 kilometers from Mizan Teferi. At that time, Mizan Teferi was reachable only by a dry-weather road from Bonga Airport, whose runway was unpaved.

My first flying adventure began. I took a small plane from Bonga to Mizan Teferi Airport and watched the world shrink—people, cars, and trees turning toy-sized as we climbed. The flight was short. From the airport, the only way to reach Mizan Teferi was by mule. The two-hour ride through lush jungle greenery gave me time to take in the beauty of the landscape. Thanks to my earlier training at Gorgora, traveling by muleback felt manageable.

On arrival, my coworker Abebech and I rented a simple two-room house with a separate kitchen and a latrine out back, sharing a wall with a veterinary clinic. On our first day, we bought a whole stalk of bananas for twenty-five cents. They were so sweet that we finished them the same day—bananas unlike any we had ever tasted. The next day we met our team: a freshly graduated health officer and sanitarian from our college, plus three local health assistants. After introductions, we toured the area as part of our orientation.

Something funny happened on day two. We tried to make pasta sauce, but we knew nothing about cooking. We chopped onions and began cooking them without adding water—they burned. We tried again the same way, and they burned again. At last, we added water and produced a tasteless sauce. The following day, we hired an experienced maid—common practice among employed Ethiopians—and order returned to our table.

Mizan Teferi resembled the Garden of Eden—lush forest, fertile soil, and wild fruit everywhere: impossibly sweet pineapples, bananas, papayas, guavas. For our coffee breaks, we picked free pineapples in the forest. The people living in the most remote parts of the area lived very simply. They spoke Gimira, one of more than 270 dialects in Ethiopia. They did not farm using oxen or plows, nor did they need to. Instead, they simply pierced the soil with a sharpened stick and placed the seed into the ground.

Their clothing recalled Adam and Eve after Eden. Abebech and I quickly became best friends in our new home. I had brought a beautiful basket with me from Nedjo, and we kept our monthly salary in it. Neither of us kept track of who used how much or for what purpose. We ate together, watched out for one another, and escorted each other wherever we went. It was as if we were conjoined twins.

The veterinary clinic attached to the house Abebech and I rented had a fenced veranda at the front entrance. One morning, as we were leaving for work, we noticed a tall, handsome man watching us. He greeted us as we stepped out of the house.

A few hours later, he appeared at the health center and introduced himself as a photographer from Jimma. He asked to take photos, saying he would develop them in his shop there. We believed him and set a time for the next day. We dressed up; he took individual and group shots and posed me exactly as he wished.

He returned with the pictures two weeks later. The following evening, he came to our house and gave us our photographs. Then he leaned toward me and confessed that he was not a photographer at all, but had come because he was interested in me and had used that excuse to gain direct access to me. He spoke in Afaan Oromo, my mother tongue—a language Abebech did not understand. She spoke Amharic, Ethiopia's official language.

I was furious at first, but I did my best to restrain my anger because I feared what he might do to us. In a calm, measured tone, I told him to return the next day at the same time for my answer. As promised, he came back the following evening, right on time, impeccably dressed for what he clearly believed was his first date with a new love. Too bad for him—he had no idea what awaited him instead. I locked the door from the inside and spoke to him through the window, warning him never to seek me out again.

He stationed himself at the veterinary clinic next door for two weeks, watching from the veranda with his elbows resting on the fence and attempting to speak to me each time I went in or out. Eventually, he threatened to have me abducted while I was traveling through Jimma, eight miles away, and then he left.

Bride kidnapping—the practice in which a man abducts a woman he wishes to marry—was a common form of marriage in the past. If a girl refused a proposal, she could be kidnapped. I remember my grandmother telling us her story of how she had been kidnapped but managed to escape on the third day. She later married my grandfather a few years afterward.

As the eldest child, I carried a deep dream of building a good future for myself, my parents, and my siblings, and I never wanted such a fate for myself. Even the thought of being kidnapped and forced into marriage against my will was terrifying.

A Powerful Pursuer and A Miraculous Escape

Unfortunately, that was not my last experience of this kind. The next attempt involved a prominent and powerful multimillionaire with significant influence. There was an elderly man on staff named Belete, a health assistant who was probably older than my father. Because of his age, we called him Abba Belete—Father Belete. He seemed to be very fond of me.

My nose could not tolerate strong or unpleasant smells, so each morning he would clean the health center before I arrived for work. "For my daughter's nose," he would say every time I came in. At the time, I had no idea why he was being so exceptionally kind to me.

One day, a tall gentleman named Asefa Wase came to the health center. He was Eritrean, just like Abba Belete. The gentleman summoned me and asked if I could sell him a can of chloroquine, a drug used to treat and prevent malaria. I later learned that he owned large coffee farms in the region, and it appeared that he was purchasing chloroquine as a preventive measure for his coffee pickers. I explained that we dispensed the medication only with a prescription from the health officer, so I could not sell him an entire can. He thanked me and left. Two weeks later, I had a dream that my grandmother, whom I loved dearly, was on the verge of death. I took the dream seriously and asked for leave to travel to Nedjo to see her. New employees were required to work for a year before qualifying for paid leave, but our boss granted me a two-week leave because I was crying nonstop.

When Abba Belete learned of my travel plans, he offered to take me to the airport on the back of his mule. I was overjoyed to receive free transportation for the two-hour muleback journey, especially since I would be escorted by a man who had always shown me such kindness. My roommate, Abebech, also accompanied me, and Abba Belete took me to the airport as promised. When we arrived at the airport, I noticed that Asefa Wase was also waiting for a flight. Abba Belete asked him a favor, saying, "Please, please take care of my daughter." He spoke as though he were not setting me up in any way, and I suspected nothing. I hugged Abebech and cried as I boarded the plane, distressed at leaving her behind alone.

After I took my seat, Asefa Wase sat next to me. Immediately after takeoff, he began trying to charm me, saying, "You are so compassionate. You cried for your friend." I began vomiting right away. That flight marked the first and last time I ever suffered from motion sickness. The plane made a thirty-minute layover in Mettu, where I had the opportunity to change seats and sit beside a woman, but that did not solve the problem. Asefa joined me there as well and sat beside me.

One of the health assistants on staff, Bula, had arranged for his friend Mitiku to reserve a hotel for me in Jimma and to pick me up from the airport. I was relieved and happy to see Mitiku waiting for me upon my arrival. Asefa Wase offered to take me to his new, luxurious hotel in

Jimma, but Mitiku told him that a hotel room had already been booked for me and instructed me to get into the taxi he had waiting.

For my own protection, I offered to share my hotel room with the other woman, and we got into the taxi together. However, my wealthy predator humbled himself to ride with his prey and entered the taxi as well.

"Drop me off at my hotel first," he ordered the taxi driver.

When we arrived at his hotel, and before stepping out of the taxi, he said to the driver, "Wait for me. I want to accompany her to her hotel. I will pay you. I will be right back." Then he went inside his hotel.

At that moment, I said in my heart, "Who is this man whom everyone obeys?" I was terrified.

Shortly after he returned and got back in the taxi, he opened up his Samsonite, which was full of money, and said to me, "Look here, all this money is yours."

I asked, "When did I make all this money?"

"All I made is yours," he replied. That didn't convince me either. I am sure he thought money would attract me, but I was panicking instead. Finally, we arrived at the hotel Mitiku that had been reserved for me.

Asefa Wase said to us, "I will be back shortly and treat you to lunch, so don't eat your lunch until I come back." Then he left in the taxi.

you to lunch. Don't eat until I return," and left.

Only then did I learn Mitiku knew him. "I'm scared," Mitiku whispered. "He is filthy rich. Everyone knows him. He can do anything. I'll go home to tell my maid I'm staying here tonight." He booked a room next to mine, took us to lunch, and brought us back. Asefa arrived and demanded to take us out. When Mitiku said we had already eaten, Asefa raised his voice: "Did I not tell you not to? How dare you?" Mitiku calmed him: "You'll have plenty of time. She has business with the Jimma health department and will be here two weeks." He lied to protect me.

Asefa Wase eventually calmed down and said, "Okay. Do not eat breakfast tomorrow morning until I come. I will take you to breakfast." We replied, "Okay," and he left.

Mitiku also left for his house, but he soon returned and went into the hotel room he had reserved. The next morning, Mitiku escorted me to the road leading to Addis Ababa so I could catch a bus. We had to wait for buses coming from two towns closer to Jimma—Agaro and Bonga.

Because it was the busiest month in Jimma due to the coffee harvest season, the first two buses were already full, and we had to wait for another one. More than a dozen other passengers were waiting as well.

"Young lady, your man is coming," one of the men said.

"Who is my man?" I asked.

"Asefa Wase," he replied. I suddenly realized these men had been on my flight the day before.

Then came a thunderous voice. Asefa demanded, "Didn't you say you were staying? Why did you lie?"

"Sorry," Mitiku cut in. "She changed her mind suddenly, but she didn't get a bus. She has no alternative now but to *stay.*"

Asefa Wase calmed down again and said, "I will be right back. Wait for me here," and left. What a relief. A bus arrived just after he walked away, and I climbed aboard for Addis Ababa. I reached Nedjo on the fourth day. Joy flooded me when I found my grandmother alive, though she was still in bed. My mother began to tell me the story. "This is truly a miracle," she said. "Your grandma was admitted to the clinic for two weeks. Two days ago, we were told she wouldn't make it, so they discharged her. Now she is doing very well."

The next day, I took my grandmother back to the clinic to be examined while I was present. I didn't know her exact diagnosis, but I was overjoyed to hear the confirmation that she was perfectly well. At that time, the Swedish head of the clinic, Lydia Larson, told me the Synod had a vacancy at the Bodji Clinic, thirty miles from Nedjo, and asked me to take the job. I explained that the Ministry of Health had required me to sign a binding contract to serve six years in exchange for my free college education, so I could not accept. I never imagined I would soon take that position—and uncover Lydia's medical incompetence. My grandmother fully recovered during my one-week stay, and I returned to Mizan Teferi the following week.

When I returned, Abebech and I received a dinner invitation from a wealthy Eritrean man named Amare, who owned a pharmacy. God bless him for the invitation. He was very rich, and the local people even called him "Amare Garamando," using a word in their language meaning "god." Because of that reputation, we felt honored to be invited; in fact, it was our first formal dinner invitation in the ten months we had lived there.

Fleeing a Powerful Pursuer Led Me to God's Purpose for My Life

We soon learned the real reason for the dinner. After we ate, Mr. Amare delivered frightening news. "Asefa Wase has made all the arrangements to kidnap you in his car," he told me plainly. "If you don't want this man, you must disappear from here as soon as possible—secretly." Abebech and I trembled. The next morning, we told our boss, and I said I was determined to leave immediately. The job offer I had received the prior week gave me hope that the Ministry of Health would not pursue me for breaking my three-year placement contract in less than a year. I had served only eleven months. I packed at once and left Mizan Teferi for good the following day. Abebech escorted me to the airport, and we cried for nearly half an hour before I boarded the plane. She feared she could not make it without me in that isolated place. As she feared, two months later she developed a peptic ulcer and was transferred to a hospital in her hometown.

I spent the night at a hotel in Jimma and took a bus to Addis Ababa the next day, arriving at the station around 6:00 p.m. The following morning, I caught a bus from Addis Ababa to Gimbi, spent the night at my uncle's home, and then rode a pickup truck to Nedjo. I returned to my parents and siblings just ten days after my previous visit. What a surprise for them! It had to be a surprise—there was no easy communication back then. Nedjo had a single telecommunication center downtown, and people went there for long-distance calls. I told my parents I was moving to Bodji for good to work as a nurse. We were all overjoyed; none of us had imagined such a turn of events.

The day after my arrival in Nedjo, I met again with the Swedish nurse, Lydia Larson, and learned that the Bodji Clinic was in urgent need of an Oromo-speaking nurse because the community spoke only Afaan Oromo. A Swedish missionary nurse and her Oromo husband, also a nurse, were scheduled to leave for Sweden in a month. The next day, I reported to the Western Synod office in Bodji and received my employment letter on the spot.

I did not realize how much I was being Westernized. The Synod administrator took me to the residence of the outgoing nurse couple. They had already been told that I would succeed the Oromo nurse and showed me the room prepared for me—my permanent bedroom. Another Swedish nurse, the wife's successor, was on her way from Sweden. The house was a beautiful three-bedroom, two-bath villa with a breathtaking view, a Western-style kitchen with a wood-burning stove, a dining room, and a wood-burning fireplace in the living room. I had become familiar with Swedish ways while attending the mission school in Nedjo from first to eighth grade, but this house surpassed anything I had known. Though I had never been to Sweden, I felt as if I were living in a Swedish home.

The male nurse gave me an excellent orientation during the three weeks I lived and worked with them. He told me they had run out of tetanus vaccine, which could be obtained only from the public hospital in Nekemte. The vaccine was critical because of the area's unsanitary conditions and the fact that most people walked barefoot. I decided to travel to Nekemte at my own expense to obtain the vaccine before the couple left. I was fortunate: a well-to-do pharmacist, Mr. Samuel Deressa, happened to be at the hospital when I picked up the vaccine and offered me a ride from Nekemte to Gimbi the next day. He set a meeting place, and I left to prepare.

Something unexpected happened as I left the hospital: I ran into the very man who had threatened to have me abducted in Jimma. He looked pleased to see me. He hugged me and said, "I was looking for you and was told you moved to Gimbi." Feeling confident I was safe, I showed him the vaccine and replied, "Yes, I came to Nekemte to get this, and tomorrow morning I will catch the bus to Gimbi." In truth, I already had a ride scheduled and was not taking a bus. "Okay," he said. "I will come to the bus station and say goodbye." I sensed he believed me because he saw the vaccine in my hand, and I suspected he planned to board the bus with me—there was only one bus between Nekemte and Gimbi at a fixed time. The next morning, however, I met Mr. Samuel as planned, rode with him to Gimbi, and took a pickup truck to Bodji the following day.

The couple in Boji left for Sweden just five days after I returned from Nekemte with the tetanus vaccine. Soon after, Lydia Larson, the Swedish nurse from Nedjo who had arranged my new job, joined me shortly after the couple left to help for a month, until another Swedish nurse could arrive. At the time, I did not know her age—she was probably in her sixties, as she had already been working there for twenty-five years. The community viewed her as kind and highly competent, and that was how she presented herself. The clinic had an outpatient department; female and male wards with ten beds each; a children's ward with ten beds; and a maternity ward with a delivery room. There was a separate unit for tuberculosis patients. The outpatient clinic contained two exam rooms, a dressing room, an injection room with a pharmacy cabinet, and a records room.

Our staff included two nurses (Lydia and me), two male health assistants, two janitors, and one clerk. The health assistants had not received the formal training required for certification. I learned that the Swedish missionary nurses had trained janitors on the job and then assigned them as practical health assistants—called "dressers" at the time. These two men interpreted for the Swedish nurses, and the clerk also interpreted when needed. One of the assistants spoke good English.

I discovered Lydia Larson's horrific malpractice during my first week with her by reviewing patient records. The first case was a beautiful young woman named Worknesh, who came for a refill of INH, a tuberculosis drug. As a nurse practitioner, I thoroughly reviewed each patient's health history before I examined them. In Worknesh's chart, I found she had been taking INH for seven years—originally prescribed by Lydia when she had worked at the clinic.

By the time the Synod hired me, Larson had been working in ways that I would later recognize as medical malpractice for twenty-six years. When I asked why she was taking INH, Worknesh showed me a deep, oozing sore on her right thigh that had left her crippled. I diagnosed cellulitis with likely extension to the bone. I wrote a referral letter to Nekemte Hospital and instructed her to see a physician. I did not refill the INH. A week later, Worknesh returned to the clinic with a medical report from a physician at Nekemte Hospital. The physician had also diagnosed her with cellulitis, prescribed eighty capsules of tetracycline, and instructed her to have her oozing bone treated by an orthopedist.

I kept encountering similar errors in charts for patients assigned to me. Lydia had often written "penicillin 2 + 2." When I asked a health assistant what that meant, he said they injected two milliliters of penicillin into each buttock—because patients praised her more when they received two shots. Only God knows how many poor patients developed penicillin resistance.

Another grave mistake I witnessed involved a woman who was brought to the clinic with a skull injury after being assaulted by her husband. Larson gave the patient her usual prescription of "penicillin 2 + 2" and dressed the wound. The woman was also instructed to return to the clinic every three days to have the dressing changed. However, she was not given the tetanus vaccine—the very medication I had traveled all the way to Nekemte to obtain and bring to the clinic before I began working there. The woman appeared fine when she returned on the third day for her dressing change. Sadly, she was brought back to the clinic the following week suffering from tetanus seizures, at which point Larson admitted her for treatment.

I could no longer contain my anger and confronted Larson, saying, "This woman is going to die because you did not give her the tetanus vaccine. What kind of police report are you going to file?"

She replied boldly, "Of course this wouldn't have happened if her husband had not hit her."

The woman died in the clinic on the second day. Her husband was arrested for murder based on Larson's police report. However, there were no repercussions or corrective measures taken regarding Larson's malpractice, and similar cases continued to occur.

On another occasion, Lydia prescribed morphine for a woman who was eight months pregnant and attending her biweekly antenatal visit. At the next checkup—assigned to me—I was shocked to see morphine recorded. I asked whether she had felt the baby move since the last visit. "No," she said. I listened for fetal heart tones and heard none. I admitted her, and the next day she delivered a stillborn by induction.

One Saturday afternoon, while I was on duty, my cousin's wife was admitted to the clinic around 4:00 p.m. to deliver her third baby. I examined her at about 6:00 p.m. and then went home. When I returned at 8:00 p.m., I was shocked and confused to find her experiencing strong, frequent contractions. It was far too early to suggest that she had entered the second stage of labor. I examined her cervix for dilation and found it as hard as stone. At that moment, I suspected that Larson had administered ergometrine.

"Did the frenji—the white woman—give you any injections?" I asked. "Yes," she said. I immediately checked the trash and found the discarded ergometrine vial. I panicked because of what I had been taught about ergometrine by my American midwifery instructor, Ms. Long. Ergometrine is used only after the delivery of the baby and placenta to reduce or stop postpartum hemorrhage. It works by intensifying uterine contractions and causing the cervix to harden. Therefore, my cousin's wife could have died from uterine rupture while the baby was still in utero.

I prayed earnestly and then administered pethidine, believing it would help relieve the severe contraction pain she was enduring and also act as a muscle relaxant to allow cervical dilation—and it worked. Praise God, she delivered quickly, but the baby was stillborn. Unfortunately, I had expected this outcome, because ergometrine causes fetal anoxia. I went home with the empty ergometrine vial that Larson had thrown into the trash and confronted her, asking how she dared to give ergometrine to a woman in labor. She remained silent.

On another Saturday, a healthy seven-year-old boy was admitted to the clinic by Larson. While making my routine rounds before leaving for lunch, I noticed that he had a nasogastric tube in place, and a female janitor—untrained and unauthorized to perform such a task—was about to feed him through the tube. When I saw blood in the tubing, I screamed in shock, "Don't do it! The tube is in his lung. This child will die instantly if you do that."

She replied, "Giftiy"—an Afaan Oromo title of honor meaning honorable—"Lydia will kill me if I don't feed him." Paralyzed by fear of authority, she pushed the milk into the syringe despite my warning. The child died instantly before my eyes.

That moment exposed the full extent of the clinic's moral and professional collapse: untrained staff forced to perform medical procedures under threat, life-saving warnings ignored, and accountability completely absent. Standing there, watching a preventable death unfold, I knew I could no longer remain silent or complicit. I said to myself, "Enough is enough," and I decided to resign. I spent the weekend reflecting on the three weeks I had worked alongside Lydia. Every evening she had asked me to pray with her, and each time she led, praying, "God, bring patients tomorrow. Protect the clinic staff, the maids, and the guards." If she had allowed me to pray, I would have asked for healing. All the Swedish missionary pastors and their wives had shown me Jesus by life and word when I was young. Lydia was the opposite, yet she was treated like a physician and revered like a queen. Everyone called her Giftiy Lydia and held her in the highest esteem.

Finally, I made the decision to leave and submitted my resignation to the Synod, along with my written report, the following Monday. After reviewing my resignation and report, the Synod's leadership met with me and asked me to remain in my position. Their only response to the situation involving Larson was to reassign her to a role as a social worker, since she did not want to return to Sweden. Years later, when I visited the folk high school she had attended before coming to Ethiopia as a registered nurse, I discovered that she had not even completed high school.

A Creative Life-Saving System Beyond Medical Practice

The Swedish nurse I had been waiting for arrived from Sweden a week later, and we began our life together as roommates. Shortly after her arrival, we hired a maid and settled into a shared rhythm—enjoying Western meals five days a week and Ethiopian food twice a week. In time, I began to rediscover a sense of fulfillment, both in my professional calling and in my spiritual life. I joined the church's women's group, which met weekly to raise funds for the church through their handicraft skills, and those gatherings became a source of encouragement and renewal.

However, one issue I observed deeply disturbed me and compelled me to seek a solution. The culture assigned women a very low status in society. They were expected to care for their husbands and children, often at great personal cost.

I observed pregnant women who came to the clinic for the weekly maternal and child health (MCH) sessions carrying their babies while walking behind their husbands, who escorted them to the clinic. This form of escorting was very different from what I had seen in the United States, where husbands accompany their wives to follow-up appointments with care and support. Here, the husbands simply walked alongside or ahead of their wives, even on long and difficult journeys, without offering any help. Watching these pregnant women struggle to reach the clinic deeply troubled me. I could not understand the purpose of escorting if it did not involve support or assistance. In addition, there was no referral system in place at the time for complicated deliveries that required cesarean sections. These two realities compelled me to work toward finding solutions for both situations.

First, I designed and launched mobile maternal and child health (MCH) clinics and demonstration centers at four new sites on the church's property, emphasizing both proximity of services and preventive health care. I organized a team composed of two health assistants and an agricultural agent, and together we provided physical examinations, health education, and immunizations. The agricultural agent offered training in horticultural farming.

My goal was to introduce horticultural crops—such as carrots and beetroot, which were unknown to the rural community at the time—so that our teaching on balanced nutrition would not remain empty preaching. Each week, we conducted food preparation demonstrations, and the following week the mothers were assigned to demonstrate what they had learned. We also distributed supplies provided by UNICEF.

Over time, the impact became visible. Mothers who once walked long distances without understanding basic nutrition began cultivating their own gardens and preparing balanced meals for their families. Preventive care reduced avoidable illnesses, and immunization rates steadily improved. What began as a response to cultural and structural challenges grew into a model of integrated community care—one that combined health services, education, agriculture, and empowerment. It was not merely a clinic outreach program; it was a transformation in how families understood health, dignity, and self-reliance.

Second, I initiated a referral program for complicated deliveries entirely on my own, because the clinic lacked any system for handling such emergencies. At the time, women in labor were transported from distant villages by ten to twenty male porters who carried them on stretchers—a practice that underscored both the urgency and the lack of medical infrastructure.

Recognizing the danger this posed, I approached Reverend Tasgara Hirpo, the Synod president, and requested permission to use his personal vehicle to transport emergency cases to Gimbi Hospital, nearly seventy miles away. God bless him—he granted permission, asking only that I take responsibility for the cost of fuel. In an environment with no budget, no ambulance, and no formal protocol, this became our lifeline.

Whenever I encountered a malpresentation requiring a cesarean section, I appealed to the porters for gas money, and they gave willingly and without hesitation. I personally accompanied each woman in labor to Gimbi Hospital and returned the same night, ensuring I could resume my duties the following morning.

Through faith, vigilance, and decisive action, not a single mother lost her life in childbirth under my care, nor did I make a diagnostic error. What began as an improvised solution became a life-saving system—one built on courage, trust, and an unwavering commitment to protect mothers and their children.

The Ethiopian Evangelical Church Mekane Yesus, Western Synod, also operated a hospital in Aira, approximately seventy miles from Bodji, and a clinic in Chalia, about twenty miles from Aira. Each year, missionaries with families in both Bodji and Aira returned to their home countries for a three-month summer break. During the summer of my first year at the Bodji clinic, I was assigned to assist a German medical doctor, Dr. Elizabeth Knoche, in Chalia for two months. Alongside my clinical responsibilities, I taught health assistant (licensed practical nurse) students who were preparing for their national certification examination. The Aira hospital housed a health assistant training center and provided the certification training required by the Ethiopian Ministry of Health.

This assignment marked a turning point in my professional journey. Teaching allowed me to pass on not only clinical knowledge, but also the ethical standards and discipline I believed were essential to patient care. When I returned to Bodji, I was told that all the students had passed their examinations with outstanding results—an affirmation that investing in proper training and accountability could transform both individuals and the health system itself.

Stepping Into My Refining Journey

My refining journey was cooking when I returned. I got a proposal from a very quiet man, the Synod accountant. He was from Nedjo too, and we had both attended the same Swedish mission school, but I hadn't known him then (he was two years ahead of me). Although he was very attractive, my heart just didn't accept him, and I avoided him. He got the chance to speak with me in private for the first time as we were on our way back from the Ethiopian Evangelical Church Mekane Yesus's (EECMY's) general assembly, which we had both attended in Yirgalem, South Ethiopia. It so happened that we stayed at the same hotel in Addis Ababa where I booked a shared room with another girl for two nights. That girl left with her fiancé the next day without telling me while I was out shopping. She was gone when I got back to our hotel.

My guy, who seemed to be closely watching for an opportunity, jumped into my hotel room as I opened the door. I was shaking in fear of what he would do to me. It was my first time all by myself in that kind of situation. When he noticed how scared I was, he said to me, "I will not touch you, trust me. I just want to ask you why you didn't want me." I spoke my mind in telling him I didn't want him because our personalities didn't match, and he went back to his room. I could see from his face that he was so sad, but he didn't express his emotions verbally. After he left, I went to the hotel's reservations desk and switched my room. I kept my distance after our return to Bodji the next day. Little did I know, this closed door would open again two years later.

The man, who had seemed to be watching closely for an opportunity, rushed into my hotel room the moment I opened the door. I was trembling with fear, unsure of what he might do. It was the first time I had ever been alone in such a situation. When he saw how frightened I was, he said, "I will not touch you—trust me. I just want to ask why you did not want me."

I spoke honestly and told him that I did not want him because our personalities did not match. After that, he returned to his room. I could see from his face that he was deeply hurt, though he did not voice his emotions. Once he left, I immediately went to the hotel's reception desk and requested a different room. After we returned to Bodji the next day, I kept my distance and believed the matter was finally settled. I did not yet know that what I thought was a firmly closed door was only temporarily shut—and that two years later, it would open again, bringing consequences I could not yet imagine.

In August 1974, I traveled to Addis Ababa once again to attend a three-day workshop entitled Training Women for Leadership, organized by Reverend Eva Zabolai-Csekme of the Lutheran World Federation in Geneva. From the moment I arrived, I sensed that this journey carried more than professional purpose—it was a divinely appointed trip.

During that visit, an unexpected door opened when I met a Swedish nurse named Alpha Fraim in Addis Ababa. She was serving with the Swedish International Development Authority (SIDA) as the director of a newly established pediatric nurse practitioner program. Although Alpha had already completed recruiting nursing students from all regions of Ethiopia, she invited me to complete an application in her office.

The following day, she placed an acceptance letter in my hands, informing me that the course would begin in January 1975 and that I was to report to SIDA in Addis Ababa one month before the program started. To me, this was nothing less than a miracle. Normally, only nurses employed by the Ministry of Health and formally recommended by their institutions were eligible for such training. Yet God made a way where none seemed possible. When I returned to Bodji, I submitted my request for a leave of absence to attend the pediatric nurse practitioner course, fully aware that this opportunity marked the beginning of a new season of preparation—one that would further refine my calling and expand the reach of my service.

The Unimagined and Shocking Regime Change

Something unimaginable happened two months before I was to travel to Addis Ababa to attend the course. The Ethiopian New Year falls on September 11—or September 12 in a leap year. On the morning of September 12, 1974, I turned on my radio to listen to the news and heard an announcement I had never imagined or expected.

The broadcast declared, "His Majesty Haile Selassie I has been removed from the imperial throne and is being taken to the place prepared for him." For the first time ever, the title His Imperial Majesty was omitted. The announcement was followed by voices shouting at the emperor, "Leba! Leba! Tafari leba! Tafari leba!"—"Thief! Thief! Tafari thief!" As someone who had personally benefited from the emperor's good deeds for his country, I knew immediately that this marked a dark turning point. I sensed that difficult days lay ahead for the nation.

Immediately after removing the emperor from his palace, the lower-ranking military group that overthrew him decreed itself the Provisional Military Administrative Council (the Derg) and took control of the government on September 15, 1974. All imperial administrative structures, the court systems, and the imperial constitution were abolished. In essence, the world's oldest monarchy, which had claimed direct descent from King Menelik I, the son of the biblical King Solomon of Israel and the queen of Sheba of Ethiopia, was put in its coffin and buried.

Located in the tropical zone of East Africa, between the equator and the Tropic of Cancer, Ethiopia, is one of the oldest countries in the world—over three thousand years old. Archaeological findings confirm that Ethiopia is the origin of humankind—a 3.5-millionyear-old complete human skeleton, Lucy, was discovered in 1974 in the Awash region, 224 kilometers from Addis Ababa, by an American paleoanthropologist named Dr. Donald C. Johnson.

Following Lucy's unearthing, archaeologists also discovered a human skeleton that the scientists named Idaltu, meaning "elder," dating back 5.8 million years. Ethiopia is also the resting place of the ark of the covenant, which lies in St. Mary of Zion's church in Axum, guarded by a succession of anointed virgin monks. The ancient Ethiopian monarchy did not have a formal constitution with religious and traditional laws as its basis until Emperor Haile Selassie I had a modern constitution adopted for the first time in the nation's history, in 1931, revised in 1955. The emperor's failure to consider that his reform system might need to be updated finally invited the coup.

Two months after Emperor Haile Selassie I was overthrown, I traveled to Addis Ababa to enroll in the pediatric nurse practitioner course. Alpha Fraim, the program director, arranged for me to stay at the nurses' residence at Princess Tsehai Hospital—now known as the Armed Forces Hospital—until SIDA secured housing for its students. There were ten students in the program: two from Addis Ababa and eight from different regions of the country.

I arrived in the capital at a moment when uncertainty had begun to seep into daily life. Although there were no widespread demonstrations in other parts of the country, Addis Ababa felt tense and unsettled. People spoke in hushed tones, watching closely to see what the new order would bring. Immediately after the emperor's removal on September 11, 1974 (September 12 in a leap year), the Derg announced the appointment of Lieutenant General Aman Mikael Andom, a widely respected military figure, as chairman and acting head of state. As I stepped into this new season of professional training, I did so against the backdrop of a nation redefining itself—uncertain, fragile, and standing at the threshold of profound change.

The Bloody Regime Change Crisis Begins

On the evening of November 23, 1974—just two days after I arrived in Addis Ababa—I was in my room when I heard what sounded like a chain of thunderstorms. It was later revealed to be heavy gunfire directed toward General Aman Andom's residence. In that moment, it felt as though the world was coming to an end. The lights were turned off in all the surrounding rooms. While the other nurses quietly hid under their beds, I found myself washing my clothes, strangely unafraid, as if a deep calm had settled over me despite the chaos outside.

The next morning, we heard shocking news on the state-controlled radio: the general had been executed, along with some of his supporters and sixty former officials of the imperial government whom the Derg[5] had arrested. Because the nurses' residence within the hospital compound was so close to General Aman's home, several fellow nurses and I ran there after hearing the announcement. The walls were riddled with holes. It looked as though a storm of bullets had battered the house from every direction—a silent testimony to the violence of the night before.

On December 20, 1974, the Derg proclaimed socialism as Ethiopia's official ideology—an ideology I deeply opposed because of my Christian faith. That was the context in which I began my new course, under a government that openly rejected the values I held most dear. Faith, which had always guided my life and work, was now viewed with suspicion, even hostility.

That same day, the Derg issued a policy document calling for public ownership of the economy. In the same month, Yekatit 66 Political School was established to train political cadres with the purpose of reshaping how people thought, spoke, and believed. By February 1975, privately owned businesses—including banks, insurance companies, and all foreign-owned enterprises—were nationalized without compensation. By the end of 1975, all private businesses, industries, and properties had been absorbed by the state.

Daily life began to change rapidly. Fear replaced trust, silence replaced open conversation, and loyalty to the new ideology was increasingly demanded. As the nation was being stripped of its freedoms, I felt the weight of a deeper test—not only of my professional path, but of my faith, my convictions, and my courage to remain steadfast in a time when obedience to God carried an unseen cost.

As part of the Derg's propaganda, mass ownership was declared, asserting that the sefiw hizb—the mass population—were the rightful owners. In practice, this socialist principle of "from each according to

---

[5] Derg: A military junta established on June 21, 1974, originally known as the Coordinating Committee of the Armed Forces, Police, and Territorial Army. Formed by junior and mid-level officers of the Imperial Ethiopian Army and members of the police, the Derg overthrew Emperor Haile Selassie I and assumed control of the Ethiopian government.

his ability, to each according to his needs" turned those who had never labored for property or investment into overseers of the very people whose assets had been confiscated. Power was redistributed not through justice, but through ideology.

Evangelical Christians, especially those actively involved in outreach, became prime targets of persecution. Many were imprisoned, interrogated, tortured, and killed for refusing to renounce their faith. Evangelical churches were closed, Christian gatherings were banned or tightly controlled, and public worship was no longer permitted. Forced underground, the church adapted—and, against all odds, grew. What the regime sought to silence instead multiplied through faith, resilience, and quiet courage.

I remained at the nurses' residence for six weeks before moving into a beautiful villa that SIDA rented for us students—a five-bedroom, two-bath home in Old Airport, about two miles from Princess Tsehai Hospital, now known as the Armed Forces Hospital. Our pediatric nurse practitioner course was held at the nation's medical school adjacent to Black Lion Hospital, where the Ethio-Swedish Children's Hospital was located. Each day, we traveled to and from school by bus or taxi, pursuing advanced medical training while the nation around us unraveled.

SIDA continued to pay us 70 percent of the salaries we had earned before enrolling in the program. These privileges, however, provoked resentment within the Ministry of Health under the new socialist government. Officials accused SIDA of spoiling its students, placing Alpha Fraim in a prolonged struggle as she defended our rights. Alpha firmly insisted that the standard of living students had before entering the program should be maintained.

The tension between the Ministry of Health and SIDA persisted until our graduation. Unable to reach an agreement, SIDA ultimately terminated the program, making my class both the first and the last to complete this course. The irony was striking: while political freedoms were being stripped away and faith suppressed, opportunities for world-class education—made possible through international partnership—were still shaping lives.

I often reflected on the legacy of Emperor Haile Selassie I and the strong relationships he had cultivated with the United States and Sweden. Those relationships continued to bear fruit even after his removal, allowing us to receive exceptional training in a time of national darkness. For me, this contrast—between oppression and opportunity, fear and preparation—became a defining lesson. It shaped my understanding that even in seasons of restriction, God can still equip His servants for what lies ahead.

I returned to Bodji immediately after graduating and resumed life with my Swedish nurse roommate. Upon my return, I discovered that everything was exactly as it had been when I first took the job at the clinic. The mobile maternal and child health (MCH) clinics I had established at the four sites had stopped while I was away attending the pediatric nurse practitioner course. The referral and accompaniment services I had put in place for women with complicated deliveries had also ceased.

It was deeply saddening and frustrating to realize that all the critical services I had worked so hard to establish had completely collapsed in my absence. Once again, I found myself rebuilding from the ground up. Restarting the four mobile MCH clinics required approval from the Synod's medical committee, which I promptly sought.

Dr. Kretchmer, the head of the medical committee, approved my application without hesitation. He even shared that the people of Bodji had submitted a complaint against the other Swedish nurse and had asked the Synod to bring me back, unaware that I had only been away on a leave of absence. That affirmation strengthened my resolve, but it did not mean the path ahead would be smooth.

About a month after my return, a Swedish missionary couple arrived with their two children and moved in temporarily with the other Swedish nurse and me. The wife, who was also a nurse, began working part-time at the clinic. At the time, their arrival seemed harmless, even welcome— but it soon became clear that this change would introduce a new set of challenges, ushering in yet another season of testing, discernment, and endurance.

One evening, while I was on duty, a woman in labor was brought to the clinic by male porters who carried her on a stretcher. Upon examination, I discovered that the baby was in a transverse position, which could only be delivered by cesarean section. I immediately asked the porters to contribute money for gas and transported the woman to Gimbi Hospital in the Synod president's car. She underwent a cesarean section as soon as she was admitted, and I returned to Bodji.

When I arrived home, it was 4:40 a.m. I went straight to bed and woke up at 8:15 a.m., ready to go to work. As I walked toward the dining room to eat breakfast, I suddenly heard what sounded like a thunderstorm. It was the new part-time Swedish nurse shouting at me, "Agitu! There are patients waiting for you on the veranda! Go to work right now!"

The tone of her voice and the way she carried herself—as someone the culture viewed as a "superior" white missionary—made me sense white supremacy for the first time in my life, and on my own soil. I had grown up accustomed to discipline and being told what to do, but this was different. There was a new quality in her words: the belief that she belonged to a higher class of human being. I did not believe that—never had.

It was deeply unpleasant to be addressed in this way, and even more unsettling to realize that I knew better. I had never experienced anything like this with the Swedish missionary teachers at the Swedish mission school in Nedjo, nor with the Swedish missionary pastors and their families. But the missionary nurses were different. That moment stayed with me.

3

ENTERING NEW CHAPTERS OF LIFE

The gate to my journey through fire opened in the very first week after I returned to Bodji, having completed my pediatric nurse practitioner course. I had assumed that the man who had shown interest in me two years earlier would have moved on after my long absence, but I was wrong. He returned with what appeared to be an angelic demeanor—quiet, gentle, and carefully composed. When I realized that neither his intentions nor my inner response had changed, I felt an unsettling weight settle over me. My heart did not welcome him. I knew I was standing at the edge of a difficult path, because our personalities were deeply mismatched.

What troubled me most was not what others saw, but what I sensed. In that small village, he was widely admired as a sober, gentle, and kind man. Scripture says, "Even a fool is counted wise when he holds his peace; when he shuts his lips, he is considered perceptive" (Proverbs 17:28). His silence worked in his favor, earning him a reputation for wisdom. Even my own father questioned how I could refuse such a man.

Yet from the beginning, my spirit was unsettled. My discernment never wavered. Beneath the calm exterior, I sensed something I could not reconcile with peace or trust. I feared entering a marriage that would demand silence from me rather than partnership. His inwardness left me unable to see who he truly was—what he loved, what angered him, what shaped his faith. I did not yet have proof for what I felt, only a quiet warning within me. But I have learned that when discernment speaks softly, it is often preparing the heart for trials it cannot yet name.

All of this reinforced my reservations about him, and I made my rejection clear. First, I did not want to marry quickly. Second, I did not believe he was the right person for me; in nearly every way, we were opposites. He came from a rural area far removed from the Swedish mission school we had both attended, and he did not share the depth of spiritual experience I had grown up with. While I was the eldest in my family, he was the youngest of four siblings, raised by his widowed mother.

We differed even in temperament and presence. He was six feet tall—introverted, handsome, and very quiet. I was five foot one, extroverted, direct, open, and deeply expressive in my faith. Spiritually, all I knew of him was that he attended church on Sundays and participated in Holy Communion once a month. Beyond that, I could not discern the substance of his inner spiritual life. After months of wrestling with these thoughts, I made the decision to marry him. Even now, I do not fully understand why.

According to our traditions, soon after I accepted the marriage proposal, elders were sent to my parents' home to seek their approval. Once my parents consented, the wedding date was set for three months later, and preparations began immediately. My fiancé took me to Addis Ababa to have a custom-made wedding dress sewn for me—one that cost twice as much as a Western wedding dress. It took a full month to complete.

As the wedding approached, I took a two-week leave and arrived at my parents' house a week before the ceremony. On the evening I arrived, I watched neighborhood girls gather at the front door, singing traditional wedding songs. In our culture, girls begin singing a month before the wedding and continue every evening until the wedding day. Their voices carried joy, anticipation, and blessing—sounds meant to usher a bride into a hopeful future.

Everyone around me was celebrating. Inside, I was unraveling. While the songs rose each evening, my heart sank lower. My inner voice warned me that by proceeding against my deepest convictions, I was walking into

Gehenna on earth. There was no premarital counseling, no safe space to seek guidance or clarity. I carried my fear alone.

That final week at my parents' home was filled with outward festivity and inward torment. I smiled when expected, listened when spoken to, and prepared when instructed—yet inside I was overwhelmed by dread, fear, and uncertainty about the life I was about to enter. As the wedding day drew closer, the distance between what was being celebrated publicly and what I was experiencing privately grew unbearably wide.

The Friday before my wedding day, I cried without stopping, as if I were being forced into something I could not escape. I feared the marriage would be difficult and felt as though I were stepping through a door with no return. But with family already gathered and the celebrations underway, there was no space left to reconsider.

Around 1:00 a.m., the woman baking *injera*[6] for the wedding found me vomiting while I wept and woke my father. He did not ask why I was crying. Instead, he said, "I see no reason for you to cry. You are marrying a man who will never disappoint you in any way. I once traveled with him and saw how he treated me. He is the best."

In that moment, I understood that my fear would not be heard. I stood alone inside a decision that had already been sealed.

As dawn broke that Sunday morning, I felt as though I were standing at the edge of my own life, watching it move forward without me. My tears had changed nothing. The songs, the preparations, the expectations—all continued, indifferent to the turmoil in my soul. In our culture, a bride's silence is often mistaken for consent, and endurance for obedience. That morning, I learned how easily a woman's fear can be hidden beneath celebration.

When the sun rose, there was no turning back. What had been decided by families, tradition, and time now carried the weight of permanence. I did not walk toward marriage with joy or anticipation, but with a heart bracing itself for survival. I did not yet know how deeply this choice would

---

[6] A Pancake like spongy Ethiopian bread

refine me, nor how costly obedience would become—but I sensed that something sacred in me was being asked to endure fire.

The groom's party arrived at 9:00 a.m. The girls who had been singing every evening for a month blocked the entrance as the groom and his party attempted to enter, chanting the traditional song, "Hinkennu balabala abbakoo, sihacufu balballi abbakoo"—"I will not give you entrance to my father's door; let my father's door spit you out." His best men offered the girls money, but they refused to relent. In the end, the best men had to push the girls aside by force to gain entry—the customary conclusion to this ritual exchange.

After breakfast was served, we walked to the church at 10:00 a.m., about eight hundred feet from my parents' house. Our wedding ceremony followed a Western style. After the officiating pastor delivered his sermon, Evangelist Djalata Negeri read a poem he had prepared for the occasion. In it, he proclaimed, "Dubbatee sihinarsu, dha'ee sillalessu"—meaning, "No offensive word from his mouth to irritate you, no battery from him to harm you." My heart, however, did not believe it.

We exchanged our vows—"until death do us part" and "for better or for worse"—immediately after the service. Even as I spoke the words, my heart knew that my portion would be "for worse." After the ceremony, we took photographs outside the church and then returned to my parents' house, where the wedding feast awaited us.

Something unexpected happened when we arrived at our hotel for the honeymoon. One man ran toward me from the hotel and gave me a tight, unsolicited hug as we were heading to the reservation desk.

"Is this man normal?" my husband asked.

One of the hotel attendants stepped between them and said, "He is drunk, sir," preventing what could have turned into a confrontation. My husband then turned toward me and said, "One man on a bus once tried to touch you while you were walking in front of me. I pulled his hand down hard through the window to punish him, and now I am facing this again."

Soon after we returned from our honeymoon, my parents invited us for mana'asseenna[7]—"coming home" in Afaan Oromo. The mana'asseenna dinner was the second feast following our wedding, and relatives and friends were invited.

The next morning, my husband told me he wanted to speak with me privately and led me to the nearest forest. I assumed it was for something important, but to my surprise, it became a conversation that ushered me into a life of pain. With a serious expression, he told me plainly that he had married me to exact revenge for what he felt was my mistreatment of him before our marriage.

At the time, I did not take his words seriously. I assumed he was reacting out of offense after seeing me have a private conversation with my father during the mana'asseenna dinner the night before. By nature, I am a positive person, and I did not believe he truly meant what he said. Yet his words stirred a memory—the warning my cousin, Hanna Geneti, had given me not to marry him, fearing that he would seek revenge after marriage. Even so, I tried to dismiss the unease. I did not yet understand that this moment marked the beginning of a painful pattern. Meanwhile, what seemed like the best "welcome gift" was already waiting for us from the Synod.

Upon our return from the mana'asseenna, we moved into the brand-new house the Synod had given us—a beautifully designed villa with a breathtaking view, surrounded by forest. It had a spacious living room with a wood-burning fireplace, a large dining room, a generous Western-style kitchen, two bedrooms, one bathroom, and a storage room attached to the right side of the kitchen entrance. There were three entrances: the front door faced east, the back door opened onto a deck, and the kitchen door was on the right side of the house. I still miss that beautiful home.

We hired a servant and began our new life together as a couple, despite our completely opposite personalities and upbringing. My vacation ended,

---

[7] The bride's side of family reunion

and I returned to work immediately after moving into our new home. It was just my husband and me living in that large house. We both came home during our lunch breaks.

My mother-in-law was often there when I returned from work in the evenings. She had once been a source of joy—lively, sociable, and warm. I loved her deeply, and she loved me as well, though that love did not come easily. I noticed her negative attitude toward me almost immediately after I married her son, but I did not take it seriously. By nature, I do not dwell on negative thoughts.

I did not realize she harbored a grudge against me until I brought her to our home to care for her when her bronchial asthma became severe. I administered her medications and injections daily and woke up at night to check on her condition. When she did not improve, I became deeply concerned and purchased a different asthma medication. Before giving it to her, I explained that I had bought it because she was not responding to the free medication.

She suddenly began to cry. Confused, I asked her, "What did I do wrong? Why are you crying?" She replied, "I am crying because I was so mean to you, yet you have still been so kind to me. I was angry that you ignored me when you left for school. Other girls were so obsessed with my son that they brought us food and drinks to impress him, but you didn't even say goodbye to me."

The truth was that I did not know her at the time, nor was I interested in her son, so I had no reason to behave that way. We both apologized to one another and forgave each other. After that, we bonded deeply. She had raised her older sons' and daughters' children together with them, and over time she treated me with genuine affection.

One day, she sat me down and spoke to me candidly about my husband's character. She offered wise counsel on how to manage my marriage with her son and disclosed behaviors of his that were unacceptable—details I do not feel comfortable sharing. She then gave me two specific pieces of advice.

First, she said, "Have him hand his entire salary to you every payday, and manage it yourself."

Second, she warned, "Do not bring these two grandchildren of mine"—she mentioned them by name—"into your marriage. They are very clever and will steal his heart and take advantage of him at the expense of your marriage."

I asked her why she had not told me these things before I married him. She replied that she had been afraid of losing me. Before our marriage, my husband's mother had lived with him, and she knew him far better than I did at the time. Unfortunately, I did not listen to her advice. My positive and kind heart led me to believe she was simply being hard on her son, and I have regretted that decision ever since.

During the first few months of our marriage, he seemed kind despite our communication problems, and I genuinely tried to be a good wife. I did my best to live by 1 Peter 3:1–2 (NKJV): *"Wives, likewise, be submissive to your own husbands, that even if some do not obey the word, they, without a word, may be won by the conduct of their wives,

Disagreements between my husband and me began soon after we started our life together. The most difficult challenge in the early stages of our marriage was my inability to cope with his sarcastic communication style. I took our conversations seriously and was deeply hurt, as I was not accustomed to that kind of joking. When my mother-in-law was present and heard us argue, she would often say, "You two turn a minor issue into a big deal." I tried to adapt by responding with sarcasm myself, but that proved dangerous for me.

One day, he said to me, "You wouldn't have found anyone to marry you if I hadn't married you."

I replied, "Yes, after a long search, I found an indiscriminate man and grabbed him quickly."

Although we were both joking, he became enraged and rushed toward me to beat me. I had to run to avoid being harmed.

My first year of marriage was extremely stressful. Alongside the physical toll of pregnancy and severe morning sickness, I carried a heavy workload at the clinic. Patients pressured me to see them, insisting that the Swedish nurse did not speak their language well enough to treat them properly. The clinic clerk later told me that patients repeatedly urged him to direct their medical needs to me instead of the Swedish nurse, though he divided the cases evenly between us.

What an unexpected shift it was. Traditionally, white missionaries were highly regarded and favored over the native population. I was therefore astonished to see patients actively seeking me out instead of the Swedish nurses. The clinic clerk later told me that they repeatedly pressured him to direct their medical needs to me rather than to the Swedish nurse, though he divided the cases evenly between us.

One evening, while the Swedish nurse was on duty, a family caring for a woman in labor came to my house, pleading with me to deliver her baby. At the time, I was five months pregnant, but I could not bring myself to refuse. I went with them.

The woman was already in the second stage of labor, and the baby showed signs of fetal distress. I had no choice but to perform a vacuum extraction to deliver the baby quickly, which I managed to do successfully. The following day, however, I became ill as a result of exerting myself during the delivery while I was pregnant.

Unexpectedly, I gave birth to my first baby five weeks before my due date, largely due to my excessive workload. On the day labor began, I started feeling pain in my lower abdomen around 11:00 a.m. The Swedish nurse was in Sweden on her long summer vacation, and the medical doctor assigned to cover in her absence was sick that day. I was stretched to my limits, moving constantly between treating outpatients and running to the labor room to check on women who had been admitted. That day, I examined 106 patients entirely on my own.

Even as the pain intensified in the afternoon, I did not recognize it as labor. I assumed it was an early symptom of amebiasis, since the sharp pain was located below my umbilicus, and I took pain-relief tablets. Instead of subsiding, the pain grew stronger and more frequent. At that point, a newly assigned female health assistant from Aira suspected I might be in labor. She convinced me to be examined, telling me that she herself had delivered before her due date. When she checked me, she said my cervix was already dilated three fingers.

Hearing that, I panicked as images of what I had learned in school—and what I had witnessed while assisting primigravida (first-time) deliveries—flooded my mind. It was then my turn to be rushed to Gimbi Hospital, since there was no one available to deliver me at the clinic. Unlike the women in labor I had accompanied before, my delivery was rapid and uncomplicated.

We arrived at the hospital around 9:30 p.m. My husband, a tall man with long arms, carried me into the labor room and placed me on the examination bed. Fortunately, I weighed only fifty-two kilograms and was not too heavy for him. The doctor arrived about ten minutes later, but my baby was born before he even had time to put on his gloves. Had my husband waited for a stretcher, I likely would have delivered in the car. It was an unimaginably easy birth.

I was overwhelmed with joy as I saw and held my beautiful baby boy. In our culture, it is considered a great honor when the firstborn is male, but that did not matter to me. I was simply grateful to have delivered a healthy baby.

The next morning, I woke up early and pleaded with the doctor to let me go home, but hospital policy did not allow discharge within twenty-four hours of delivery. I had to wait until the following morning before I was released and could return home to Bodji. Returning home to Bodji with a newborn did not bring rest. Instead, it marked the beginning of another season of endurance. My body was still weak from childbirth, yet the demands of life and work did not pause. I had entered motherhood the same way I had entered so many other roles in my life—carrying responsibility before recovery, duty before rest.

As I cared for my infant son, I also continued to care for a community that relied heavily on me. There was little space to slow down or heal. Looking back, I see how that early pattern of self-sacrifice followed me into motherhood, just as it had shaped my marriage and my calling. I did not yet know how to ask for help, nor did I believe I was allowed to stop. Even so, holding my baby reminded me why I endured. In the midst of exhaustion and strain, his presence became both comfort and strength—a quiet assurance that life, even when born under pressure, could still be a gift of grace.

Returning home to Bodji with a newborn did not mean I was left without care. In our culture, a mother is traditionally nursed for one full month after giving birth. During that time, servants and family members attend to her needs so she can rest, eat, and regain her strength. Before delivery, multigrain flour and special food items are prepared in advance, ensuring the mother is nourished properly during her recovery.

I, too, was surrounded by this care. My body was given time to rest, and I was supported in ways our culture values deeply. Yet even within this season of nursing and protection, responsibility waited just beyond the threshold. I knew that once the month passed, I would return to a life already heavy with expectation—motherhood layered onto marriage, work, and calling.

Those quiet weeks of rest were a gift. They allowed my body to heal and my heart to bond with my son. Still, they also marked the brief pause before endurance was once again required. In my life, even seasons of care were often preparation for what lay ahead. Just three weeks after I gave birth to my first child, my husband left for Addis Ababa and enrolled at Addis Ababa University to complete his degree program, leaving his newborn son and me behind.

When I Encountered Prejudice on My Own Soil

After completing my one-month maternity leave, I returned to work and immediately faced an unacceptable situation on my very first Thursday back. The health assistants were out running the mobile MCH clinic I had established, since I was breastfeeding and unable to travel. That day, only the new Swedish nurse, the clerk, and I were at the clinic.

When I arrived at 8:00 a.m., the new Swedish nurse instructed me to administer medications, injections, and treatments until the 10:00 a.m. coffee break, while she examined patients and wrote prescriptions.

I politely asked, "What about the language barrier?"

"Etana will translate for me," she replied.

Etana, the clerk, spoke very limited English. Normally, the two health assistants took turns translating when she saw patients. I sensed prejudice in the arrangement but simply said, "Okay."

The patients who came to me with prescriptions complained, yet I did my best to calm and reassure them.

At 10:00 a.m., I went home to breastfeed my baby during the coffee break. The Swedish nurse did not take her break. Instead, she continued clearing outpatients before I returned, apparently so she would not have to treat the patients I examined afterward.

When I returned to the clinic, the injection and dressing rooms were overflowing with patients waiting for me and holding their prescriptions. I was overwhelmed and deeply disappointed. I said to her, "What are you doing? I can't take this." Then I left for home, determined to submit my resignation to the Synod the next day.

At 5:00 p.m., she came to my house. The first words she spoke upon entering were, "I didn't even have a coffee break or lunch."

I told her I was deeply upset by the prejudice I sensed and that I had decided to resign. Only then did she apologize and ask me not to quit. I questioned the sincerity of her apology, since it came only after I mentioned resigning. Still, I accepted it and chose to remain in my position. My decision to stay did not ease the weight I was carrying. My husband was away in Addis Ababa, absorbed in his studies, while I remained in Bodji with a newborn, a demanding job, and a growing sense of isolation. The absence of a partner at home made the pressures at work feel heavier. There was no one to share the day's burden with, no place to set down my exhaustion.

I was returning to full responsibility too soon—emotionally and physically. Breastfeeding, caring for my baby, managing a household, and serving a community that depended on me left little room to recover. The strain I felt at the clinic was not separate from my personal life; it flowed directly from it.

That period marked the beginning of a pattern I would come to recognize later—being left to carry heavy responsibilities alone, both at home and at work, while trying to maintain peace, professionalism, and faith. At the time, I did not yet name it as such. I simply endured, believing that perseverance was the right response and that relief would eventually come.

Wise Counsel that Changed my Future

In December 1976, three months after my husband left for college, my father came to visit my baby and me.

After dinner, he sat me down and asked, "Isn't this house beautiful?"

I proudly replied, "Yes, it is."

He leaned closer and asked, "You like it, don't you?"

"Very much," I answered.

Then he said something that changed the direction of my life: "But it is not yours, and its beauty will not elevate the status of your life. If you wait for your husband to return and plan to stay here in Bodji permanently, you will be no better off than your mother, who is illiterate. Think about the future of your children. You must move to Addis Ababa before your husband returns. Buy a plot of land there and build a home for yourself and your family."

After he left, I reflected deeply on his words. I decided to move to Addis Ababa as soon as possible, trusting that my husband would accept my decision. At that time, our marriage was still stable. I was fortunate to secure a ride with members of the Synod administrative staff who were traveling on official business to their headquarters in Addis Ababa.

A week later, we began our journey at 10:00 a.m. I sat in the front passenger seat, holding my four-month-old baby for the 470-kilometer trip. There were no car seats for children in those days. We had to spend the night at the Synod guesthouse in Nekemte because it was impossible to reach Addis Ababa in one day.

The next morning, we resumed our journey at 6:00 a.m. We continued our journey to Addis Ababa, which was still 317 kilometers (197 miles) away. As we drew closer to the city, the driver informed us that we would be stopped at a security checkpoint and that everyone would have to get out of the car to be searched. At the time, tensions were escalating because of internal power struggles within the Derg, the new socialist government. Eventually, the bearing of arms was prohibited, and all travelers entering Addis Ababa were required to pass through security checkpoints located at the north, south, east, and west entrances to the city.

As expected, we were stopped by armed, uniformed officers at a checkpoint about thirty miles outside Addis Ababa. The officers instructed the driver and the three men seated in the back to get out of the car so it could be searched. Because I was holding a baby, they allowed me to remain seated.

Before the officers conducted their search, I had hidden my husband's pistol in the diaper bag beneath my feet. Surprisingly, I felt no fear. Praise God—they did not touch the diaper bag, and I remained safe. After completing the search, the officers thoroughly checked the four men from head to foot and then allowed them to return to the car.

We continued on and arrived in Addis Ababa at 2:30 p.m., stopping at the German Mission guesthouse of the Ethiopian Evangelical Church Mekane Yesus. Upon arrival, I was assigned a fully furnished, Western-style guesthouse with a living room, dining room, bedroom, bathroom, Western-style kitchen, and even a bottle warmer for my baby.

My husband stayed at the Mekane Yesus Hostel at Arat Kilo, within walking distance of the university he was attending and approximately fifteen miles from the guesthouse. After settling in, caring for my baby, and preparing dinner, I sent a messenger to ask my husband to come. He did not have a telephone in his room, so this was the only way to reach him. He then came to the guesthouse right away. The first thing he said upon his arrival was, "What a surprise!" Dinner was already on the table, and my baby was asleep when he arrived. After we ate, I explained how I had decided to move to Addis Ababa, and he agreed with the plan. That evening, he returned to his hostel and brought back his belongings so he could stay with us.

The following week, my husband switched to evening classes and accepted a full-time position as an accountant at the Mekane Yesus headquarters—the same role he had held at the Western Synod in Bodji. He needed to do this in order for us to be eligible for housing, since Mekane Yesus provided housing only for missionaries and Ethiopian employees holding key positions. That same week, I began looking for work in Addis Ababa. I applied for an opening at the Defense Industries of the Ethiopian Ministry of National Defense to serve as head of the clinic.

We stayed at the German mission guesthouse for three weeks before moving to a fully furnished two-bedroom American mission guesthouse in a gated compound in Mekenisa. The administrator of the American mission guesthouse, Mrs. Lorene Blisi, gave us a custom-made adjustable bed for our son. She explained that it had been made in America and brought from there. The compound also included a two-story unit where two Ethiopian pastors and their families lived, another two-bedroom guesthouse next to ours, and a conference hall. A roundabout in front of our house separated the different buildings.

The first week in our new location felt especially fortunate for me. I was invited to take a pre-employment test at the Addis Ababa University Testing Center for the position I had applied for two weeks earlier. I took the test alongside several other candidates and received a job offer two weeks later.

The employment process surprised me. Despite the newly established socialist government's strong opposition to Christianity, I was required to place my right hand on the Bible and be sworn in for the government position. Defense Industries consisted of eleven departments, including the clinic, and I was appointed head of the clinic.

Stepping into my new role as head of the clinic marked another turning point in my life. Once again, I found myself entrusted with leadership in an unfamiliar and demanding environment. The responsibility was significant, not only because of the position itself, but because it came within a government system that openly opposed the faith that shaped my life.

I entered the clinic with a deep sense of duty and humility. My training and experience had prepared me professionally, but I was keenly aware that wisdom, discernment, and integrity would be just as necessary as medical skill. Leading under a socialist government required caution, balance, and restraint—especially as a Christian woman in a position of authority. Even so, I was determined to serve with excellence. I believed that competence, fairness, and compassion would speak louder than ideology. I did not know then how quickly my leadership would be tested, but I understood that this position was not accidental.

4

SWEET AND SOUR

I was beginning a new life as a government employee in the nation's capital, transitioning from a rural life rooted in a Christian setting to a more secular environment. Although our personal lifestyle did not change much after moving to Addis Ababa, the character of the city itself was entirely different from that of Bodji.

Addis Ababa offered features that did not exist in the small, isolated rural village—taxis and buses, electricity, potable water, convenience stores, and other urban amenities. In Bodji, however, the Synod had already provided electricity, clean water, and modern housing within a quiet, protected setting. For that reason, city life did not particularly appeal to me. I genuinely liked my new, stress-free job. The respect and appreciation I received from the director of Defense Industries, General Alemayehu Agonafer, during my first three months of employment made the position even more satisfying.

At that time, new employees were required to complete a six-month probation period and undergo evaluation before becoming permanent staff. However, I was granted permanent employee status after just ten weeks. The clinic provided first-aid services to civilian employees only. Although Defense Industries was a large operation with heavy machinery, workers were well trained in safety precautions. As a result, very few employees visited the clinic, and those who did usually came for minor ailments such as headaches. Employees with more serious conditions were referred to the army hospital.

Sweeter than I Imagined

The bloody revolution I mentioned earlier was unfolding steadily by the time we settled into the American Mission guesthouse in Mekenisa. Despite the ongoing political tension, everything aligned well for me as I resettled in Addis Ababa. The bloody revolution I mentioned earlier was unfolding steadily by the time we settled into the American Mission guesthouse in Mekenisa. Despite the ongoing political tension, everything aligned well for me as I resettled in Addis Ababa.

A few weeks after we moved into the American mission guesthouse in Mekenisa, a Norwegian missionary visited our home and offered to sell me a baby walker and a unique stroller. The stroller included a diaper bag and springs on both sides that allowed it to rock gently and soothe the baby to sleep. It could also be used as a bed. At that time, strollers were not common in Addis Ababa, even years later when I left the country. This one was especially unusual—I had never seen anything like it, not even in the United States.

My Mother Vising Us at the American Mission Guesthouse

In that same month, my husband found a timely opportunity to buy a used Renault car in excellent condition from another missionary. After moving to Addis Ababa, our workplaces were no longer within walking distance. We had to rely on taxis, city buses, or driving. We bought the car immediately, even though neither of us knew how to drive at the time.

Obtaining a driver's license in those days was not easy. A driver had to pass all three required tests—the written exam, mesenakel (obstacle course), and the road test on city streets—to be licensed in Addis Ababa. The mesenakel and road tests were the most difficult. During the road test, stopping on a hill without using the brake—without letting the car roll backward—was especially challenging. It required carefully balancing the clutch and gas pedal halfway so the car would hold its position. To make matters worse, many examiners were corrupt. As a result, many applicants had to retake the tests several times. By God's grace, I passed all three on my first attempt. Praise God!

More blessings followed our car purchase. A few weeks later, a British woman offered to sell me a very fine car seat for my six-month-old baby, which I gladly bought. I was likely the first Ethiopian to own a car seat for a child. Car seats were not common in Addis Ababa until long after I left the country. Both the stroller and the car seat were of excellent quality and were later used by all five of my children. In many ways, my children had what Western children have today, even back then.

I also maintained a high standard of childcare, shaped by my training as a pediatric nurse practitioner and the hygienic lifestyle I learned from my grandmother early in life. I fed my babies on a strict schedule and breastfed until my milk dried naturally—usually around nine months. Bottle-feeding quantities were carefully measured according to age. I used sterile techniques when handling feeding bottles and nipples, including forceps, and required any nannies or relatives with colds to wear masks when caring for the baby. I used white cotton cloth for diapers, which were thoroughly washed, boiled until spotless, and ironed. I also used plastic diaper liners and diaper rash cream imported from Sweden.

Order became my shield. In a world that often felt uncertain—politically, professionally, and personally—I found comfort in structure, discipline, and excellence. Caring meticulously for my children was not merely routine; it was my way of creating stability in the midst of instability. Cleanliness, schedules, proper nutrition, and safety were things I could control.

Motherhood gave me purpose beyond survival. While other areas of my life were shifting, I poured my energy into raising my children with intention, dignity, and high standards. I wanted them protected, prepared, and positioned for a better future. Yet even as I built this carefully ordered life, subtle cracks were forming elsewhere. Stability on the surface did not always mean peace underneath. In time, circumstances within my marriage would begin to challenge the very structure I had worked so hard to establish.

Another opportunity came my way amid the adversity the city was enduring under the brutal communist government. As mentioned earlier, the EPRP's White Terror provoked the Derg into an immediate and violent counteroffensive against the EPRP and all those it considered enemies. I watched on Ethiopian television as Colonel Mengistu Haile Mariam delivered a speech at Revolution Square—formerly and presently Meskel Square—in Addis Ababa, officially endorsing a savage campaign against the EPRP and his other opponents. The final slogan shouted during that speech was, "Yankee, go home!"

Soon afterward, Western missionaries began leaving Ethiopia. The administrator of the American mission guesthouse informed us that they were departing the country and needed to sell the furniture we had been using. I took out a bank loan and purchased the furniture and appliances, all of which had been imported from America. I handled the purchase myself because my husband was unwilling to contribute. I could not ask for his paycheck, as my mother-in-law had advised, and I did not know how much he earned.

Miraculous Survival After Our New Car Accident

Two months after we purchased our car—but before either of us had obtained a driver's license—something dangerous occurred. We needed to travel to Nedjo for my sister Tsehai Wodajo's wedding, and my husband decided to drive. We each took a one-week leave from work and began our journey at 5:00 a.m. on a Thursday.

We arrived safely in Gimbi at 5:00 p.m. without being stopped by traffic police. Because the eighty-kilometer stretch of road between Gimbi and Nedjo was unsuitable for automobiles, we left our car in Gimbi. Around 6:00 p.m., we boarded a pickup truck and reached Nedjo by 10:00 p.m. that same evening.

We spent Friday and Saturday in Nedjo preparing for the wedding with our families. My primary role was cooking for the celebration and helping prepare my sister—the bride—for her wedding day. As the eldest sister, she looked up to me and was happy to have me there for such an important moment. The groom had been my high school classmate, and they had come to know each other through me.

The groom and his party arrived at our house at noon on Sunday. As they tried to enter, young girls blocked the doorway, singing the traditional song, "Hinkennu balabala abbakoo, sihacufu balballi abbakoo," just as they had done at my wedding. In keeping with custom, the best men eventually pushed the girls aside so the groom could enter, and we proceeded immediately to the wedding lunch.

After the meal, my parents and the elders blessed the bride and groom according to tradition, and the groom then took his bride to his home. As we prepared to return to Addis Ababa the next morning, an elderly man named Sirriqa Jaldu came to my parents' house and asked my husband for a ride to Addis Ababa so he could receive medical treatment.

I looked at the old man and asked, "What are you going to be treated for in Addis Ababa?"

"I have heart disease and high blood pressure," he replied.

Because he was overweight and suffering from serious medical conditions, I immediately feared the risk of taking him on such a long journey—especially since we did not yet have driver's licenses. I did not even know how he had learned that my husband was driving. I explained the danger to my husband and urged him not to take Mr. Sirriqa with us. My nursing training had made me acutely aware of the risks involved.

My husband reacted angrily and shouted at me, "It's none of your business!" in front of Mr. Sirriqa and the relatives who had accompanied him.I fell silent rather than argue further. Shortly afterward, we left for Gimbi, bringing Mr. Sirriqa with us, along with a nanny for my baby. We arrived in Gimbi around lunchtime and ate there. After lunch, my husband told us to get into the car so we could continue on to Addis Ababa.

I refused to sit in the front passenger seat, telling him I was afraid and uncertain about what might happen to Mr. Sirriqa during the journey. The nanny and I sat in the back seat, while Mr. Sirriqa took the front passenger seat beside my husband. We spent the night in Nekemte and resumed our journey early the next morning. By midmorning, we reached a point overlooking Ambo, about ten kilometers away. Ambo lies 115.3 kilometers from Addis Ababa.

As we followed the winding roads around the hills, my husband turned toward me and said, "You said we wouldn't make it safely. See—we made it!"

I replied, "If you are boasting in your own strength instead of giving glory to God for His protection, we still might not make it."

No sooner had I finished speaking than he missed the road, and the car plunged into a deep ditch. I was thrown from the back seat into the front. My forehead struck a mirror my husband had earlier fixed to the dashboard, leaving two straight cuts between my eyebrows. I weighed fifty-two kilograms at the time, and I believe that helped prevent more severe injury, though I was left with a scar that made me appear as if I were constantly frowning.

Immediately after the crash, the nanny cried out, "Why did you say we might not get home safely? This wouldn't have happened otherwise!"

I told her I had not known this would occur.

God protected us. Three of us came out of the car unharmed, but Mr. Sirriqa had to be pulled from the wreck. I was also eleven weeks pregnant at the time, yet I was unharmed—praise God. I could only imagine what might have happened had I been seated in the front passenger seat, or if Mr. Sirriqa's body had been thrown onto me from behind.

We climbed up from the ditch to the road and waited for transportation to Ambo. It was nothing short of a miracle. As soon as I reached the roadside, I saw Tarressa—my former high school classmate from Gimbi— running toward me. When he recognized me, he shouted in disbelief, "My Agitu! Are you okay? I stopped to see what happened, and I can't believe it's you!"

Tarressa was driving a government truck, and he took Mr. Sirriqa, the nanny, and me to Ambo Hospital. My husband stayed behind to find a guard to watch the car and did not accompany us.

Mr. Sirriqa was pronounced dead upon arrival at the hospital. I received a dressing for the minor injury on my forehead. A few minutes later, my husband arrived and asked, "Is Sirriqa okay?"

"He died," I replied. "We must leave quickly and find transportation."

By God's grace, we found transportation immediately and left Ambo that same evening. My husband, however, now faced two serious and costly obligations the very next morning: arranging to deliver Mr. Sirriqa's body to his son and having our damaged car towed to a mechanic shop in Addis Ababa. The most important thing was that we were alive, and my pregnancy had not been affected by the deadly accident. That was how our trip to Nedjo ended, and I returned once again to my mixed-up life.

The joy of my sister's wedding had faded behind us, replaced by an unspoken tension that filled the car. What had begun as a family celebration was now turning into a journey shadowed by fear, silence, and risk. I sensed that we were moving toward something dangerous, though I did not yet know how close that danger was—or how quickly events would unfold beyond our control.

God protected us. Three of us came out of the car unharmed, but Mr. Sirriqa had to be pulled from the wreck. I was also eleven weeks pregnant, yet I was unharmed—praise God. I could only imagine what might have happened had I been seated in the front passenger seat, or if Mr. Sirriqa's body had been thrown onto me from behind.

That journey marked more than a medical emergency. It marked another step into a pattern I was beginning to recognize—where my knowledge, discernment, and concern were pushed aside, and where consequences followed swiftly. I could not yet see where this path would lead, but I knew that something had shifted irrevocably.

The Atrocities Intensifying Under the New Socialist Ideology

We were living in a moment when the nation desperately needed God's mighty power to withstand the atrocities of the new socialist government. As I mentioned earlier, the EPRP's White Terror provoked the Derg to retaliate with what became known as the Red Terror. Colonel Mengistu Haile Mariam's counterterror campaign made life unbearable for ordinary citizens. Civilians were organized through their respective kebeles (neighborhood administrations) and armed by the Derg to go door-to-door, disarm Ethiopians, and track down suspected members of the EPRP.

On the day the disarmament campaign began, the government announced over Ethiopian radio and television that all employees were to remain at home. I was already at work when I heard the announcement and had no choice but to return home. Along the way, I witnessed a horrifying sight—a Volkswagen burned to ashes with the driver still inside. The image of the driver slumped behind the steering wheel, reduced to charcoal, was seared into my memory. I gave birth to my second child—a daughter I named Jalale, meaning "my beloved" in Afaan Oromo—about a year after we moved into the American Mission guesthouse in Mekenisa.

I was on maternity leave during the height of these atrocities and did not witness them directly. When I returned to work in early April 1978, however, I saw a dead body lying at a distance near Mexico Square in Addis Ababa. To avoid forming a lasting mental image, I did not go closer. When I arrived home, I was told that a disarmament squad had already searched our house for weapons. By God's mercy, I had persuaded my husband to sell his pistol—the same one I had smuggled in my baby's diaper bag on our journey to Addis Ababa—early enough that nothing was found.

Many young people suspected of being EPRP members were dragged from their homes during the night; others were seized from the streets of Addis Ababa and executed. Their bodies were dumped on the doorsteps of their parents' homes or left in the streets as warnings. In some cases, parents were forced to walk over their children's corpses, under threat of execution themselves. Families were forbidden to mourn or bury their dead. Those deemed "fortunate" were allowed to pay for the bullets that had killed their children and then reclaim the bodies.

I was on maternity leave during the height of these horrors and did not witness them firsthand. When I returned to work in early April 1978, however, I saw a dead body lying at a distance near Mexico Square in Addis Ababa. To avoid imprinting another painful image in my mind, I did not go closer. Troubled and searching for understanding, I asked God why such things had been allowed. When I opened my Bible, I came across a passage I had never noticed before. It read:

> "For thus says the Lord: 'Do not enter the house of mourning, nor go to lament or bemoan them; for I have taken away My peace from this people,' says the Lord, 'My lovingkindness and mercies. Both the great and the small shall die in this land. They shall not be buried; neither shall men lament for them, cut themselves, nor make themselves bald for them. Nor shall men break bread in mourning for them, to comfort them for the dead; nor shall men give them the cup of consolation to drink for their father or their mother.' (Jeremiah 16:5–7, NKJV)

The Derg's counterterror campaign did not target the EPRP alone; it also targeted Christians. Communism—the ideology driving the terror at the time—was aimed not only at President Mengistu Haile Mariam's political rivals but also at evangelical believers. Many evangelical churches were closed, and Christian gatherings were banned, monitored, or tightly controlled. As a result, churches were forced underground, where they grew tremendously despite severe persecution. Many Christians were imprisoned, interrogated, tortured, and killed for refusing to renounce their faith. Let me give a few examples.

One morning, Mulu Elala, a high school student at Yekatit 12 (formerly Menen High School) in Sidist Kilo, boarded Bus 31 on her way to school, as she did every day. As the bus approached Arat Kilo, she began to hear an inner voice repeatedly saying, *"Mulu, return!"* When she reached the area near St. Mary's Church in Arat Kilo—only a few meters from her school—she decided to get off the bus and pray instead of attending class that day. She entered the church compound and spent the entire day there in prayer.

When she returned home around 6:00 p.m., she found her parents dressed in black, mourning. With overwhelming relief, they told her they had believed she was among the students executed at Yekatit 12 High School that day. In those years, families learned of executions through the media, and the whereabouts of the victims were considered none of their concern.

The second example is Misrake-Tsehai Debebe, a second-year college student who was targeted because of her Christian faith. In one incident, she was taken from her home, detained for twenty-four hours, and interrogated. In a later and more severe incident, armed men entered a room where she and other Christian students were worshipping. They waited silently until the service ended. One student then chose a song by a rural Ethiopian lay singer that proclaimed, *"Victory belongs to our Lord, our God. The enemy's roaring is nothing for Jesus, for He is in control."*

The song enraged the armed men. All the students were immediately arrested and taken to prison, where they were tortured severely. The student who had chosen the song received the harshest treatment. Misrake-Tsehai herself was flogged until her clothes were torn to pieces. She later testified that her suffering was minor compared to that of others and thanked God for sustaining her.

The third example is Ato Erjabo, a Christian teacher from Shashamane in southern Ethiopia. He was imprisoned and tortured in an attempt to force him to betray Christ and renounce his faith. When he later shared his testimony with me, he showed me the soles of his feet, which were blackened like charcoal. He had been hung upside down and beaten on the soles of his feet with electric cords. At intervals, his captors offered him strong alcoholic drinks—something he had never consumed—but he refused. Each refusal resulted in further beatings.

As horrific as these acts were, I believe that Ethiopians, bound by cultural and moral values, imposed certain limits even in cruelty. Pregnant women, for example, were not tortured or executed in Ethiopian prisons, and rape was not permitted. From what I later learned about the persecution of Christians in other communist countries, such as Russia, I do not believe Ethiopian torturers dared to inflict the same extreme forms of degradation described by Richard Wurmbrand in *Tortured for Christ*.

In one account from Russia's Pitesti prison, Christians were tied to crosses and laid on the floor for days while hundreds of prisoners were forced to relieve themselves on their bodies. The crosses were then raised, and the guards mocked them, saying, *"Look at your Christ—how beautiful He is, what fragrance He brings from heaven."* In another instance, after being driven nearly insane by torture, a priest was forced to consecrate excrement and urine and distribute it as Holy Communion to imprisoned believers.

When I read the words from Jeremiah, I felt as though Scripture had stepped out of history and into our present moment. The land was filled with fear, silenced grief, and unburied sorrow, just as the prophet had described. God was not absent, yet His peace seemed withdrawn from the nation. I could not comprehend why such suffering was permitted, but I sensed that Ethiopia was passing through a season of severe testing—one that stripped away false security and revealed what faith truly meant.

Even as terror spread across the country and believers paid a heavy price for their loyalty to Christ, God was quietly at work in my own life. While I did not witness the worst atrocities firsthand, their shadow loomed over everything. And yet, in the midst of national darkness, God began to reveal His compassion to me in deeply personal ways. What followed was not political, but intimate; not public, but profoundly private. Out of fear and uncertainty, blessings began to unfold—leading into divine healing and miracles that would mark the next chapter of my journey.

Blessings Growing into Divine Healing and Miracles

In the third year of my marriage, I gave birth to my second child—a girl. I named her Jalale, meaning "my beloved" in Afaan Oromo. Jalale survived a car accident before she was born, and she escaped death once again at the age of two.

When Jalale was twenty-one months old, she began to lose weight. She showed no signs of pain—only steady weight loss—so I took her to Professor Demissie's specialty clinic at the Ethio-Swedish Children's Hospital. After examining her, he found nothing abnormal, and we returned home.

Over the next two months, however, Jalale continued to lose weight. One day, during my own physical examination of her, I discovered that her liver was enlarged. Alarmed, I rushed her back to the Ethio-Swedish Children's Hospital, where I had the opportunity to see Professor Nebiyat in his office. Both professors had been my instructors during my pediatric nurse practitioner training.

Professor Nebiyat asked me, "What is wrong with your child?"

I explained her history and told him that I had found her liver to be enlarged.

"How did you know?" he asked.

"I palpated," I replied.

He then examined her himself and said, "You are right. Her liver is enlarged."

Jalale was admitted immediately. Professor Nebiyat ordered chest X-rays and blood tests, including a sedimentation rate, white blood cell count, and bilirubin levels. The chest X-ray revealed partial atelectasis of her right lung, and on the second day of her admission she was started on cloxacillin. The blood tests indicated infection, and I was told she would receive antibiotics for one week and then be discharged.

I was deeply troubled by that plan. Fearing that my concerns might be dismissed as overconfidence—*"a little knowledge is dangerous,"* they might think—I approached a Swedish pediatrician, Dr. Gunnar, and begged him to ask Professor Demissie to perform a biopsy on the enlarged liver. Thanks to Dr. Gunnar's intervention, the biopsy was done. As soon as the sample was drawn, 250 cc of pus drained from her liver. The biopsy results later came back negative, and Jalale was discharged on the ninth day after her admission.

Upon her discharge, Professor Demissie ordered weekly chest X-rays and blood tests, meaning I would have to bring Jalale to his special Thursday afternoon clinic every week. Words cannot describe how devastating that was for me. I could not sleep at night. Most evenings, I sat with her on my lap, holding her and weeping quietly. I will never forget how she gently wiped away the tears that fell onto her face as I cried. She never complained. She never became irritable. Yet I lived in constant fear of losing her.

At her third Thursday follow-up, the chest X-ray revealed a total collapse of her right lung. The blood test results had not improved either. That day, Professor Demissie told me he would schedule an appointment with the pediatric surgeon, Dr. Johnson, to operate on Jalale within two weeks.

I asked him, "What is the prognosis for lung surgery on a two-year-old child in this condition?"

He answered briefly, "We will see."

I left his office deeply frustrated and disturbed. I sensed that he knew the outcome was uncertain but did not want to alarm me. When I arrived home that afternoon, I called my sister Rahel and told her my firm decision:

"This child is a gift from God, not from man. No stethoscope will rest on her chest again—let alone a surgeon's knife. This Sunday, I am taking her to the healing program I have heard about."

I had been told that an anointed minister named Daniel Mekonen, who was known for a gift of healing, was in the city. Since childhood, my spiritual formation had been within Lutheran teaching, and I had regarded Pentecostals with suspicion—believing they were overly emotional and lacking theological depth. But this time, I was desperate. As a mother standing at the edge of losing her child, I was willing to go anywhere and try anything.

My miracle was on the way. I obtained the address of Meserete Kristos Church, where Pastor Daniel Mekonen was ministering, and prepared to take my child to the healing service that Sunday. I asked my sister Rahel to accompany me, and we arrived around 10:00 a.m. I assumed we were on time, but the church—and all three overflow shelters—were already packed with people from all over the country. We nearly turned back, unable to find a seat. Eventually, we squeezed into the back overflow shelter.

I did not know exactly when the service had begun, but almost immediately after we sat down, Pastor Daniel began praying for the sick. He asked all those in need of healing to place their right hand on the affected part of their bodies. I tried to place Jalale's right hand on the right side of her chest, but she resisted.

Then I heard the pastor say, "There is one *bilat na*"—a female child—"with tuberculosis in this congregation." (*Bilatena* is a biblical word for "child" in Amharic.)

I leaned toward my sister and whispered, "Could that be my child?"

"Yes," she whispered back. "Stand up."

I hesitated. I doubted. I remained seated.

After about a minute, the pastor asked again, "Is that you?"

It seemed someone else inside the main church had responded.

Then he said, "But there is another female child."

I whispered again, "How old is a *bilatena*?"

My sister replied firmly, "Why does that matter? Stand up."

I whispered back, "It's my first time here. If the Lord wills, let Him heal her."

Immediately after those words left my mouth, the pastor said, "All right, let us pray," and he prayed briefly:

"You tuberculosis present in this child, be burned this very minute and second in the name of Jesus of Nazareth!"

At that exact moment, Jalale screamed, "I am in pain," and instinctively grabbed the right side of her chest. She then lifted her dress and touched the right side of her bottom. I would not understand the significance of that second gesture until later that evening, when I undressed her to bathe her and discovered—and drained—an abscess that had been present on her bottom for two days.

On Friday, I had applied ichthammol dressing to the abscess I had discovered on the right side of her bottom, but when I removed the dressing on Sunday evening to drain it, the abscess was gone. I stood there in disbelief. Her skin was completely normal—there was no swelling, no wound, not even a trace of the ichthammol ointment. At that moment, I knew I had received confirmation that she had been healed. I was overwhelmed with joy.

Through His divine gift, Pastor Daniel had diagnosed what neither the pediatricians nor I had considered. In Ethiopia, all newborns are routinely vaccinated with BCG against tuberculosis, and Jalale had received that vaccine. Because of this, none of us had imagined that she could have TB. Only later did I realize that I had unknowingly contributed to her suffering. After her birth, I had her receive the TB vaccine twice before discharge because I did not see the expected vaccination scar on her arm and assumed the vaccine had not taken.

Three days later, my husband said to me, "I know you took Jalale to Meserete Kristos Church last Sunday."

Surprised, I asked, "How did you know?" I had not told him, fearing he might ridicule me or prevent me from returning to the church.

He replied simply, "Because she is completely healthy. She plays, eats well, and is happy."

The following Thursday, I took Jalale back to the hospital for her scheduled weekly checkup. The chest X-ray and blood test results confirmed what we had already witnessed at home—Jalale was healed. The X-ray showed a fully restored lung. Her sedimentation rate dropped from 95 mm to 5 mm, her white blood cell count decreased from 11,500 to 5,000, and her lymphocyte count fell from 8,000 to 4,500.

This miracle transformed my spiritual life completely. The following Sunday, I returned to Meserete Kristos Church carrying Jalale's chest X-ray and test results. I stood before the congregation and gave my testimony, confessing how God had shown me His power over the sophisticated childcare practices and medical knowledge I had trusted so deeply. Proverbs 3:5 came alive for me: *"Trust in the Lord with all your heart, and lean not on your own understanding."*

I continued attending Meserete Kristos Church until the Derg shut it down.

That healing marked the end of one season and the beginning of another. God had confronted me lovingly but firmly, showing me that professional knowledge, discipline, and best practices—valuable as they are—can never replace complete trust in Him. I had relied on what I knew, what I could measure, and what I could control. In His mercy, God reminded me that life itself remains in His hands.

The miracle did not simply restore my child's health; it reshaped my faith. I was no longer content with inherited beliefs or theological assumptions. I had encountered the living power of God in a way that demanded surrender, humility, and obedience. From that point forward, my spiritual walk deepened—not through emotion, but through awe. Yet miracles do not remove trials; they prepare us for them. While God revealed His healing power in my family, pressures were intensifying in other areas of my life—my marriage, my work, and my calling. The same hand that healed my daughter would soon begin refining me through fire. The next chapter unfolds how faith, once awakened, was tested in ways I never anticipated.

After churches were closed by the socialist government, I continued worshipping with fellow believers underground. During that season, God also blessed me with a personal gift of divine healing, which I continue to enjoy to this day. I will mention a few examples.

I was healed in my own home from gastritis and severe migraine headaches that I had suffered from for five years. I was also rescued from a surgeon's knife. One Saturday morning in 1982, I was rushed to the army hospital in Addis Ababa at 6:00 a.m. with severe pain in my right lower abdomen and persistent vomiting. The nurses on duty prepared me for surgery and called the surgeon to perform an appendectomy.

When the surgeon arrived, he angrily asked the nurses, "Why did you call me in on a weekend for a civilian?" I responded calmly, "Doctor, don't be angry. God wanted to save me from your knife." Then I turned off the intravenous drip I was receiving, removed the needle from my vein, and got out of bed. Immediately after those words left my mouth, the pain and vomiting stopped completely, and I went home healed.

In July 2008, I experienced seven hours of intense kidney pain. Having been hospitalized with the same symptoms four years earlier, I recognized it as a kidney stone. I laid my hands on my affected kidney and commanded the stone to be expelled in the name of Jesus, and it happened instantly.

Later, in March 2012, after suffering knee pain for two months, I was diagnosed with arthritis in both knees. The next morning, I prayed for healing—and I received it immediately. I do not share these testimonies to elevate myself or to suggest that healing follows a formula. I learned through experience that divine healing is an act of God's mercy, not a reward for faithfulness or effort. Sometimes He heals instantly; other times He sustains us through suffering. What mattered most was not the healing itself, but the deepened trust that grew from surrendering control and acknowledging God as the ultimate healer.

These experiences reshaped my understanding of faith. I no longer saw God only through doctrine or tradition, but as a living, present power who intervenes according to His will. At the same time, I learned that spiritual gifts do not exempt one from hardship. Healing in one area of life does not prevent trials in another.

As God continued to work in me spiritually, my personal life was moving toward a season of intense testing. The faith that had been strengthened through miracles would soon be required to endure prolonged suffering. The next chapter tells how the refining fire intensified—and how obedience was tested beyond anything I had known before.

When the Sweet Was Challenged by the Sour

The sour part of my life during this season was mostly internal. Marriage, as I was living it, fell far short of its true meaning—a union of two people. My husband never consulted me on matters concerning our daily life or finances. One day, while we were driving home, I asked him to pay the electric bill. In response, he scratched my left arm deeply with his nails, right in front of our three children sitting in the back seat. From that moment on, I was afraid to ask him for money for our living expenses. Throughout the eighteen years we lived together, I never knew how much he earned until I finally left the country.

It was his legal and moral responsibility to provide for his family, and I could have taken legal action against him. But I wanted my children to grow up with clean minds, free from bitterness and conflict, and I chose to maintain peace. God did not fail me. I always had enough to provide a comfortable life for my family.

When I gave birth to my third child, I endured a particularly painful trauma related to finances. It was Ethiopian Christmas week, and my due date—January 5—fell three days before my payday. Government employees were paid at the end of the Ethiopian month, but my husband, who worked for a private company, was paid on January 3. That day, he came home with a pair of new shoes—for his nephew.

I asked him whether he had set aside money for my hospital admission. He shouted at me, "Are you jealous that I bought him shoes? You will get out of here, and I will raise him spoiled." That moment crushed me. Medical care at the time was inexpensive—less than one hundred Ethiopian birr, equivalent to about forty-eight dollars—but even that small amount mattered more to him than my delivery.

The following morning, a Saturday, he said he had an appointment with a woman from work and left with our car. My labor began later that afternoon while he was still away. He returned home at 7:20 p.m. and took me to the hospital. At admission, the hospital clerk asked him for one hundred birr to retrieve my medical record. He told the clerk, "I don't have the money." At that point, I asked whether I could give my husband power of attorney to collect my salary from my workplace on Monday to cover the cost. The clerk agreed, kept a copy of the document I wrote, and admitted me.

My husband did collect my salary on my behalf—but I never asked what he did with it. I neither confronted him nor held a grudge. I let it go to preserve peace. Because my first two deliveries had been uncomplicated, I allowed my husband to go home after I was admitted. Shortly after he left, the doctor discovered that the baby was in brow presentation and ordered an immediate cesarean section, even though my cervix was fully dilated. I went through the surgery completely alone.

As I began to wake from anesthesia, I was disoriented and unconsciously tried to remove the dressing on my lower abdomen. In doing so, my intravenous line became disconnected, and by the time I regained full consciousness, my bed was soaked. Only then was I able to call the nurses.

My nurse-friend, Alemitu Etafa, who lived in the nurses' residence within the hospital compound, was upset that I had not called her when I was admitted. From that point on, she came early every morning to care for me. I believe her kindness played a significant role in my quick recovery. My stitches were removed on the fifth day, and I was discharged. At home,

I often heard my husband tell the children, "I bought you a mother," or promise them "tomorrow" whenever they asked him for something. Our third child would ask the next day, "Is today tomorrow?" still hoping for what had been promised.

I never complained. God's grace sustained me, and my salary was enough for our family to live comfortably. One day, however, I asked God why He seemed silent when my husband failed to fulfill his responsibility as a provider. His answer came through Scripture—Genesis 3:17–19—regarding the division of labor. Adam was assigned the role of provider, and Eve that of childbearing. My husband did not share my labor pains, and I realized it was not right for me to take on his role.

I felt convicted for violating the division of responsibility God had established at creation, and I resolved to stop complaining. One day, I posted a proverb on the notice board in our bedroom: *"Sismut yineksal, siyazlut yaleksal"*—*"He bites when kissed; he cries when carried on the back."* When my husband saw it, he laughed and tore it down. Nothing changed.

I had convinced myself that I made a wrong decision to marry him against my inner voice in the first place and shouldn't complain. I could not see how such opposite personalities might blend, yet his patience and the gentler aspects of his introverted nature appealed to me. He was calm and reserved. While many men spent their evenings at bars after work, he was sober and consistently home. Perhaps those qualities—along with his appearance—quieted my deeper spiritual misgivings.

That decision marked a turning point in my life. It was the moment when discernment yielded to endurance, and caution gave way to compliance. What followed was not simply a marriage, but a refining fire—one that tested my faith, reshaped my calling, and exposed strengths I did not yet know I possessed. When I asked God at last why this mismatch happened He revealed to me that He created me to serve Him, yet I would only live to please my husband and remain a Sundy Christina.

When the Internal Thorn Met the External One

The sour part of my life did not remain internal for long. In the third year of my employment at the Defense Industries, I began facing serious difficulties at my workplace. Political departments were established in all government institutions for the purpose of ideological indoctrination. Derg cadres were assigned to brainwash Ethiopians into accepting Marxism–Leninism and to spread propaganda through a mandatory program called *wuyiyit kibeb*[8]

All employees of the Ministry of National Defense were required to attend four hours of political training each week, while other government employees attended two. At the end of every *wuyiyit* session, participants were forced to raise their left hands and shout slogans such as: "Down with feudalism!" "Down with bureaucratic capitalism!" "Down with imperialism!" and "Revolutionary motherland or death!"

As a Christian, I abhorred the ideology behind these slogans and regarded them as curses. Instead of attending the *wuyiyit kibeb*, I remained in my office during those hours. Employees were not permitted to leave the compound at that time, so staying in my office was my only option. The cadres frequently intimidated me for refusing to participate.

Eventually, the harassment escalated. One day, the head of the political department came to my office and said he had something "confidential" to discuss with me. Assuming he might be seeking medical advice for a personal issue, I stepped with him into the corridor near the clinic entrance.

He leaned close to my ear and whispered, "I want to take you out to lunch."

Startled and offended, I replied, "Oh my goodness! What would people say if they saw me with you, when they see me with my husband?"

He walked away without saying a word. I had spoken deliberately to demoralize him. Compared to my husband, he was not an attractive

---

[8] *A political discussion group organized by the socialist government to promote and reinforce communist ideology among citizens.*

man—but I soon realized how dangerous my response had been. Heads of political departments wielded enormous power under the socialist system—power to destroy lives without accountability.

A few days after I rejected his advances, he followed me into the director's office and shouted at me in front of the executive secretary, "It is bad enough that you never attend the *wuyiyit kibebe*"

"Making it worse," he continued, "you give Hussein"—the health assistant I supervised—"permission to leave during *wuyiyit* hours. You will suffer the consequences!"

I replied calmly, "I have the right to grant Hussein the off-duty privilege he has earned as an employee. If you believe you have the authority, you may instruct the gate security not to let him out." Then I walked away.

After that confrontation, he mobilized four of the six cadres under his supervision to retaliate against me.

Their first attack was to go to the director, General Alemayehu Agonafer, and falsely accuse me of tribal favoritism. They claimed I favored the Oromos—my own ethnic group—over other employees and granted them sick leave unjustly. The director convened a meeting with all department heads to address the complaint along with other agenda items. The accusation against me was listed first.

God gave me wisdom and composure. I explained that certain department heads had pressured me to issue sick leave to employees who were not ill, and that I had refused in order to preserve professional integrity. When I finished, the director pointed toward those department heads and said, "If you act under the direction of these men, then you are insulting your profession."

They fell silent. It was clear that the director had defended me.

The second accusation soon followed. I was charged with violating clinic policy by treating employees' children. It was true that I had been seeing employees' children for two hours twice a week. What my accusers did not know was that I had obtained written authorization from the director beforehand.

General Alemayehu summoned me and asked, "Would you die if you stopped treating these children in the clinic?"

"No, sir," I replied.

"Then stop," he said.

Two weeks later came a third accusation. This time they claimed I was treating non-civilian security guards using the civilian employees' clinic budget. There were twenty-one senior veterans serving as security guards at the time. I was unaware of the accusation until all the guards came to the clinic to thank me for my care. They told me the director had summoned them and instructed them not to use the clinic any longer because I was being accused of serving them.

What appeared to be a setback became a hidden blessing. I had not realized that serving those veteran guards would earn me their deep respect—and later, their loyalty. Each morning, they saluted me at the gate just as they saluted the director and his deputy, both high-ranking army officers. More importantly, they became a source of unexpected support during a severe food shortage in the city.

The shortage resulted from rationing policies imposed by the Agricultural Produce Marketing Corporation (APMC), which controlled agricultural markets under the socialist system. The corporation purchased grain from farmers at low prices, imposed quotas, and fixed food prices. Predictably, this led to scarcity. Long lines formed daily for basic necessities. Government employees organized group trips to Gojam—456 kilometers away—to buy grain and share transportation costs.

Yet I was spared those exhausting journeys. Thanks to the security guards, I was included in the military food distribution list. Because they received supplies directly from government storage, they arranged for grain, cereals, sugar, and coffee to be delivered to our workplace at a discounted rate. Their quiet solidarity sustained my family during that difficult time.

When the cadres realized their accusations had failed at the director's level, they stopped appealing to authority and began targeting me directly.

One morning during a coffee break, one of them entered my office, clearly intending to provoke me into saying something dangerous. In front of the clinic staff—likely positioning them as witnesses—he opened the conversation by declaring, "There will be a coup soon."

But God continually put wise answers in my mouth. I replied calmly, "You announce the news, and you debate it yourself. It's none of my business."

On another occasion, he pointed to the posters on the clinic wall—pictures of Marx, Lenin, and Engels—and said, "These posters will be taken down and burned."

I answered, "You are the ones who put the posters up, and you are the ones who will take them down and burn them. It's none of my business."

For his final attempt, however, he crossed a line I could not tolerate. He pointed his thumb downward and said, "Down with God's mother!"

That statement enraged me. I shouted back, "Stop loitering during business hours! Get out of my office immediately!" Then I ran straight to the office of the new director, General Gugsa Mekonnen, who had recently succeeded General Alemayehu Agonafer, to file a formal complaint.

When I entered his office, I asked angrily, "Your Highness, can't I live freely in my own country and worship God?"

He replied calmly, "What happened?"

I repeated my question.

He then said, "Just tell me who is troubling you. I have high regard for you because I have heard that you are a woman of strong moral character and a diligent professional."

At that point, I told him everything the cadre had done to intimidate and harass me. General Gugsa instructed me to submit my complaint in writing and assured me that he would do everything in his power to protect me. After receiving my written statement, he ordered security personnel to accompany him to my office and confront the cadre with the report. Somehow the information reached the cadre in advance, because he stopped coming to the clinic altogether. Two months later, he came to my office and apologized for his actions.

The attacks did not stop there. Another cadre soon took his turn to intimidate me. He organized a separate *wuyiyit* session for department heads—including the director and his deputy—and scheduled it in the sales hall, which shared a wall with the clinic. My instinct told me he was trying to use my superiors as witnesses against me for not attending the *wuyiyit kibeb* sessions. So I decided to attend the meeting next door.

The cadre opened the session by saying, "Today's topic is democracy. I will begin with a question: What is democracy, and when will it become practical? Sister Agitu, will you answer?"

"Sister" was the professional title used for nurses in Ethiopia.

An inner warning rose within me. I sensed that his plan was to trap me—to associate me with MESON by pushing me to declare something politically dangerous. MESON had already been crushed by the government for proclaiming, "Democracy for the oppressed—now!" Being Oromo made me even more cautious. I took it as confirmation to trust that inner voice.

So I remained silent.

After about a minute, he pressed again. "Sister Agitu, we always hear the word democracy—freedom of speech, freedom of expression. What is democracy, and when will it be practical?"

He was placing the answer in my mouth. I was certain he believed he had cornered me.

Sounding almost childlike, I replied, "I don't know."

I do not know what he felt in that moment, but he proceeded to answer his own question   the very answer he had tried to extract from me   and continued his lecture.

I had escaped the snare that day.

But the pressure did not end there.

The following Saturday, the head of the political department called for a general assembly for the regular weekly *wuyiyit* session. The meeting was held in the cafeteria, large enough to accommodate all employees. I attended because my superiors were present, and I feared being identified again for my absence.

I deliberately sat in the second-to-last row at the back.

At 11:55 a.m., the siren announcing the end of work hours rang before he had finished his lecture. Those seated in the front rows began pushing toward the exit, eager to pass through the security checkpoint and leave the compound.

Enraged, he shouted at the crowd, "This is anarchism! Trying to leave before shouting slogans is very rude!"

Then he singled me out.

"For example—Sister Agitu! Sister Agitu! Come to the front and say the slogans!"

I did not move. I remained seated at the back.

Then I raised my voice and said clearly,

"I will not."

I had to shout in order to be heard because I was seated far from the stage and had not been given a microphone.

He shouted back, "How come?"

I replied, "Tekotitehegn askorifehegn new ende tadya? Kewuste sigenefil new enji." ("Should you shout at me and offend me first? Words should flow willingly from within.") The entire audience burst into laughter because my expression in Amharic was humorous. He calmed down and said sternly, "This is not funny, comrades. It is a lack of political consciousness." Then he led the slogans himself.

Praise God—I was safe once again. No one else would have dared to respond to him the way I did, because he wielded immense power. Yet God protected me.

A few weeks later, a notice was circulated announcing the removal of the head of the political department from his position and the appointment of his successor, Captain Shiferraw. I posted the notice on the clinic wall and quietly allowed myself a moment of relief—using their own political language to savor his downfall.

"What a relief," I thought—unaware that my troubles were far from over.

Soon I would discover that the most dangerous threat was still ahead—my immediate superior, a colonel. The colonel moved out of his spacious office—located about two hundred feet from the director general's office—and relocated to the salesroom next to the clinic. We now shared a wall. To be honest, both the salesroom and the clinic resembled a warehouse and were poorly constructed. At the time, plans were underway to build a new clinic, which was completed after I left.

Not long after he moved next door, the colonel summoned me to his office. The purpose was not professional. He simply told me that he wanted to take me out for lunch.

In Ethiopia, a man inviting a woman to lunch or dinner is often a coded advance.

I replied, "Thank you, but I don't think I can," and I left his office.

That was the most frightening offer I had ever received.

For the first time, I was genuinely afraid. This man had the power to retaliate, to harm me professionally—or worse. And what I feared would later begin to unfold. I cried out to God for help, and He answered me through His Word:

> "Do not say, 'A conspiracy,' Concerning all that this people call a conspiracy, Nor be afraid of their threats, nor be troubled." (Isaiah 8:12, NKJV)

That verse became my anchor. I did not know how the threat would unfold, but I knew I was no longer facing it alone. God had begun preparing me—not by removing the danger, but by steadying my heart within it. Until then, every attack I had faced came from outside my immediate authority—cadres, political operatives, strangers emboldened by ideology. This time, however, the danger had moved closer. It now stood within my chain of command, armed with rank, power, and unchecked entitlement.

I continued my work as faithfully as I could, outwardly calm but inwardly watchful. I had learned that in those days, silence could be safer than speech, discernment more valuable than confrontation, and prayer more powerful than resistance. What I did not yet understand was that this moment marked a turning point. The protection God had granted me thus far would soon be tested in a far more personal way. The next chapter reveals how internal resolve and external pressure collided—and how obedience to God would demand a courage I had never before been required to summon.

But the fear did not leave me. I knew that reporting him to the chief executive—his direct superior—could have serious consequences for him, yet I had no evidence. His advance had been verbal and made in private. Although I was well regarded at my workplace, I no longer felt safe. I therefore made the difficult decision to resign from the prestigious position I had held for more than seven years. I was fully aware that my decision went against government policy. Department heads and military personnel were not permitted to resign, and no employer was allowed to hire an individual without a formal release letter from their previous employer. Even so, I resolved to try.

Almost immediately after beginning my job search, I saw a vacancy announcement from the Commercial Bank of Ethiopia for the position of clinic director. I submitted my application. Two weeks later, I received an invitation to sit for a preemployment test at the Addis Ababa University Testing Center. The recruitment process was strikingly similar to the one I had gone through years earlier when I was hired by the Ministry of National Defense.

On the day of the test, I sat alongside thirty-one health officers. I was the only nurse in the group; the position was officially intended for a health officer with a Bachelor of Science degree. Still, I applied with confidence. The exam felt remarkably easy to me, and I completed it in half an hour.

Through my years of clinical practice, I had memorized the dosages, side effects, and contraindications of every medication I prescribed. I also kept detailed drug leaflets on file for reference. That discipline served me well during the exam.

That evening, one of the health officers who had taken the test called me and said, "You did the right thing by leaving early. None of us finished the exam. They collected our papers before we were done."

"What are you talking about?" I replied. "I completed the entire test and submitted it. It was very easy."

Surprised, he asked, "What are the side effects of prednisolone?"

I listed them from memory. When I finished, he asked, bewildered, "What do you mean when you say, 'The patient will become drug-dependent?'"

Two weeks later, I received an invitation for an interview with Dr. Iyasu, the former dean of the School of Public Health where I had studied.

I arrived at Dr. Iyasu's office full of anticipation, hoping for good news. I believed I would not have been invited for an interview if government policy had truly been an obstacle. As soon as I sat down, Dr. Iyasu told me that I had scored 100 percent on the examination—and that none of the health officers had even come close.

He then asked, almost incredulously, "How did you dare to take the preemployment test for a position posted for health officers when you are a nurse?"

I replied calmly, "I proved myself through the test, but I do not have the paper."

Dr. Iyasu laughed and said, "But we need the paper."

That was his indirect way of telling me I would not be offered the job. I left his office deeply disappointed. It was clear that they would not hire me without a release paper, yet I had taken the test in faith, hoping for a miracle. After that, my hope faded, and I stopped searching for another position. I remained in my job, even though my immediate supervisor continued to pose a threat. Still, my desire to leave that workplace was about to be fulfilled—though in a way I could never have imagined.

I left Dr. Iyasu's office with a quiet heaviness in my heart. I had done everything within my power, proven my competence beyond question, and yet the door remained closed. For the first time, I stopped striving. I remained where I was, even though the environment had become unsafe and my spirit uneasy.

At that point, I understood that this season was no longer about professional advancement or human approval. It was about endurance, obedience, and trust in God when every visible path seemed blocked. The internal wounds I carried and the external pressures I faced had converged, pressing me into a corner where only divine intervention could make a way.

Though I could not yet see how deliverance would come, I sensed that God was preparing an exit—one not initiated by my effort, but by His sovereign hand. What lay ahead would test me more deeply than anything before, yet it would also mark the beginning of a decisive turning point in my life. That chapter of my journey closed with unanswered questions—but not without hope. For even in silence, God was at work, arranging what I could not yet imagine.

5

A REFINING JOURNEY

I began discovering the bitter reality of my marriage shortly after my husband accepted a position with a private pharmaceutical corporation. As a result, we had to leave the American mission guesthouse because we no longer qualified for housing once he stopped working for Mekane Yesus.

Once again, however, blessings followed me in my search for a new home. While looking for a rental property, I found a beautiful house surrounded by a concrete fence, located just one block from my workplace. It was one of the nationalized properties overseen by the urban housing administration. Since the nationalization of urban homes in late 1975, private ownership had been abolished, and houses could only be rented through the government. These nationalized homes were highly desirable because rent was extremely low under the Derg's "mass ownership" policy.

Before nationalization, the house had belonged to the daughter of Colonel Tesema Ezeneh, the late director of Defense Industries—the very institution where I was employed. Securing such a property should have been nearly impossible. I was competing against high-ranking government officials who were political party members and wielded significant influence. But the Almighty God has the final say.

General Alemayehu Agonafer, then director of Defense Industries, provided me with a letter of support addressed to the director of the urban housing administration. I scheduled an appointment and presented the letter. As soon as the director finished reading it, three men entered his office. He asked me politely to step outside for a few minutes.

I waited for about half an hour. When the men left, the director called me back in and began with an apology.

"I'm sorry for the interruption and the long wait," he said. "They are high-ranking government officials. By the way, they are bidding on your house—but I told them it has already been taken. I will give the house to you."

I cannot describe my joy. The house was beautiful, in a prime location, close to everything—and just steps away from my workplace. We moved in that same week. At the time, I had three children, the youngest only three months old. Two months later, I enrolled in the evening program at the science faculty of Addis Ababa University. My goal was to complete the prerequisite courses for medical school and eventually become a physician.

A few months after settling into the house, I opened a small home-based clinic to generate additional income. My salary alone was no longer sufficient. I was repaying a bank loan I had taken to purchase furniture from the American mission guesthouse, and now rent and university tuition added to the financial strain. Asking my husband to fulfill his responsibility would provoke anger, so I carried the burden myself in order to preserve peace. Yet beneath the surface, something far darker was unfolding.

Many unacceptable and deeply painful violations had already occurred in my marriage, but I will focus on the incident that ultimately set me on the path that led me to where I am today—with purpose.

About a year later, the house we were renting was returned to its original owner, and the urban housing administration relocated us to another fenced compound that contained two houses. One evening, something unusual happened. I returned home around 6:00 p.m. after visiting a sick friend. I stood at the gate for more than five minutes, ringing the bell repeatedly, but no one responded. Finally, a relative who was living with us to help with the children opened the gate.

Hearing God Speak to Me for the First Time Transformed My Life

I walked in, sat down on the sofa in the living room, and tried to shake the strange feeling rising inside me.

Then I heard a voice in my right ear, in Amharic:

> "Abdi is playing in your bedroom. Go and ask him where your relative was when you were ringing the bell at the gate."

I immediately ran to our bedroom and asked my son where my relative was when I had been ringing the bell at the gate.

He replied, "My dad dragged her into your bedroom and locked the door behind them. I couldn't open the gate for you because my dad locked the front door and the door to the servants' quarters."

After he finished speaking, I returned to the living room and said to my husband, "I know what you have been doing behind my back, but I have left it to God."

He shouted at me, "What are you trying to say?" and continued cursing at me, twisting his words in a way that made it sound as though I were the one at fault.

Though I was shocked and deeply outraged, I did not react impulsively. Hearing the voice of God speak to me for the first time in my life had filled me with awe and restraint. My son had his own room and had no reason to be in our bedroom—yet God had orchestrated events so that the hidden sin would be exposed. I resolved to handle the matter in a godly way. I told my relative to pack her belongings and leave the house early the next morning.

That night, I had a dream that revealed exactly what had happened between my husband and my relative. In the dream, our next-door neighbor, Shiferraw (an Amharic name meaning "thousands fear him"), stood in the roundabout garden in front of our house. He threw two hoes into the soil—one painted blue and the other dirt brown. (The blue represented my relative, and the dirt brown represented my husband.)

Immediately, the hoes turned into snakes. They coiled together and then stretched upward toward heaven. The tongue of the blue snake kept moving as both lifted their heads upward, as if it were speaking. After a minute or so, the snakes separated. They then fell back to the ground.

Shiferraw picked them up, carried them into our house, and threw them onto a shelf in a dark room. When I entered that dark room to see what had happened, the snakes bit my side and my finger. But because it was dark, I could not tell which snake had bitten me. I did not understand the dream, so the next morning I went to my dream interpreter at work.

After listening carefully, he asked me, "Is she your sister?"

"No," I replied.

"Your dream clearly shows that she is," he said.

He explained that the blue color represented a saddened and wounded heart, while the brown represented shame. He said, "Your husband had sexual relations with your relative. This has already taken place, and you will soon find out. Because your relative is deeply hurt and disheartened by what happened, she has lifted her head toward heaven and prayed, 'God, please bring to light the crime committed against me in the dark.'" He then told me a similar story of how such a prayer had once been answered, to affirm the accuracy of his interpretation.

What struck me most was that he did not know the incident had already happened. I had not told him. Yet his interpretation aligned with what I had just discovered. At first, I had blamed my relative. But after hearing the interpretation of the dream, my perspective shifted. I began to see that she, too, had been wounded. That same morning, I reported the matter to Reverend Benti Garba, the pastor who had officiated our marriage, and to my godfather, Mr. Asfaw Ayele. I sought their counsel before proceeding with a divorce.

My godfather immediately placed my three children and me in the American mission guesthouse in Gullele, Addis Ababa, and connected me with the church's lawyer to begin the divorce process. I was deeply grateful for his intervention. In those days, women who experienced spousal abuse in Ethiopia were the ones forced to leave the marital home, while the offender remained. Any woman who filed for divorce on the grounds of adultery was required to bring eyewitnesses to court. Judges would ask the witnesses, "Did you see them in the form of thread and needle?"—*Kirrenna merfe honew agnetehachewal?*—meaning, "Did you actually see them having sexual intercourse?"

Who could ever witness such an act in public?

While the pastor and my godfather began mediating the situation, I worked with the lawyer to prepare my case. I weighed carefully the cultural and religious consequences for both my relative and myself. My husband was highly regarded for his outwardly admirable character. He was generous, sociable, and quick to help others financially. Many would believe I had fabricated the accusation to destroy him and would label me a wicked wife.

My relative, too, would suffer devastating consequences. If the rape became known, she would be ostracized, deemed adulterous, barred from church participation, and likely never find a husband. After a month of one-sided mediation, Reverend Benti pressured me to forgive and return home. I quoted Matthew 19:9—*"except for sexual immorality"*—and insisted that we at least remain separated until my husband truly repented.

Reverend Benti responded sharply, "Agitu, don't argue theology with me. I will counsel him and bring him to repentance. But do not pray, 'Forgive us our trespasses as we forgive those who trespass against us,' if you are unwilling to forgive him and go back today." I cannot fully describe how painful and devastating those words were. I replied, "You are emboldening my husband not to repent. But I will return to my fire, because I fear God—the God who will be with me in the fire. May He repay you for what you have done to me."

The mediators then summoned my husband to apologize. I do not know what was discussed with him privately, but when he entered, he fell at my feet and said, "I am sorry for the attempt I made. It was only an attempt. I am sorry for the attempt." So, that very day, I returned home—armed with a false apology that only emboldened him to continue the worst assaults. This situation filled me with hatred and made me increasingly judgmental. Yet God was preparing me to be delivered from that state of heart.

One evening, while attending a conference at Entoto Mekane Yesus Church, I heard evangelist Negash Gebreyus preach from Micah 7:5–7. He emphasized this verse: *"A man's enemies are the members of his own household. Therefore, I will look to the Lord."* Then he exhorted the congregation, "Stop fixing your eyes on others. Fix your eyes on Jesus."

That message pierced me deeply. I realized my eyes had been fixed on my enemy, watching and waiting for God's judgment upon him. The next day, I contacted Meserete Kristos Church and asked them to pray for me. They referred me to a young female evangelist named Mulu Elala. I called her immediately and scheduled a meeting at my home the following Tuesday after she finished work.

When Mulu arrived, she asked me, "What do you want us to pray for?"

I answered honestly, "I hate my husband for what he did. The message I heard revealed to me that my heart is wrong. Now I feel guilty for hating him and being judgmental." I then explained everything that had happened and how deeply wounded I was.

Mulu bowed her head briefly and said, "I will pray for you."

I asked her, "Will I ever be able to love him as if he did nothing wrong?" I hated him so much that I did not want to live with him, and that is why I needed serious prayer.

"Yes," she replied calmly. "You will. I will pray for you."

She shared Scripture and prayed for me. We agreed that she would come every Tuesday after work to pray with me.

The second Tuesday came—nothing changed. The third Tuesday—still nothing. Before Mulu left on that third visit, I told her I had decided to leave my house until my situation changed and that I had begun looking for another job. She prayed for me regarding this decision and left.

The following week, I passed a job interview with Redd Barna, the Norwegian Save the Children Federation, and was hired as Supervisor of

Community Development and Health. I was assigned to a rural village called Bale Gadula, in the Bale region of southern Ethiopia. After receiving the offer, I went to General Gugsa's office to inform him of my resignation. He told me plainly that he did not want me to leave.

"The respect you receive here is worth more than the money you are chasing," he said. "I advise you not to go." He did not mention that resigning was illegal. Perhaps God was already showing me that the "respect" he spoke of would soon disappear. I thanked him sincerely and told him my decision was final.

On the sixth Tuesday of our prayer meetings, I shared the good news with Mulu—that I had been hired by Redd Barna. Though I feared the unknowns of this new journey, it was heartbreaking to leave my three young children—six, five, and three years old—behind in the care of a servant. At the same time, I felt relief at escaping the danger at work and the tension at home. Sadly, I had yet to learn that things would not unfold as I hoped.

On August 1, 1983, immediately after receiving my employment contract, I was assigned to attend a two-week orientation at the Integrated Holistic Approach Urban Development Project in Charkos, one of Addis Ababa's slum areas. The project was founded by Dr. Jember Tefera, a woman who dedicated her life to serving the poorest of the poor through housing, health care, and income-generating programs, in partnership with Redd Barna.

After completing the orientation, I prepared to leave for Bale Gadula. Early the following Monday morning, the organization's driver arrived with a truck to take me on the journey. Along the way, we picked up the secretary, Emebet Tesfaye. We arrived in Bale Gadula that evening. Redd Barna provided accommodation and food for its employees, including a male chef. However, our rooms were still under construction, so Emebet and I were temporarily assigned to sleep in the office.

The next day, the executive director introduced us to the five staff members—all men. Only Emebet, the chef, an employee named Mesfin, and I were from Addis Ababa; the remaining staff were locals. After orientation, the director took us sightseeing.

Everything I saw unsettled me. Bale Gadula was nothing like I had imagined. It felt as though I had returned twelve years earlier to my first post in Mizan Teferi after graduating from public health college. There was no electricity, except for a generator that ran from 6:00 to 10:00 p.m. There was no road accessible to vehicles between Bale Gadula and Goro, twenty-five miles away. There was no telephone service. Employees were not allowed to use the organization's vehicle. It felt less like employment—and more like confinement.

The week I arrived in Bale Gadula, something unusual happened. One morning around 5:00 a.m., I felt two large fingers—an index finger and a middle finger—pressing hard into my right rib cage. I woke up instantly.

I thought Emebet had woken me and immediately jumped out of bed, but she was still in a deep sleep. I reached for the candle beside my bed to see what was happening, but I hesitated, not wanting to disturb her, and returned to bed instead. I began rebuking the spirit, repeating, "In Jesus's name," over and over again. Even so, I could not fall back asleep until Emebet woke up around 6:00 a.m.

When she awoke, I asked her, "Did you wake me up?"

She replied, "What happened?" and I told her everything.

"What did you do when you felt the two big fingers waking you up?" she asked.

"I kept saying, 'In Jesus's name,' over and over again," I replied, "but I still couldn't go back to sleep."

"You were supposed to get on your knees and pray," she said gently. "It was God who woke you up."

At that moment, I realized that God had placed Emebet in my life to shape my communication with Him. With my Lutheran background, I had never experienced God in this way. I then told her that I often had visionary dreams but no longer had access to my dream interpreter, Hussein, and asked her what I should do.

She advised me to pray and ask God for dreams that were direct. Though she was younger than I was, Emebet was spiritually more mature. She came from Full Gospel Church, the first Pentecostal church in Ethiopia. That evening, we began worshipping together every night—a practice we continued until I left Bale Gadula for good. Always hungry for God, I started listening to Trans World Radio and Family Radio broadcasts from the United States. These radio programs became my church in the wilderness, surrounded by an overwhelmingly Muslim population. I listened daily.

During my second week in Bale Gadula, I finally found the quiet time my soul longed for. I fasted and prayed from September 7 to 9, 1983, asking God to reveal the end of my marriage. On the second day of fasting and prayer, around 5:00 a.m., I received a clear answer through a dream.

It was a long dream, but here is a glimpse of it: I returned home from Bale Gadula to visit my family. When I arrived, I found my husband sitting on our bed. I sat beside him and said, "God has been so good to us. Please change your ways so we can live a good life together."

He replied, "I have nothing to change."

Then I saw a man say to me, "I am taking you and your children abroad with me. Let's go."

I responded, "But I am pregnant." (In reality, I was not.)

He answered, "The child in you is mine," and took me and my children onto a flight routed through Nairobi.

When I woke up, I knew it had been a dream—but it felt incredibly real. Immediately, Isaiah 54:5–6 came to my mind:

> "For your Maker is your husband… For the Lord has
> called you like a woman forsaken and grieved in spirit,
> like a youthful wife when you were refused," says your
> God.

I became convinced that Jesus Himself was preparing to take me out of this unfixable marriage. In time, that belief proved true. Soon after,

I learned that God had already placed an external witness to the hidden evil in my home.

During my third week at Bale Gadula, I returned home to Addis Ababa to celebrate the Ethiopian New Year. When I arrived, the servant I had entrusted with my children's care was gone. I asked my husband what had happened to her. "I sent her away," he said. "She was not good for the children." He added that his nephew and niece, who were living with us at the time, were helping instead.

The Hidden Sour Began to Surface

The following day, my neighbor Kasech—who lived next door— invited me to lunch. It was the first time she had ever done so, and I was surprised. After we finished eating, she began telling me what had happened in my house while I was away.

"One night," she said, "your servant jumped through the window and came knocking at our door, trembling. She told me your husband was assaulting her, and I let her stay with us for the night." Kasech continued, her face tightening as she spoke. "Early the next morning, the servant went back to make breakfast for your family. I opened the door and watched her knock to be let in. Your husband came out shouting, 'This is your excrement!' He threw your dog's feces at her from the garage and beat her. She left with nothing."

Kasech then told me that she had also learned the truth about my relative—how she, too, had been assaulted by my husband. She wondered aloud how I could remain in such a marriage. Hearing that she had discovered the shame I had hidden left me deeply embarrassed. Yet because I had resolved to endure until what I had seen in my dream concerning the end of my marriage came to pass, I replied, "The God who declared that adultery is sin has been silent about it. I leave it to Him."

The following day, I asked the servant to come to our house to collect her belongings and her wages. I paid her twice the amount she was owed. I did not ask her what had happened, nor did I mention it. Then I called

Reverend Benti—the mediator I mentioned earlier—and explained the situation, seeking his help. To my shock, he said, "Agitu, he is your cross. You must carry him. I will continue to counsel him." His words saddened me deeply. I had always understood a husband to be a partner with whom one carries life's burdens—not the burden itself. Still, I trusted my husband and believed he would never repeat such behavior toward servants in our home. That trust, I now know, was painfully misplaced.

Three years later, Reverend Benti called me unexpectedly and said, "I am calling to tell you that I have given up on your husband. You may obtain a letter from the church and file for a divorce."

I replied, "It is too late. I prayed immediately after you ended the mediation the way you did, and God gave me my answer."

Sadly, I turned down that opportunity and endured further torment. From that point on, I no longer believed God wanted me to stay, but I was confused. The crimes that followed in our home left me with lifelong regret. In truth, God had already intervened in our relationship the night I conceived my last-born son in 1986—before Reverend Benti gave me the option of divorce. I will explain this later. That intervention alone was proof enough that I should not have stayed. Reverend Benti died a few months later. Learning from a nurse friend—who provided his postmortem care—that he had died of HIV/AIDS made me feel that he had called in repentance and further confirmed to me that it had been wrong to listen to his counsel and return home.

Before returning to Bale Gadula after my one-week holiday, I hired a servant. I could not trust my children to my husband's nephew and niece, who were living with us for their own advancement. After returning to Bale Gadula, I continued listening faithfully to Christian radio programs. A message on the call of Abraham, which I heard on September 23, 1983, touched me deeply. As I listened, I sensed that God was calling me to serve Him. Still, my circumstances made it impossible for me to equate that calling with leaving my family, as Abraham had done. I wrote everything I heard in my journal. That call would take me on a journey—when the time was right.

I visited my children on the last weekend of every month. During my second visit after my September holiday, I begged my husband to attend church with me. We arrived late and could not find seats, so we stood outside in the overflow area. Shortly afterward, the preacher made an altar call: "Those of you who hate your brother because of sin committed against you, stand up and repeat after me." My husband and I were already standing.

Preacher led those responding in this confession:

> "First John 3:15 says, 'Whoever hates his brother is a murderer.' I confess that I hate my brother, and I am a murderer. God, please forgive me. I choose to love my brother from now on, and I am freed from living as a murderer."

As I recited the words, conviction pierced my heart.

The preacher then instructed, "Those of you who prayed this prayer, wash your brother's feet when you get home. Forgive him—and forgive yourself." That evening, I washed my husband's feet and asked him to forgive me for hating him because of his wrongdoing. It did not change him. In fact, it seemed to embolden him to become worse. But it changed me.

I was freed—released from hatred, judgment, and bitterness. I learned to forgive those who harmed me and to pray for them. In time, I even became his defender. Let me share one example. One day, while praying for him, I came across Book of Isaiah 26:10:

"Let grace be shown to the wicked, yet he will not learn righteousness; in the land of uprightness he deals unjustly and does not behold the majesty of the Lord."

Then I turned my prayer into a question:

""Lord, King David committed far greater sins—adultery and even murder—yet You forgave him. Why, then, do You seem to take my husband's wrongdoing so seriously?" That very afternoon, while reading a book I had purchased in London, my eyes fell immediately on this statement:

"To human judgment, David's sin appears far greater than that of Ananias and Sapphira, since they only sold their own property. But in God's eyes, their pretense—their attempt to appear as something they were not—was the greater sin."

The weekend ended, and I returned to my job feeling relieved. Foolish me—I believed things would improve.

Although living conditions at my new assignment were far below my standards in Addis Ababa, I was initially grateful to work for a Pentecostal Christian. Yet the problems I soon faced under his leadership led me to conclude, painfully, that *it was better where it was worse*. The atmosphere I had despised at my former workplace was far healthier than the one I now found myself in. One day, a senior employee asked me what our boss's religion was. When I replied, "Full Gospel," he sputtered angrily and shouted, "Not even a quarter—let alone full!"

Spared from Unsurvivable Car Accident Without a Scratch

My new boss was such a difficult person that the other employees eventually prepared a petition against him. I refused to sign it and instead decided to leave quietly. On the morning of May 12, 1984, I asked the tractor driver to give me a ride to Goro, where I could find transportation to Bale Goba—the capital of Bale—and then continue by bus to Addis Ababa. The tractor was my only option because my boss did not allow employees to use the organization's car and was rarely on site.

It was my first time riding on a tractor, seated behind the driver. It felt like riding a mule behind its handler. When we reached Goro, I found a double-cabin pickup truck heading to Bale Goba and boarded it. I was assigned the front passenger seat, with another passenger sitting between the driver and me. The driver was speeding far beyond what was safe. Suddenly, the door flew open, and I was thrown out of the moving vehicle onto the roadside field. The driver sped away without stopping, leaving me unconscious.

I do not know how much time passed. Another driver coming from behind saw me lying there, unconscious. He pursued the fleeing driver, forced him to return, and made him take me to a hospital in Bale Goba. I regained consciousness on the way back and found myself seated in the same place I had occupied earlier. Confused, I asked the passenger beside me, "Where am I?"

He explained what had happened and told me the driver was taking me to the hospital. Strangely, I felt completely well at that moment. I immediately remembered Emebet's warning the day before. When I had told her I was leaving, she said she had seen a troubling dream and feared I was in danger. I had not listened. Now, I believed this accident was confirmation that my trip had been against God's will.

I told the driver I did not want to go to the hospital and asked him to return me to Goro instead. He pulled over. Within minutes, a bus heading to Goro passed by. The driver stopped it and secured me a seat—clearly relieved to be rid of me. He paid for my fare, and I returned to Goro, arriving around 7:00 p.m. I checked into a hotel immediately.

That night, when I lay down, the room began spinning violently. I could not sleep. I checked my scalp and felt a large swelling on the right side of my head, near the junction of the coronal and sagittal sutures. Panic set in. I called the hotel attendant and explained my situation. He reassured me that help would come in the morning. By God's grace, my condition stabilized around 4:00 a.m.

Early the next morning, the Norwegian mission's medical team knocked on my hotel door. Before examining me, the nurse asked if I had swelling on my head. I said yes and lifted my hand to show her—but the swelling was gone. I was astonished that such a large swelling had disappeared overnight. Still, I was no stranger to God's miracles in my life. After examining me, the nurse instructed me to rest for three days, warning that failure to do so could result in lifelong headaches. Fortunately, my boss heard about the accident and sent the organization's driver to pick me up. I returned to Bale Gadula and rested for three days as instructed. Glory be to God—I have never suffered headaches since.

Awaited by Diverse Trials Upon My Return from Bale

What a surprise it was when the very difficulties I faced with my boss created the way for my exit. Although I had refused to sign the petition against him, my boss reported to the head office in Addis Ababa that I had conspired with the other employees and encouraged them to petition against him.

I did not learn of this until I was summoned to Redd Barna's head office on July 16, 1984. Upon my arrival, the administrator handed me a letter terminating my employment, having accepted my boss's false report as fact. The decision did not disturb me—I had already been preparing to resign, waiting only for God's direction. However, I calmly told the administrator that I wanted to understand the reason for my termination.

After he explained that I was accused of conspiring against my boss, I asked him to check the petition itself and look for my name among the signatures. When the administrator could not find my name on the employees' petition, he offered me the option to resign and receive an additional three months' salary. He had to do this to avoid the legal consequences of terminating me unlawfully. Unknown to me at the time, the best was yet to come. Above all, God was opening a door with a purpose in mind. For that reason, I did not place blame—and still do not blame—my former boss who harmed me. Later, I learned from the administrative staff that he had acted out of fear, believing I might replace him if he were dismissed.

I was overjoyed to be home again with my sweet children—then seven, six, and four years old. They were obedient, respectful, loving, and well-disciplined. Our family life appeared peaceful until the outrageous immorality in my home came to light. On weekends, we enjoyed outings with our children—picnics at expensive hotels where my husband covered the expenses (the only times I ever saw his money). Although the tension between my husband and me was hidden from the children, it did not deprive them of these moments until we eventually left Ethiopia for good.

They especially loved swimming at the Ghion Hotel in Addis Ababa on Saturdays. During summer breaks, I rented suites at the Adam Ras Hotel in Adama (Nazret), fifty-six miles from Addis Ababa, where they swam and played joyfully. These memories remain precious to me.

Yet despite my joy at being reunited with my children, the situation at home was far from welcoming. The retaliation I had feared after leaving the Ministry of National Defense arrived just one week after my return. I did not know that an arrest warrant had been issued for me until two armed police officers appeared at my door one morning.

They ordered me to come outside. One of them said curtly, "You are wanted. Let's go!"

I was shocked and terrified. I could not imagine what crime I had committed, but I had no power to resist. My husband followed as they escorted me to jail. I was first taken to an investigator's office at the correctional facility.

The investigator sat me down and asked, "Do you know why you are here?"

"No," I replied.

"You are charged with violating the law by quitting your job illegally," he said.

By God's mercy, my husband managed to bail me out that same day. I did not tell him the reason for my arrest.

The following morning, I went to the office of the head of civil administration, Mr. Tamerat, at the Ministry of National Defense headquarters to appeal my case.

As soon as I entered his office, I spoke boldly:

> "Would I be considered a citizen in a country that does
> not respect my right to life?"

He responded calmly, "Please sit down and tell me what happened," ringing the bell on his desk to summon his *telalaki* (messenger).

After I sat down, Mr. Tamerat said, "Let me order a tear-wiper," referring to a drink meant to calm someone. He asked, "What would you like—coffee, tea, or a soft drink?"

"Coffee," I answered—and truly, I began to calm down.

I then told him everything my former boss, the colonel, had done to me. As I spoke, I sensed God's favor. Mr. Tamerat listened attentively and without interruption. When I finished, he made a lengthy phone call to the appropriate government authority, explaining my case in detail. I prayed silently throughout the conversation.

At last, the official on the other end instructed Mr. Tamerat to issue me a release letter, copying three relevant government departments. Mr. Tamerat asked me to wait while the letter was typed and signed. When it was ready, he handed it to me.

Before I left, he added, "Your former boss has been demoted. He is now in that small office in the shelter," he said, pointing. "You may see him if you wish."

I did not. I simply left.

That day was one of the happiest of my life. Words cannot express my joy. Against all odds—and in defiance of government policy—God intervened on my behalf, and everything turned in my favor. While I completed this chapter of my life with victory, my home situation continued to deteriorate, and my journey through fire grew even more intense.

How Assault by My Husband's Niece and Nephew— With My Husband's Support—Shaped My Spiritual Life

When I returned from Bale Gadula, the servant had already left— though she had lasted longer than the previous ones. My husband claimed he had sent her away because his nephew and niece could help around the house. Later, I learned the truth, which did not surprise me. Contrary to his claim, his nephew and niece soon turned against me for reasons I could not understand.

One day, while I was hospitalized following surgery to remove hemorrhoids, his niece stood at the foot of my bed and shouted at me, "May you never rise from this bed!" before storming out. Shortly afterward, my nurse-friend, Alemitu Etafa, came to visit me. I told her what had happened, and she was deeply saddened. I then called my husband to come to the hospital and told him what his niece had done.

To my utter shock, he responded, "She did the right thing! Good job! That's what you deserve!" and walked away.

It was devastating and humiliating to realize that Alemitu showed me more compassion than my own husband. I did not want to return home at all. But God spoke to me clearly, instructing me to go back to my children, promising that He Himself would take them to places they did not yet know. Obedience mattered more than my pain, so I returned home after being discharged.

As God had promised, my husband's niece left the country on a scholarship just one month later. However, the nephew soon took his turn in escalating the abuse. One day, after I asked him why he had not cleaned the house, things turned dangerous.

When my husband returned from work that evening, I heard him shouting, "I will break her into pieces!" I did not know what his nephew had told him, but my husband came charging toward our bedroom from the detached unit where the nephew stayed. I locked myself inside and cried out through the window, "I need help!" again and again, until our neighbors, Kasech and her husband Yakob, came to my rescue.

They brought us together in the living room and summoned the nephew to join us. Kasech began by saying she had long wondered how we tolerated two young adults who contributed nothing to the household. Both she and Yakob urged my husband to value his marriage above all else and asked him to send his nephew away.

I knew my husband would not heed their advice. Immediately, I remembered what God had spoken to me in the hospital—that He would handle matters in His time. I repented for speaking when I should have remained silent and trusted God's word to come to pass.

My repentance did not stop there. I called Mrs. Muluberhan Djote, a member of my women's monthly prayer group and a former instructor, and shared what had happened. She referred me to evangelist Fetlework Tefera (now a pastor) and gave me her phone number. I called Pastor Fetlework immediately and visited her home the next day.

After offering me refreshments, she asked, "What brings you here?"

"I want you to pray for me—that God forgives me," I replied, explaining the confrontation with my husband's nephew.

She looked at me kindly and said, "When you arrived at the gate, God showed me an open heart. I had been praying about the stone hearts that come to me for prayer. You did nothing wrong. God wanted to show me that He still finds hearts like yours."

She prayed for me, and I left deeply comforted. That very evening, my husband's nephew apologized, and peace was restored.

The following week, two police officers arrived at our home to draft the nephew into military service. By God's mercy, their truck was already full, and they told him they would return the following week. That night, as I prayed for him, I came across Proverbs 24:11:

> "Rescue those being led away to death; hold back those staggering toward slaughter."

God answered that prayer. The nephew enrolled in nursing school immediately and left before the officers returned.

One month after leaving Redd Barna, I resumed the weekly Tuesday prayer meetings that had previously been held in my home. I also began searching for work once again. World Vision in Addis Ababa became both my first stop—and my last.

It so happened that my friend Hamelmal Yalew's husband, Eshetu Yimer, was the personnel head at World Vision. He told me they were looking for a nurse for their project in Alamata, Northern Ethiopia, and encouraged me to apply. I told him I would pray about it first and left his office.

That evening, as I prayed, I came across Psalm 127:1–3. I read it first in Amharic and then in the New International Version:

> "In vain you rise early and stay up late, toiling for food
> to eat—for he grants sleep to those he loves. Children are
> a heritage from the Lord, offspring a reward from him."

The message felt precise and timely. I understood it as God's answer—not to take the job out of fear of financial need, and not to leave my children in pursuit of provision. My children were my true inheritance.

The next day, I called Eshetu and declined the offer. World Vision provided attractive salaries and benefits, but I had to obey what I believed God was telling me. Later, I learned that the nurse who accepted the position I declined was killed during a shootout between government troops and Eritrean Liberation Front guerrillas. She died from bleeding. I had not known the location was that dangerous when I declined the offer. Once again, I saw God's protective hand over my life.

In the third month of my job search, I received a surprising phone call from Dr. Jember Tefera. She informed me that the Agricultural Equipment and Technical Services Corporation had a contract opening for a clinic director and suggested I apply. Within hours of our conversation, I was invited for an interview—and I was hired.

The position was similar to the one I had held at the Defense Industries. I provided first-aid treatment for employees on duty, and only a few visited the clinic for medical care. However, this job offered even better benefits: transportation to and from work and full health insurance coverage. During my employment at Defense Industries, I had only the standard government health coverage and no transportation privileges.

The transportation benefit was especially timely. Without informing me or seeking my approval, my husband had sold our car. I had no idea what he did with the money. Our culture gave him full authority over such decisions, and my moral convictions did not allow me to fight over it. I simply endured it in silence. Despite all that, I was overjoyed to receive such a fulfilling position. Once again, God had opened a door at exactly the right time.

Looking back, I see how every closed door, every narrow escape, and every painful delay was woven together by God's hand. When fear urged me to move, God told me to stay. When survival tempted me to compromise, God called me to trust. I did not always understand His ways, but again and again He proved faithful—protecting my life, preserving my children, and opening doors no human authority could shut. I ended this chapter not because my trials had ceased, but because I had learned to listen for God's voice and obey it, even when obedience cost me comfort, certainty, and peace. What lay ahead would test me further, but the foundation had been laid: God was my refuge, my provider, and the One who ordered my steps.

6

ENDURANCE REWARDS

Soon after I started my new job, a passage from Isaiah 65:23 began to speak to me with unexpected force:

> "They shall not labor in vain, Nor bring forth children for
> trouble; For they shall be the descendants of the blessed
> of the Lord, And their offspring with them."

The message stirred something deep within me and pointed me toward what I had never planned to do. It affirmed that God wanted me to have another child. At first, I paid little attention. I had already decided that the three children I had been blessed with were enough. Then the message came again—this time in a dream—clearly revealing the gender of the child, a girl, and giving me a glimpse of her future. When I woke up, I reflected on the dream and remembered another dream I had received earlier, on September 8, 1983, which had also included my next conception.

The impression was so strong that the very next day I went to the Ethiopian Family Guidance Association and asked to have my intrauterine contraceptive device removed. The nurse advised me not to do it, but I insisted. I did not want to appear foolish by telling her that God had spoken to me. Ironically, she had once been my instructor during my family-planning training and certification eight years earlier, and we knew each other well. Sure enough, I conceived that same month. My relationship with my husband improved after I started this new job, and throughout the pregnancy things remained peaceful—though that season of calm would not last long.

At the same time, the call I had received in Bale Gadula in 1983 to serve God began resurfacing in my heart with increasing urgency. Eventually, I joined the choir at Addis Ababa Mekane Yesus Church, since music ministry had been part of my life from a young age and was what I loved most. I was five months pregnant when I joined the choir, and I never missed a single Thursday practice.

When my due date arrived, I was admitted to the hospital to deliver my baby. Earlier in the pregnancy, I had known the baby's gender through what I call a "divine ultrasound," but by the sixth month I had forgotten and began preparing for a boy—to balance my children, since I already had two girls and one boy. As labor began, an inner voice spoke clearly to me: "Your baby is a girl, and her name is Bethel." Sure enough, I gave birth to a girl. My original plan had been to give her an Oromo name, but I obeyed the inner prompting and named her Bethel.

Bethel arrived as a blessing in every sense. During the final month of my first year at the Agricultural Equipment and Technical Services Corporation, I came across a job posting for an organization called the International Coordinating Committee for Welfare and Development Programs (ICC) in Addis Ababa. Since my current position was contract-based, I was actively seeking permanent employment. I applied immediately and was invited for an interview the following week.

The interview took place at ICC's office in the city council. I was interviewed by representatives from five international organizations—including UNICEF—along with the chairman of Higher 21 Kebele 23. After the interview, I was told they would contact me with their decision, and I returned to my job. Two days later, I had a dream in which I was hired by an organization in Zurich. When I woke up, I could remember only that the city's name began with the letter "Z." I even looked it up on a map.

Bethel and Menase: My Reward for Endurance—and the Job That Followed

Two weeks after the interview, I received a phone call from ICC asking me to come in to hear their decision. When I arrived, a representative from UNICEF was present to share the news. He told me that thirty-three candidates had applied for the position, but that I had been selected as the best fit. He then handed me my employment letter. Mr. Getahun Belay, the executive director of ICC, explained that I had been hired as a project officer to run the Students for Kids International Projects (SKIP)—a program of Pestalozzi Children's Village in Zurich, Switzerland—under ICC's sponsorship at Higher 21.

I submitted my resignation to the Agricultural Equipment and Technical Services Corporation and joined ICC the following week, rejoicing—unaware of the battle that lay ahead. ICC was strategically designed by top Addis Ababa City Council officials to gain access to— and exploit—humanitarian and relief aid funds and supplies. To achieve this, ICC formed a consortium of officially recognized international humanitarian and governmental organizations under its umbrella, placing a senior city council official as an executive committee member and chair of the social affairs committee of the consortium.

Among ICC's members was the Christian Relief and Development Association (CRDA), an indigenous umbrella organization of NGOs and faith-based organizations in Ethiopia. Established in 1973 by thirteen faith-based and secular humanitarian organizations, CRDA was an experienced and trustworthy relief-coordinating body. In reality, there was no practical need to create ICC at all. Through its structure, ICC systematically maintained direct and indirect control over the funds allocated to programs within the listed organizations. It also exercised direct control over humanitarian projects that were not ICC members— including SKIP, the program that employed me.

Before the end of 1986, the SKIP project was scheduled for evaluation by external evaluators from Switzerland. However, despite allocated funds,

ICC had failed to provide a vehicle for the evaluators because the money designated for that purpose had been misused. Since the Swiss government partially funded SKIP, the Swiss Embassy in Addis Ababa intervened and purchased a brand-new vehicle for the evaluators' use.

Two evaluators soon arrived from Switzerland and conducted a thorough evaluation. Two full pages of their report were devoted to my work with SKIP, and I received an excellent assessment. Still, this did not protect me from further attacks by ICC for my refusal to cooperate with corruption. After the evaluators left Ethiopia, SKIP decided that I should use the new vehicle for project operations.

That decision, however, placed me in serious danger. The government official overseeing ICC coveted the vehicle for two reasons. First, it was only the second of its kind in the entire country—Comrade Colonel Teka Tulu, a Central Committee member, owned the other. Second, as part of the Derg's strategy to discourage church attendance, the government had banned both private and government vehicles from operating on Sundays. NGO vehicles, identifiable by their yellow license plates, were exempt.

To gain access to the car, the city council assigned a driver to me— even though I was fully capable of driving myself and had no need for one.

One Thursday morning, the official overseeing ICC summoned me to his office for the first time. He asked politely whether I needed anything. I replied honestly that the project was at a standstill because ICC had failed to submit the required progress report to the donor agency, which was necessary for the release of funds. He assured me the issue would be resolved and encouraged me to make further requests. I later realized that this part of the conversation was merely an attempt to establish rapport.

He then shifted the discussion and asked whether I needed the car for the upcoming weekend. I told him I was embarrassed to use the car even on weekdays because there was not enough project activity to justify it. Despite that, he said *he* needed the car for the weekend and asked to use it. I told him I would let him know and left. After praying at home, I returned the next day and told him he could use the car—but only if he recorded the mileage in the logbook and purchased fuel, since the use was personal. It was a bold statement.

The following month, the same official summoned me again—this time on a Friday. He repeated the same opening conversation and then asked, once more, to use the car that weekend. As before, I said I would let him know. That evening, I prayed earnestly for guidance on how to deal with a corrupt authority. God answered me through Scripture:

> "Better to be of a humble spirit with the lowly than to divide the spoil with the proud." *(Proverbs 16:19)* The answer was unmistakably *no*.

The next day, I told the official plainly that I could not lend him the car. The driver, who overheard the exchange, was visibly alarmed and asked me, "Do you want to die?"

I replied calmly, "I have done what pleases God."

My driver was deeply troubled. In those days, no one dared to challenge powerful officials—doing so could cost a person their life. I was fully aware that my decision would have consequences, yet I was not afraid. My faith in God made me bold enough to fear Him rather than any man in authority.

My New Job Positioned Me to Confront Corruption

The official was furious. The following week, ICC sent me a letter demanding that I surrender the car immediately. Instead of retreating, my resolve only strengthened. I responded without compromise. I wrote back to ICC and copied the Swiss Embassy, stating plainly that the demand was retaliation for my refusal to allow the official to use the car for his personal purposes. I further informed them that I was returning the vehicle to the Swiss Embassy—the original donor—and advised ICC to obtain the car from the Embassy if they still desired it.

I then drove the car to the Swiss Embassy and delivered my letter. However, the ambassador explained that they could not accept the vehicle from me. Because the car belonged to SKIP, he said, removing it from a SKIP employee could be construed as a human-rights violation under Swiss law. I returned home with the car and parked it in my garage, where it remained until the SKIP director and the Ethiopia program coordinator arrived from Switzerland to address the matter.

Three days after their arrival in Addis Ababa, they asked me to meet them at the Ethiopian Hotel at 8:00 p.m. I suspected they feared being seen with me during daylight, which is why the meeting was scheduled for the evening.

I drove the contested car to the hotel to hand it over. The first words the director spoke to me were, "Agitu, you are boxing against a wall."

I replied calmly, "The wicked are never protected by a wall. I do not want to be judged by God Almighty."

I ended the conversation by telling them not to worry about me, but rather about their project, which had remained stagnant for more than four years. Two days later, ICC issued a letter terminating my employment after thirteen months of service. A week after that, ICC's coordinator—my immediate supervisor—summoned me to his office. Instead of discussion, he shouted at me in anger:

"The Swiss ambassador holds you in such high regard that he sent a mediator on your behalf! Who do you think the Swiss ambassador is? We can expel him from this country within twenty-four hours!" They never did.

God Was Building My Future While I Battled ICC Over My Dismissal

I had to wait for God's go-ahead before suing ICC for illegally firing me. During the twelve months that followed, while I was waging a legal battle with ICC, God was quietly building my future. He astonished me with circumstances that defied natural explanation. On one hand, I was uncertain about the future of my already difficult marriage. On the other, I was unemployed. Yet in the midst of that instability, God showed me—in a dream—the process through which I would acquire land and build my own home.

At that time, under a new socialist policy, the government allocated five hundred square meters of land to citizens. Though this seemed impossible, I remembered a dream I had three years earlier, during my final year at Defense Industries. In that dream, I saw myself in a newly built house, but the ceiling was covered with newspaper blackened like charcoal. My dream interpreter explained, "You will indeed have a new home built for you. The charcoal-black newspaper covering the ceiling means that your husband's sins will continue and will be exposed for all to see." That interpretation encouraged me.

The very next afternoon, at 1:00 p.m., I went to the office of the urban land administration head, Colonel Mamo, to apply for land. He did not arrive until 4:15 p.m.—almost exactly matching the time I had seen in my dream (4:10 p.m.). When I handed him my application and he finished reading it, he said, "Go find a pocket lot and report back to me so I can assign it to you."

That was extraordinary favor. It meant I could receive land—possibly even larger than the standard 500 square meters—in a prime location in Addis Ababa. I returned home filled with joy and shared the news with my husband, asking him to help me locate a suitable pocket lot. Instead, he told me to go back and ask Colonel Mamo to assign me any available lot.

That same Sunday, before I returned to Colonel Mamo's office, I received a powerful confirmation. As I was entering church, Evangelist Negash GebreYesus stopped me and said, "I have been looking for you. The Lord gave me a message for you from 1 Samuel 25:28: *'The Lord will certainly make for my lord an enduring house, because my lord fights the battles of the Lord.'"*

I was astonished. I had not seen Negash for two years, and his message directly affirmed what God had already shown me.

On Monday morning, I returned to Colonel Mamo. Without delay, he assigned me a 500-square-meter plot in a new development area adjacent to Bole International Airport and instructed me to submit a house plan for his approval.I prepared a modest 70-square-meter plan and brought it to him the following week. He glanced at it and said, "The land I gave you is in a first-class location, with the city's ring road running in front of it. This plan does not qualify." He threw it into the trash, took my application, and wrote in red ink across the top: *"Submit a 115-square-meter plan for approval."*

Although I had no money to build such a house, I went upstairs to the architects' office, selected a modern three-bedroom, two-bath design that met his requirement, and brought it back to him within the hour. He approved it before noon. Later that afternoon, his secretary issued me a support letter addressed to the city council so I could obtain my land title. Quietly, she then revealed a critical secret: a new policy reducing land allocations from 500 square meters to 250 was scheduled to be implemented within two weeks. She urged me to act immediately.

The next morning, I arrived at the city council office before it opened at 8:00 a.m. I was the first person there. The officer told me to return the next day. When I did, he said, "Come tomorrow." That "tomorrow" stretched into more than a week. But I had time—I was not employed.

After eight business days, perhaps weary of seeing me every morning and afternoon, he finally issued my land title. As he wrote it, I asked him to include my husband's name as the household head. He snapped, "I don't know this man!" Yet I persisted until he added my husband's name alongside mine. To this day, I do not understand why I insisted on that.

Confronting God's Justice in My Marriage Spared My Husband's Life

Bethel was five months old when I was fired from ICC. That same month, I conceived my fifth child—unexpectedly. What seemed accidental would soon prove to be part of God's sovereign plan, filled with miracles. Two months earlier, on April 12, 1986, I had a deeply troubling dream. In it, I saw my husband and one of our sons die as a result of God's anger over an affair my husband had engaged in the previous night, Friday, April 11, with a woman from Ambo. When I awoke, the dream felt more like a vision. I locked myself in the bathroom and prayed fervently for mercy, weeping before God.

Afterward, I quietly laid my right hand on my husband and asked God to speak to him directly. Within seconds, he jumped out of bed. When I asked what happened, he told me he had just woken from a dream—brief, but confirming the one I had seen. That night, shortly after I fed Bethel and put her to bed around midnight, the skin beneath my wedding ring began to itch intensely. The itching worsened until the skin started peeling. I woke my husband and showed him. He told me to remove the ring, which I did, and I was finally able to sleep. From that day on, I could no longer wear my wedding ring without pain. Eventually, my husband took it, and I never knew what he did with it.

Because the physical sign followed the dream within hours, I decided to fast and pray for my husband that day. After dinner that Saturday, I prepared warm water, washed my husband's feet, and then told him about the dream I had seen that morning. I said to him, "Please don't die. We need you," trying to express love and to remind him of his value before a merciful God. He paused for a few seconds and then said, "One woman—who I think was from Ambo—tempted me yesterday while I was using a public telephone outside the courthouse in Lideta, but God protected me." He then read a passage from the Bible and prayed with me—for the first time in our marriage.

I did not jump with joy. My heart already knew the truth. As my fear deepened, I begged him to go to church with me the next morning. When we returned from church on Sunday, I was met by a troubling sight. Our wedding picture frame, which had been on the end table, lay shattered on the floor. My husband's framed photograph had also fallen from the entertainment center and was broken in pieces. That scene unsettled me deeply.

The following day, Monday, I went to the home of Evangelist Fetlework (now Pastor Fetlework) and shared my dream with her, asking her to pray for us. I knelt as she prayed in tongues for two hours. Since I did not have the gift of interpretation, I asked her what she had received from the Lord. She said, "Your brother will not repent. To confirm this, ask him tonight to repent."

I chose not to do so, knowing he would deny everything. Instead, I prayed that God Himself would speak to him. The God who forgave King David is always ready to forgive anyone who humbles themselves and truly repents. The very next day, at our Tuesday prayer meeting, my prayer was unexpectedly answered. At that time, Evangelist Tadele (now Pastor Tadele) led our Tuesday prayer gatherings. That evening, however, the program took an unusual turn. He began by saying:

"Today's program will be different. I came with a hard message. We must repent for conforming to the world through wickedness and adultery. Tonight, this will be a repentance meeting only. I ask each of you to tell us what you need to repent for, so we can pray together. I will begin with—" and he called my husband by name.

My husband replied that he had nothing to repent for. I trembled with fear, wondering if he thought I had spoken to Evangelist Tadele. Yet he never mentioned it afterward. That moment confirmed what Pastor Fetlework had told me the day before. Though discouraged, I did not lose hope. At the same time, I lived in fear of my husband. Whenever he sensed that I had discovered his wrongdoing, he would turn against me, defending himself with words that made me feel guilty and at fault. I am not perfect. At times, I blamed myself for not knowing how to handle our marriage from the beginning.

Two months later, what I had seen in my dream—the warning of death—seemed to manifest. My husband suffered a severe asthma attack, and I rushed him to Zewditu Hospital. He was treated and discharged with medication, but by the next morning, Sunday, his condition worsened drastically. He could barely breathe and managed to say, "Take me to

Nazret (Adama), or I will die." Nazret is about one hundred kilometers away and has a warmer climate than Addis Ababa.

Fear gripped me. I remembered the events of the previous week and worried he might die on the way. That Friday morning, he had accused me, saying, "You infected me with gonorrhea."

"How dare you?" I cried, running to the front door and shouting, "God, come in and judge!"

Later that day, he returned home with long-acting penicillin and asked me to inject both of us. I injected him but refused to take the medication myself. On the following Monday, I had laboratory tests done at Arsho Laboratory, which confirmed that I was negative. When I showed him the results, he later admitted that he experienced similar symptoms whenever he had direct sexual contact with me. When his asthma worsened the following Sunday, guilt overwhelmed me. I feared that my cry for judgment had invited death. Yet faith rose in me. I told him I needed to go to church before taking him to Nazret, and I left.

At Addis Ababa Mekane Yesus Church, I sat on the front veranda beside one of the pillars. Wrapping my right arm around it, I wept and cried out to God: "Please heal my husband and deliver me from being a murderer." When I returned home from church, I found my husband sitting calmly in a chair on the veranda—completely healed.

The Pregnancy Dream Fulfilled, but the Baby's Life Spared by Fervent Intercession

My last pregnancy, mentioned above, followed this incident. Because of the dream, my pregnancy began with a deep fear of losing a male child. As soon as I realized I was pregnant, I decided to seek an abortion, justifying my decision by what I believed I had heard from the Lord. But God was about to show me that no sin is ever justifiable, and that His mercy endures forever.

Abortion was illegal in Ethiopia at the time, but I devised a way around the law. The gynecologist I contacted instructed me to bring him my pregnancy test result so he could terminate the pregnancy. However, while I was driving home with the test result in my hand, I heard a voice shout clearly in my ears: "It is hard for you to kick against the goads."

These were the very words spoken to Saul in Acts 9:5, at the moment of his conversion.

As soon as I arrived home, I repented and decided to keep my pregnancy. Yet the fear did not leave me. You may consider this foolish, but even before I knew the gender of the child, I named my unborn baby Menase—Manasseh, the son of King Hezekiah, who was born after God extended his father's life (2 Kings 20). I hid myself indoors throughout the pregnancy and cried out to God continually, pleading for mercy over the life of my unborn son.

This pregnancy and delivery were unlike any of my previous ones. I had no morning sickness, and the labor was remarkably easy. I gave birth to a ten-pound baby boy with only slight lower abdominal pain. When I told the midwife that the baby was coming, she argued with me and delayed putting on her gloves. I had to rely on my nursing skills to prevent injury during delivery.

Although I rejoiced at having a brother for my older son, the uncertainty surrounding this child's life continued to haunt me—until God performed what I consider one of the greatest miracles of my life, three weeks after Menase was born. Here is what happened:

I asked Evangelist Fetlework to take me, though I was unwell, to a Thursday prayer program. I had not attended for nearly ten months and did not know the location, so she accompanied me. Shortly after we arrived and took our seats, the minister announced, "I have only ten minutes before I must leave. Those of you who are sick or troubled, kneel around the coffee table so I can pray for you."

Mrs. Fetlework whispered to me, "You kneel," and I obeyed.

The minister moved around the table, laying hands on each person. When he reached me, he placed his right hand on my shoulder and asked,

"Do you have a male baby?"

"Yes," I replied.

"What is wrong with him?" he asked.

"The Lord and I know," I answered.

Then he said, "The Lord says He has removed what was on the child," and gently patted my shoulder before moving on.

I was overwhelmed. I had never met this minister before, nor had I shared my burden with anyone present. Words could not express my joy. When I arrived home, I held my baby tightly and kissed him again and again. When I look at my two precious children, Bethel and Menase, I often say, *"We would never know what we missed, because we would never have seen what we lost."* God honored my obedience and counted it, in His mercy, as faith—much like that of Abraham.

Five months after Menase was born, the construction of our new home was completed, and we moved into our beautiful villa. Providentially, a former colleague of mine had become the manager of a brick factory in Addis Ababa, which enabled us to obtain building materials quickly and complete the work in a short time.

Divine Guidance Led Me to a Remarkable Victory over ICC

Seven months later, I finally received God's permission to file a lawsuit against ICC for terminating my employment illegally. The full story is lengthy, but briefly: at the time, a labor court existed under the Ministry of Labor and Social Affairs (MOLSA), where petitioners were not required to have legal representation. However, employees in leadership positions were barred from using that court. As a result, I hired an attorney to file the lawsuit. At our final meeting, my attorney collected my hire and termination letters from the ICC and prepared to file my case in federal court. From there, I went directly to my weekly prayer meeting. Just as everything appeared ready, the Lord spoke to me that afternoon during our underground fellowship, instructing me **not** to proceed with an attorney.

Confident that God was in control, I decided to take my case to the Ministry of Labor and Social Affairs (MOLSA). The next morning, I asked my lawyer to return the court documents he had prepared for filing.

However, he attempted to prevent me from terminating our contract. Without my knowledge, he withheld my hire and termination letters—documents essential for pursuing my case at MOLSA. I only discovered this later that evening when I reviewed the papers at home.

Fortunately, God gave me the wisdom to retrieve the documents from him the very next morning. Unfamiliar with the legal process, I wrote a letter to Mr. Shimeles Adugna, the Minister of Labor and Social Affairs, briefly explaining my situation. I had no idea then that this very unfamiliarity would ultimately work in my favor. His secretary, Mrs. Tsega Legessie, received the letter and instructed me to return in three days. When I returned on the appointed day, she handed me the minister's response in a sealed envelope and directed me to deliver it to Comrade Abba Saba, the Executive Director of the Workers' Labor Court.

When I asked for the office number, she realized I assumed his office was in the same building and redirected me to a different location. At that point, I knew neither the process nor the physical location of the Workers' Labor Court. That was when an extraordinary miracle began to unfold. After reading the minister's letter, the Executive Director instructed me to proceed with filing my case and to inform him which judge it was assigned to. After four months of legal struggle, I finally won the case. Let me explain how: One morning, before leaving home for my labor court hearing, I received this word from Scripture:

> "Say to him, 'Be careful, keep calm and don't be afraid.
> Do not lose heart because of these two smoldering
> stubs of firewood—because of the fierce anger
> of Rezin and Aram and of the son of Remaliah.'"
> *(Isaiah 7:4)*

When I arrived at court, I saw two men ICC had brought as witnesses against me. One was the kebele chairman and also the SKIP project supervisor. I said to myself, *These are the two smoldering stubs of firewood*

I was warned about this morning. I resolved not to fear or lose heart. After listening to their false testimony, I said calmly,

> "Many seek the ruler's favor, but justice for man comes from the Lord." *(Proverbs 29:26)*

Although public expressions of Christianity were forbidden at the time, I quoted Scripture without hesitation, knowing that God's authority surpasses every human system. At the end of the hearing, the judge made a startling disclosure. He told me that he worked closely with the sister of a city council official and the wife of the ICC coordinator—my former boss—and that both women had been pressuring him daily to rule against me. However, he had been warned by his superior, Comrade Abba Saba, to render a just and timely verdict.

At that moment, I understood that Minister Shimeles Adugna was fully aware of the corruption at ICC and had intervened to ensure justice in my case—despite having no personal acquaintance with me. My only contact with him had been the letter I wrote. I knew him only through his public reputation, particularly the story I mentioned in the previous chapter about his deep compassion for famine victims. The God who knows all things had guided me exactly where I needed to go.

The court ruled that ICC must pay my salary for the four months my case had been under litigation and immediately reinstate me to my former position. Unfortunately, the law did not allow compensation for the seven months between my dismissal and the filing of the case. When I presented the court's decision to the ICC coordinator, he looked at it and shouted at me, "You should be ashamed of yourself!"

Before he could continue, I replied, "Mr. Getahun, you are against me because you know whom you trusted. I am strong because I know whom I trust. We will see who the winner is." My boldness grew, and I added an Amharic proverb that declared my confidence in God:

"Balebetwan yetamamench beg läte'a dej yädral."
A sheep that trusts her owner spends the night outside.

With that, I closed his office door and left.

ICC filed an appeal, forcing me into a second round of legal battle. According to the law, I was entitled to resume my duties during the appeal process. I went to the court handling enforcement matters every working day for two months, requesting that the judgment be executed. Finally, one day, the judge shouted at me, "Leave my office! Go away!" without offering any explanation.

It was humiliating and more frustrating than anything I had endured before. It appeared that the matter had reached a dead end. Yet I did not lose my trust in God, for I had learned—again and again—that His grace is greater than every obstacle. Returning home, I prayed earnestly. During that time of prayer, I was reminded that Colonel Tesfaye Woldeselassie, the Minister of Internal Affairs, heard petitions every Thursday. The following Thursday morning, I went to his office with my plea. His office was located in the building the Derg had confiscated from the Ethiopian Evangelical Church Mekane Yesus (EECMY). I arrived at 9:00 a.m., but the waiting room was already full. I did not gain entrance until 4:55 p.m.

When my turn finally came, I handed him my written plea and said:

> "I stand before you because the action I took in the fear of
> the Lord has worked against me and placed my children's
> lives at risk. I earnestly plead with you to examine my
> case. If you find me guilty, have me executed—because
> my life means nothing if I cannot provide for my
> children."

He read my letter carefully and told me to check back in three days.

Within a week, a court messenger delivered a summons to my home. I was ordered to appear before the very judge who had previously denied me justice. What followed was an astonishing victory. On the court date, the ICC coordinator and I stood before the judge. The same judge who had humiliated me earlier picked up his phone and said angrily to the ICC coordinator:

> "Do you know where you are? I can call the police right now and have you jailed for six months if you fail to satisfy the court's judgment in favor of this woman."

The ICC coordinator lowered his head and replied, "Your Honor, she will go with me right now and resume her work."

After we left the courtroom, I followed him to his office. He wrote me a check for one month's salary and instructed me to collect my paycheck at the end of each month until the appeal was settled. He added that it would be difficult for me to return to the office during that period. He was already demoralized by what had happened to the city council official who had orchestrated the retaliation against me. He had no heart left to fight. It was then that I realized the importance of waiting for God's timing.

The city council official who oversaw ICC left Ethiopia just one week after I filed my lawsuit. According to the security officer assigned by the Minister of Internal Affairs to monitor my case, the official had accepted employment with the South African Red Cross Society without the knowledge of Colonel Mengistu Haile Mariam. His employment was terminated, and he fled to Canada. The officer further informed me that, as a central committee member, the official was not permitted to leave without authorization and was expected to be brought back for trial.

That evening, as I opened my Bible, I read:

> "Weep not for the dead, nor bemoan him; weep bitterly for him who goes away, for he shall return no more, nor see his native country." *(Jeremiah 22:10)*

Through that verse, I understood he would not return. ICC proceeded with their appeal, assigning a lawyer from the city council to represent them. One day I told him, "You cannot win this case because Jesus is my lawyer." He did not understand what I meant. After seven months, during the final appeal hearing, the judge warned ICC that they would face consequences for their actions. He gave us two weeks to reach a settlement before issuing a final judgment.

Three days later, ICC sent three mediators to my home. They offered two options:

1. Return immediately to my previous position, or
2. Resign and receive one year's salary plus a recommendation letter.

The compensation included the seven months that had not previously been awarded. I asked for three days to pray. After careful prayer, I chose to walk away with the one-year salary and begin the next chapter of my life. Looking back, I learned that the greater the challenge, the greater the opportunity hidden within it. Those difficult months deepened my fellowship with God. I read Scripture more, prayed more, and gained clarity about my future. The same person who defamed me with the letter that fired me ended up signing the recommendation letter that released me. Walking closely with God helped me finish that chapter well. The compensation from ICC became the financial bridge to my next season.

Temptation After the Victory

While I was discerning my next steps, a health officer in my neighborhood approached me with a proposal to open a clinic together. He had the professional title; I had the capital. The idea seemed timely. We signed a partnership agreement, leased a property from a woman named Almaz Guta, located about a mile from my home, purchased medical equipment jointly, and opened the clinic. But for two months, not a single patient came. Frustrated by paying rent without income, I asked to dissolve the partnership. I even offered to leave my share of the equipment behind. He refused and became angry. Soon,

I would face the consequences. The health officer and his wife persuaded our neighbor to poison me. One day, a woman named Amsale and her husband invited my husband and me for lunch. The health officer and his wife were part of this small social circle that met monthly.

After lunch, coffee was served. Mrs. Amsale knew I did not take sugar in my coffee. Pointing to a specific cup, she instructed the servant, "Agitu doesn't take sugar. Here is her cup."

As I glanced at the bottom of the cup, I noticed something white—like snow—but never imagined it was poison. I drank it. Soon after returning home, unbearable pain seized my body. I lay on the bed screaming and rolling in agony. My husband kept repeating, "They poisoned you." Within minutes, I felt I was dying. I prayed: "Jesus, take me in Your arms. Let my soul rest with You." Immediately after that prayer, I felt an urgent need to use the bathroom. What passed from me was disturbing and unnatural, yet there was no stool—nothing ordinary. As soon as it left, the pain vanished completely.

I did not die. God had not preserved me through court battles, corruption, humiliation, and injustice only to let me perish there. He had a greater plan—and my life was not yet finished. The poison that was meant to silence me became another testimony of preservation. In that moment of excruciating pain, when death felt imminent, I did not fight for breath—I surrendered my soul to Jesus. And it was in surrender that life returned.

The same God who had defended me in court, exposed corruption, secured land for my future, and preserved my children now proved once again that my life was not in the hands of men. It was in His. If He had allowed me to survive humiliation, legal battles, false accusations, marital torment, and political persecution, He certainly was not going to let a cup of poisoned coffee determine my destiny. That day I understood something deeper: when a person walks in obedience, attacks may intensify—but so does divine protection.

Looking back on that season, I see clearly that every battle had a purpose. The courtroom humiliation, the corrupt officials, the firing, the appeals, the land acquisition, the miraculous pregnancies, the broken marriage, the poison—none of it was random.

While I thought I was fighting for survival, God was shaping endurance.

While I thought I was defending myself, God was establishing testimony.

While I feared loss, God was building legacy.

My endurance produced Bethel and Menase—living proof that obedience births reward.

My legal battles produced financial provision.

My suffering produced boldness.

What I did not yet understand was that these trials were only preparation. The fire I walked through was forging something in me that comfort never could.

The chapter of fighting ICC had closed. The chapter of surviving poison had ended.

But the greater war—the one that would define my calling—was still ahead.

And this time, I would not fight merely to survive. I would fight with purpose.

7

HEEDING THE CALL WHILE GOING THROUGH FIRE

In spite of the hardships I was enduring, the call I had received to serve God grew stronger. At first, I thought that joining the church choir in response to that call was enough. But then a persistent message kept returning to my heart: "Move one step forward." Around the same time, Pastor Fetlework gave me a direct message one day. Quoting Proverbs 31:26, she said, *"She opens her mouth with wisdom, and on her tongue is the law of kindness. This message is for you. The Lord says your heart is kind, and He will make you a solution."* Still, I did not fully understand what that meant. Then the Lord revealed His will to me clearly through a dream—to serve displaced women and their families living in ramshackle shelters in my own neighborhood.

The Dream

In the dream, I was standing inside my house, looking out through my French door. Outside, I saw a woman living in a shelter made of plastic. I went out toward her, and as I passed by, she directed me to a public telephone and asked me to help her as an interpreter for a long-distance collect call to a man abroad. She spoke Amharic, Ethiopia's official language. When I placed the call, the man answered in English and asked me to ask the woman what she wanted him to bring her.

She replied, *"I only want you to come. Your coming is enough for me."*

I conveyed her answer to him, and immediately I woke up. Though it was a dream, it felt so real that I broke down in bitter tears. I repented for my indifference toward the poorest women—women who loved the Lord more than material things, just like the woman I saw in the dream. Because I lived in what was considered a wealthy neighborhood, I had never imagined that such poverty existed so close to me.

That same morning, at 9:00 a.m., I went to the local kebele (neighborhood administration) office to inquire. I asked one of the officers whether families like those in my dream existed in our kebele.

"Yes," he replied. "We have families displaced from famine-affected areas who are living in temporary shelters at two locations." Without delay, he took me to see them. I could not believe my eyes. The shelters I visited were exactly like those in my dream—small structures made of corrugated iron sheets, partitioned with cartons. Each family lived in a space no larger than ten square feet, with an average family size of five. Although these shelters were meant to be temporary, some families had lived there for over fifteen years. The roofs were old and leaking, and the conditions were heartbreaking. The government's slogan at the time was *Hullun neger wedetor ginbar!*—"Everything to the war front!"—and as a result, there were no resources left to help the very people the government claimed to serve.

The Call was Unfamiliar and Confusing

Still, the call of God confused me. I believed serving God meant spiritual work only—singing in the choir, preaching, or working within church settings. With that understanding, I applied for enrollment at Moody Bible Institute in Chicago. Yet I continued to seek clarity, remaining spiritually alert and discerning. I had no intention of leaving Ethiopia until I received God's answer regarding my marriage. Since the call to serve God was unfolding alongside my personal struggles, I needed unmistakable guidance. Finally, I fasted and prayed for three days, asking God to reveal His will. The answer came clearly the next day:

"Counseling—helping people through their problems."

In response, I prayed earnestly:

"Lord, if You want me to help people through their problems, please do not let it be merely asking them what is wrong and telling them I will pray. Please, Lord—tell me their problems Yourself, and make me a solution."

Ramshackle Shelters (40 Families Lived Here)

After examining the situation more closely, I received a clear vision to address the families' needs holistically—meeting both their spiritual and physical needs through self-sufficiency projects. In Ethiopia, the more familiar form of aid consisted largely of handouts and Band-Aid approaches that fostered dependency among the poor. I was determined to challenge that mindset by promoting economic independence among these women.

With that goal in mind, I met with the women at my house to discuss possible options. Afterward, we conducted a door-to-door survey and a needs assessment. Based on our findings and the women's own recommendations, we decided to launch three income-generating projects: leatherwork and crafts, sewing, and food processing. I then grouped the fifty-five women into three categories. The twenty-one women who had completed literacy classes and could read and write were assigned to leatherwork and crafts training. Twelve high school dropouts were assigned to pattern construction and sewing, while the remaining twenty women were delegated to food processing.

We named our group the Women's Self-Reliance Association (WSRA). Three women were elected as group leaders, and I began working toward the initiation of the proposed projects, starting with research into training opportunities and funding sources. I also concluded that conducting a marketing study was essential to achieving long-term economic independence for the women. To that end, I visited leather factories and a large sewing factory in Addis Ababa. During my visits, I asked where their workers had received training. I was told that those engaged in leatherwork were trained at the Productivity Improvement Center of the Ethiopian Management Institute, while those involved in sewing attended classes offered by the Handicraft and Small-Scale Industries Development Agency (HASIDA). These were the only two skills-training centers available in Addis Ababa at the time.

My next step was to visit these two training centers and arrange the necessary training for the women's group. I also decided to seek funding from international donors in the city and wrote my first grant proposal to the Swedish International Development Agency (SIDA). It so happened that a Swedish friend, Regmore Slomonson, was in Ethiopia with her husband, who worked for SIDA at the time. Regmore submitted my proposal on behalf of WSRA.

Soon after we submitted the proposal, the compensation I had received from ICC was exhausted. I was completely broke. For the first time in my life, I briefly experienced what poverty truly meant before moving forward with my mission to help the poor. I had never imagined myself in such a situation.

One Saturday, April 7, 1990, I went to the office of my friend Fantaye Alemu to borrow money so I could buy teff, Ethiopia's staple grain, because I had nothing left to feed my children. Saturday was market day, and I could not bear the thought of my children going hungry if I missed that opportunity. I arrived at her gate at 9:00 a.m. and asked the security guard to let me in, but he told me she was in a meeting and that I would have to wait until noon.

At that moment, the words of Deuteronomy 28 came to my mind: "Blessed shall you be in the city, and blessed shall you be in the country… You shall lend to many nations, but you shall not borrow." I also remembered an Amharic proverb: YeAbayin lij wuha temaw—"Even the child of the Nile can become thirsty." I said to myself, "I am a child of God. I will not borrow. May God's will be done concerning my children," and I left.

From there, I went directly to a women's monthly fasting and prayer meeting that I regularly attended. That afternoon, Evangelist Yisihak Bahilibi preached from 2 Kings 7 about how God turned a famine in Israel into abundance in a single day. The opening verse spoke directly to my situation: "Hear the word of the Lord. Thus says the Lord: Tomorrow about this time a seah of fine flour shall be sold for a shekel, and two seahs of barley for a shekel, at the gate of Samaria." The message was so precise and timely that I went home filled with hope—not for some distant future, but for the very next day.

God was so real. My hope for tomorrow did not wait until tomorrow; it had already begun to unfold by the time I arrived home. My husband's niece, who was staying with us then, ran toward me with a radiant smile and began telling me about the miracle that had taken place.

> "A farmer came to the house around 10:00 a.m. with 115 kilograms of teff—fifteen kilograms more than a full quintal—loaded on his donkey," she said. "He asked, 'Is etye [madam] home? I brought this teff for her to buy.' I told him you were not home. He unloaded the teff anyway and said, 'That's fine. I will come back next Saturday to collect the money,' and he left with his donkey."

She continued, "But about ten minutes later, he returned and said, 'I remembered that etye will need transportation to take the teff to the millhouse and have it ground. I came back to do that for her.'" She explained that he then took the teff to the millhouse, had it cleaned, sifted, and milled, and brought the flour back himself. He even paid for the milling.

This was truly astonishing. I did not know the man at all. The Teff required extensive cleaning and sifting—labor-intensive work—and he did everything without being asked.

When God Calls, He Also Provides

Another miracle followed just two days later. During the last week of May 1990, I had borrowed fifty birr (about $24.15 at the time) from a relative to buy groceries. When she began calling me daily, demanding repayment within less than two weeks, I finally told her to collect the money from my friend Ertra Namarra. As soon as Ertra gave her the money, she called me and asked to come see me. She arrived at my house on April 10, 1990, at 8:00 a.m.

As we talked, Ertra said she could not believe I had struggled to find fifty birr and asked whether everything was all right. We had not spoken for some time, so she had no idea what I had been going through. After listening to my story, she asked, "Why did you keep this from me?" Then she added, "I would have shared my groceries with you."

Before Ertra finished speaking, an expert who had reviewed the proposal we submitted to SIDA called from the Inter-African Committee on Traditional Practices (IAC) in Ethiopia. Their office was located at the United Nations Economic Commission for Africa (UNECA) headquarters in Addis Ababa. She shared the good news that SIDA had approved our proposal for funding. Then she surprised me with even more news: "IAC wants to hire you immediately. Can you come today?"

Joyfully, I replied, "Yes." She told me she would send a gate pass to security so I could enter the compound. I turned to Ertra and shared the good news, thanking her for offering to share her groceries with me. I said, "God saw your kindness and spared you from having to buy me groceries. Let's go."

We were both moved to tears. That very afternoon, IAC hired me as a program coordinator for the Inter-African Committee (IAC), National Committee on Harmful Traditional Practices Affecting the Health of Women and Children in Ethiopia. Because of my background as a community nurse and the women's self-reliance project proposal they had reviewed, I was hired on the spot.

The mission of IAC was to eradicate female circumcision/genital mutilation (FGM) through community education and by creating alternative income-generating opportunities for circumcisers who depended on this harmful practice as their livelihood. There are three main types of FGM:

- clitoridectomy (partial or total removal of the clitoris),
- excision (removal of the labia minora and majora), and
- infibulation (stitching the cut labia together, leaving only a small opening for urination).

At that time, approximately 95 percent of girls in Ethiopia were subjected to FGM due to longstanding cultural pressure. It was widely believed to control female behavior, and girls were compelled to undergo the practice to maintain social acceptance. Those who were not circumcised were often ostracized and ridiculed. While the type of FGM practiced varied by region, clitoridectomy and excision—often performed together—were the most common in Ethiopia.

After joining IAC, I continued working with my women's group as a volunteer. The following day, I received the SIDA grant check in the amount of 4,500 Ethiopian birr to launch the leatherwork and sewing projects. The flour mill SIDA had purchased for the food-processing project was already enroute from Denmark.

Because the cash grant was insufficient to send the women to formal training centers, I devised an alternative plan. I approached trainers from the two government training institutions and asked whether they would provide on-site training during their spare time. They agreed to conduct two-hour training sessions on weekday evenings and six-hour sessions on Saturdays.

The Kebele 20 administration (now Kebele 02) in Bole generously allowed us to use their conference hall free of charge for the training sessions. The hall resembled a warehouse, with both the roof and walls covered in corrugated iron sheets. We rented two sewing machines, purchased the necessary hand tools and supplies, and began the training.

Because my goal was to serve the whole person—addressing both physical and spiritual needs—I invited evangelist Wegayehu Zewde to minister to the women before the training sessions each morning. During the first week, as Wegayehu began one of the services, an evil spirit was cast out from one of the women.

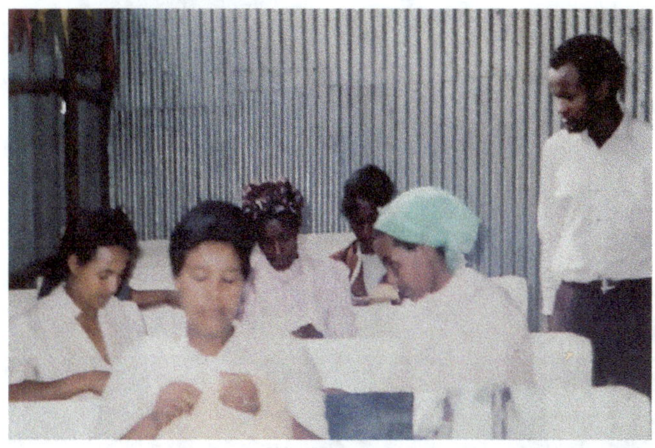

Leather Work Training

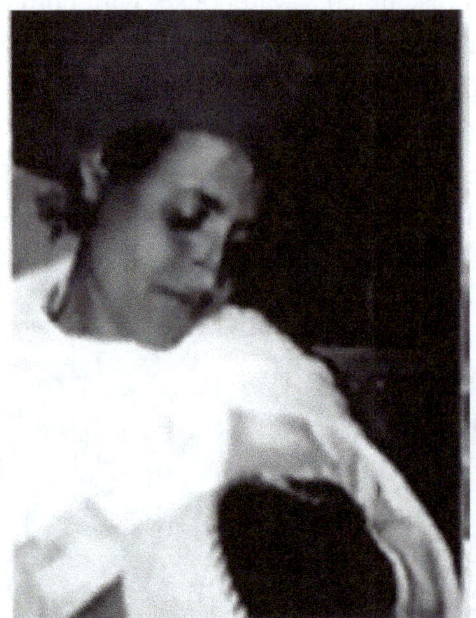

Leather Crafts

Pattern Drafting and Sewing

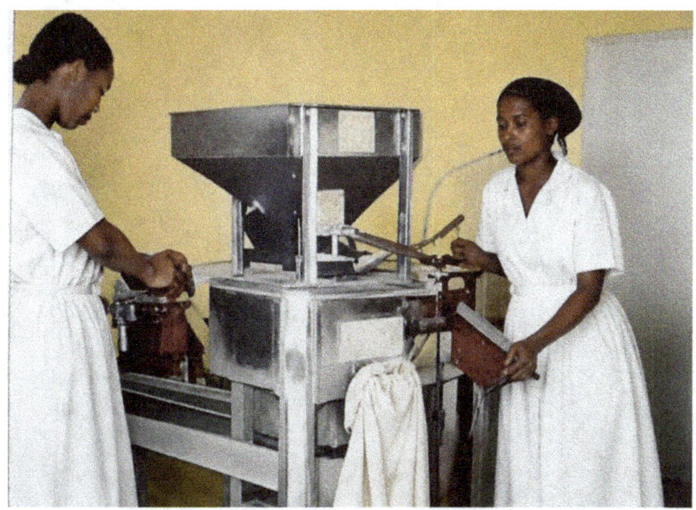

Milling and Food Processing

Although we had resolved the issue of training, another challenge remained: the women had no source of income to support themselves while participating in the program. To address this, I turned to the Christian Relief and Development Association (CRDA) for humanitarian assistance. By that time, the 1984 famine crisis had ended, and relief supplies from Western nations were in surplus. As a result, CRDA had sufficient humanitarian aid available.

Eventually, I secured enough support for our women's group. We used the food and relief assistance provided by CRDA as compensation for the women's hours of hands-on training. This approach—using initial handouts while intentionally working toward "hands up"—accomplished two important goals. First, it met the women's immediate needs and enabled them to participate fully in the training with motivation and diligence. Second, it fostered dignity, self-worth, and a growing sense of self-reliance among the women.

WSRA Leather Works Design Group at our Family Event

Everything fit together like a puzzle, and the work of the WSRA progressed remarkably well. At the same time, I thrived in my new role at the Inter-African Committee (IAC), where I was tasked with reviving what had become a struggling national committee.I recruited national committee members from twenty-two different government institutions, including UNICEF, and organized them into subcommittees aligned with specific program activities. Through consistent encouragement and clear direction, I motivated them to participate actively. We conducted three-day workshops across the country for community representatives, including women, youth, religious leaders, and health workers. I collected detailed reports from presenters on the traditional practices prevalent in each region and compiled them into a handbook, which was printed by Tesfa Printing Press.

Swedish Save the Children (Rädda Barnen) provided generous funding to cover workshop participants' per diem, as well as workshop and printing expenses. The national committee initially operated under the umbrella of the Maternal and Child Health Division of the Ministry of Health, and ICC secured office space for us within that department, where I managed the program. Before leaving the organization, I helped the IAC national committee obtain legal recognition as an independent NGO, secure its own office, and begin functioning as an autonomous entity. The impact of IAC's work was significant. According to findings later published in the British Medical Journal (BMJ), the prevalence of female genital mutilation/cutting (FGM/C) among girls under the age of fourteen in East Africa declined from 71.4 percent in 1995 to 8.0 percent in 2016.

The women of WSRA also made me immensely proud. They completed their training in six months with outstanding results. We held a modest graduation ceremony and invited representatives from the United Nations, donor agencies, and relevant government institutions. The women displayed the items they had produced during training—leather crafts such as sandals, handbags, belts, coin holders, key chains, coasters, wallets, and other products from the leatherworks group, as well as garments and handicrafts, mostly children's clothing, from the sewing group. The items were sold during the event and generated unexpected income for the group, affirming both their skill and their growing self-reliance.

Leather Work Product Sample

The sky was my limit before I noticed it. One morning in July 1990, just a few weeks after we held the event described above, a staff member from the United Nations Fund for Population Activities (UNFPA) came to my office at the UNECA Women's Center. He informed me that our organization had been selected as a best-practice model and would be visited by Dr. Nafis Sadik, Undersecretary General of the United Nations and Executive Director of UNFPA in New York, in just three days.

He went on to explain that several ministers and high-ranking government officials had been invited and that the Ethiopian Hotel would provide refreshments for the occasion. He urged me to begin preparing a draft speech on the Women's Self-Reliance Association (WSRA) immediately, as we had only two days to prepare.

At first, I asked whether he meant my work at the UNECA, because WSRA was still new and small. He assured me that it was indeed WSRA that had been selected. Without delay, he rushed me to the UNFPA office— located in the older building parallel to the new one where my office was—to draft my speech. After I completed the draft, I handed it to him and left immediately for our project site to prepare the WSRA women's group for the visit.

My women's group and I were well prepared for the colorful and prestigious visit on July 7, 1990. We were all extremely excited. The Ethiopian Hotel provided finger foods, coffee, tea, and soft drinks. We proudly displayed all the products the WSRA women had produced, along with a blueprint of the WSRA Women's Empowerment Center, which included a skills-training workshop, a retail store, a clinic, and a daycare center. We had also applied for a plot of land in the kebele—about five hundred meters from my house—to realize this vision.

By God's grace, my speech went very well, and the women sold most of the products they had displayed. Dr. Nafis Sadik herself ordered and paid for a pair of sandals, even though we did not have her size available at the time. That single act greatly boosted the women's morale.

Dr. Nafis Sadik left the following remark in the guest book: "This is a wonderful initiative of self-help by women to improve the lives of their families. It deserves all our support."

We had arranged for a professional videographer to record the event. However, I made what I later recognized as a grave mistake: I assigned my husband to take photographs. The pictures he took cut off Dr. Sadik and the other high-ranking officials above the chest. To this day, my greatest weakness remains trusting people.

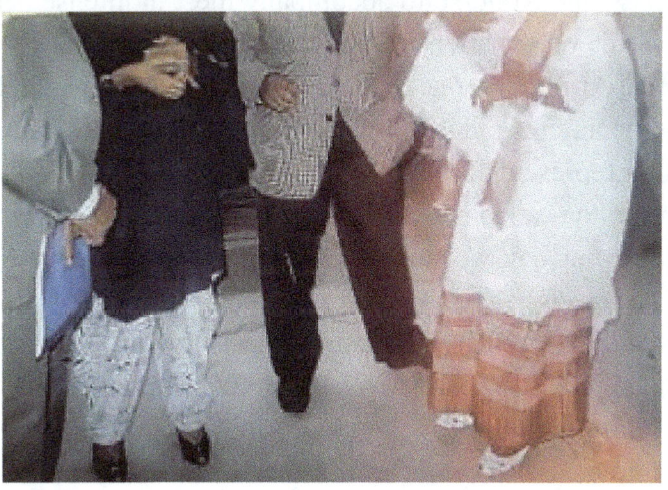

Left to right UNFPA Country Representative, Dr. Nafis Sadik,
Dr. Getachew, Minister of Health, Agitu

An Unexpected Study Visit that Sparked a National Transformation

I was about to experience an unimaginable outcome from that remarkable event. After visiting WSRA and before returning to the United Nations headquarters in New York, Dr. Nafis Sadik instructed UNFPA in Addis Ababa to arrange for me to visit the Ministry of Women's Affairs and Social Promotion in Niger under UNFPA sponsorship.

Four months after her visit, I received an official invitation from UNFPA in Addis Ababa for a five-day study tour in Niamey, Niger. I was instructed to obtain a passport for the trip. My model of integrating maternal and child health and family planning into economic development initiatives had been found commendable, leading to UNFPA's sponsorship of my visit. I was deeply excited about this opportunity because I had never traveled outside Ethiopia before. After I received my passport, UNFPA processed my visa and handed it to me along with my per diem—U.S. dollars in my hand for the first time in my life.

In December 1990, I traveled to Niamey. The Ethiopian Ministry of Health assigned a nurse to accompany me. An intense heat unlike anything I had ever experienced greeted us upon arrival at Diori Hamani International Airport. As one of the hottest cities in the world, Niamey's average temperatures range between 90 and 100 degrees Fahrenheit. A driver and a representative from the Ministry of Women's Affairs and Social Promotion welcomed us and escorted us to our hotel.

The following day, we met with the Minister of Women's Affairs—a woman—and received a full briefing about our visit. Niamey lies along the east bank of the Niger River, the third-longest river in Africa, stretching approximately 2,600 miles. It was fascinating to witness women's issues integrated into national development programs at the governmental level. I completed the five-day study tour successfully and returned to Ethiopia with broader vision and renewed confidence regarding women and children's empowerment.

An Impactful Foreign Journey Extends into Europe

Six weeks later, another opportunity followed. Through my work with IAC, I was selected to attend a one-month intensive Training of Trainers program at the ILO International Training Centre in Turin, Italy. Six representatives from the IAC national committee and I were chosen.

My adventure began immediately upon arrival at Fiumicino International Airport in Rome. Coming from the small and modest airport in Addis Ababa to such a vast, modern facility felt overwhelming. The long corridors, moving escalators, and organized systems were entirely new to me. A vehicle arranged by the training center transported us to Turin. The cold weather shocked me. I came from a climate that ranged between 50°F in winter and 75°F in summer year-round. After dinner that evening, our training sessions began the next day.

On my first morning, I returned to my room after breakfast and was surprised to find a white woman cleaning it. In Ethiopia, I had never seen a white person doing housekeeping work. That image challenged many assumptions I did not even realize I carried. Another cultural shock was seeing couples openly kissing on the streets. In my culture, such behavior was considered shameful. Each time I saw it, I whispered to myself, "Oh my goodness." My Ethiopian colleagues teased me whenever it happened, saying, "Agitu, here you go again!"

The open markets, however, reminded me of Merkato in Addis Ababa—vendors calling out loudly, displaying their goods. I heard merchants shouting "Diecimila! Diecimila!" meaning ten thousand lira. At the time, the exchange rate was about 1,500 lira to one U.S. dollar, so ten thousand lira equaled roughly six or seven dollars. The large numbers confused me at first, especially since Ethiopia's exchange rate had once been far smaller during the reign of Emperor Haile Selassie I. On weekends, we had opportunities for sightseeing. I experienced my first tram ride—something we did not have in Ethiopia. Some areas of Turin reminded me slightly of Piazza in Addis Ababa.

On our first Saturday, we visited a replica of the Shroud of Turin displayed in a glass case. We were told that the original fourteen-foot linen cloth, believed by some to bear the image of the crucified Jesus, had been housed in the Cathedral of St. John the Baptist in Turin since 1578 and was shown publicly only on rare occasions. I purchased a postcard and took a picture, but I did not believe it was the actual burial cloth of Christ. The face depicted resembled the familiar Western artistic portrayals of Jesus and did not align, in my understanding, with Isaiah 53:2, which says, "He had no beauty or majesty to attract us to him." Furthermore, during my later visit to Israel, I neither saw nor heard credible evidence confirming its authenticity.

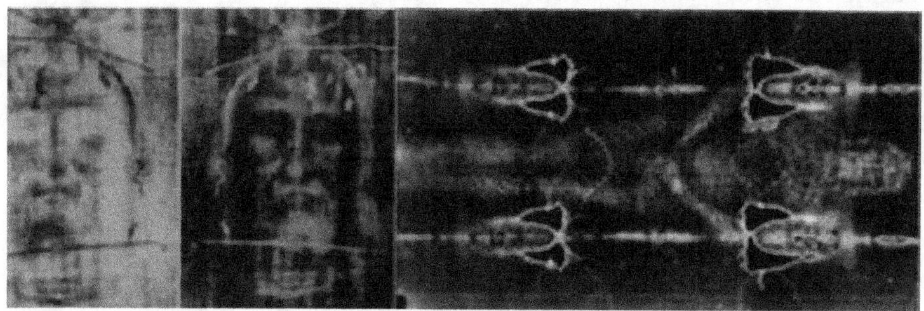

The Shroud of Turin

Walking Where Jesus Walked: A Sacred Journey

Of all the countries I have traveled to, my journey to Israel—walking where Jesus walked—was the most sacred and renewing experience of my life. I did not need physical proof to believe the Bible; faith had already taken root in my heart. Yet God, in His kindness, allowed me to see with my own eyes the places I had read about for years. The pages of Scripture seemed to come alive beneath my feet, and what I had once imagined in prayer now stood before me in stone, soil, and sky.

Jerusalem, the city of King David: In Jerusalem, the City of King David, I stood before the archaeological remains of the Temple and reflected on what Jesus had foretold in Mark 13:1–2:

> "Then as He went out of the temple, one of His disciples said to Him, 'Teacher, see what manner of stones and what buildings are here!' And Jesus answered him, 'Do you see these great buildings? Not one stone shall be left upon another, that shall not be thrown down.'"

As I looked at the massive stones scattered and displaced, I saw the fulfillment of His words. What once stood in glory now lay in ruins—a silent testimony to prophecy fulfilled. Later, walking among the ancient olive trees in the Garden of Gethsemane at the foot of the Mount of Olives—the very place where Jesus prayed before His crucifixion—I felt overwhelmed. The thought that He had knelt there in anguish humbled me deeply. Luke 22:44 came alive in my heart:

> "And being in agony, He prayed more earnestly. Then His sweat became like great drops of blood falling down to the ground." Standing there, I sensed the weight of His suffering in a new way. My own tribulations, which once felt unbearable, seemed small in comparison to the agony He endured. In that sacred garden, my perspective shifted. Pain was no longer something to resent, but something to surrender.

Temple Ruins

The archaeological remains of the Jerusalem Temple reveal what Jesus foretold in Mark 13:1–2, "Then as He went out of the temple, one of His disciples said to Him, 'Teacher, see what manner of stones and what buildings are here!' And Jesus answered him, 'Do you see these great buildings? Not one stone shall be left upon another, that shall not be thrown down.'"

These paving stones and fallen blocks are often associated with the destruction of Jerusalem in 70 CE. Some stones still bear signs of burning and impact.

Golgotha: Garden Tomb, often called "Gordon's Calvary," and Golgotha inside the Church of the Holy Sepulchre

The rock face near the Garden Tomb, often called "Gordon's Calvary," whose skull-like formation has led many to associate it with Golgotha (Matthew 27:33). For me, its setting outside the city walls and near a garden resonated deeply with Scripture.

The traditional site of Golgotha inside the Church of the Holy Sepulchre, venerated by Christians since the fourth century as the place of Christ's crucifixion.

Gethsemane: Walking among the ancient olive trees in the Garden of Gethsemane, at the foot of the Mount of Olives—where Jesus prayed in agony before His crucifixion—moved me profoundly. Knowing that He had sweated drops like blood in that very place made His suffering feel real and near. As I stood there, I sensed the weight of His anguish and began to see my own tribulations in a different light.

Luke 22:44 says, "And being in agony, He prayed more earnestly. Then His sweat became like great drops of blood falling down to the ground."

In that sacred garden, my burdens felt lighter. If He endured such agony for my salvation, how could I measure my suffering against His?

Gethsemani

Before I left Gethsemane to visit Bethlehem, I asked my Muslim Palestinian tour guide who took me to Bethlehem, "Do you guys believe in Jesus?" "Yes, we believe in Isa. He is a prophet. He will return, and his feet will step on the top of that mountain," replied the tour guide, pointing at the Mount of Olives.

Bethlehem: It was Christmas season when I visited Bethlehem, the Christmas City. Visiting the manger stirred up my heart with a memory of the lyrics I grew up singing, "Away in a manger, no crib for a bed; the little Lord Jesus laid down His sweet head."

At the Manger

The forty-foot-tall Christmas tree was amazing. It was my first time seeing this kind of Christmas tree.

Bethsaida: Situated by the Sea of Galilee and known as the home of the apostles Peter, Philip, and Andrew, Bethsaida made me visualize the gospel stories—the place where Jesus performed many miracles, walked on water, gave sight to a blind man, and fed five thousand people with two fish and five loaves. My visit to the Mount of Beatitudes on the northwestern shore of the Sea of Galilee, between Capernaum and Gennesaret on the southern slopes of the Karazin, reminded me of Jesus's word in Matthew 11:21: "Woe to you, Chorazin! Woe to you, Bethsaida! For if the mighty works which were done in you had been done in Tyre and Sidon, they would have repented long ago in sackcloth and ashes."

At the Sea of Galilee

Jordan River: Visiting the Jordan River, the border of the land that God gave to Israel and the place where John's baptism of Jesus took place, was the most uplifting moment for me. I wanted to take my second water-immersion baptism in the river where John baptized Jesus, but it was winter and too cold for me to do so.

At Capernaum

During our stay in Turin, we were also able to visit nearby cities and even neighboring Switzerland on the weekends. One weekend, the president of IAC, Mrs. Berhane Raswork, took two of the Ethiopian participants and me to Geneva, where she lived. We did not have time to tour the city then, but I later returned for a guided tour of the United Nations in Geneva. The day before we left Turin, our instructors told us to throw a coin into a fountain, saying it would bring us back to the city. We laughed and did it, yet none of us returned. I visited Rome the following year, but not Turin.

The program provided buffet breakfast and $30 per day for lunch and dinner throughout the one-month training. The schedule was intensive; sessions ran from 8:00 a.m. to 6:00 p.m. with only a one-hour lunch break. I completed the training and received my diploma as a program officer on March 15, 1991. I cannot pass over the two most important lessons I took from this training.

The first was the discipline of self-evaluation. Each trainee gave a presentation based on a grant proposal we prepared for fundraising. Our presentations were videotaped. We were then required to watch our recordings and evaluate ourselves before the group. Afterward, the group evaluated our self-evaluation. I remember one participant becoming very upset when the group rated her self-assessment poorly. She had overestimated her performance and struggled to accept the feedback.

The second key lesson was innovative multimedia modular training and the systems approach to training design and communication. In one session, a female anatomical module was used to support campaigns against female genital mutilation. We also learned to design educational materials. After returning to Addis Ababa, I adapted these multimodular training packages to Ethiopia's regional context, coordinated printing and distribution of educational aids, and made these materials available nationally.

Another opportunity awaited me after completing the training. The Swedish friend who had helped submit WSRA's first grant proposal to SIDA invited me to present at a folk high school cultural event in

Gothenburg, Sweden. When I arrived in Gothenburg, I encountered a winter unlike anything I had seen before. It was colder than Italy, and for the first time in my life I watched snowflakes fall from the sky. It brought Psalm 147:16 vividly to mind: "He spreads the snow like wool and scatters the frost like ashes."

My Swedish friend and her husband, an anthropologist, prepared a lovely dinner that evening. We enjoyed a pleasant conversation until an argument unexpectedly arose. He became upset when I remarked that the U.S. dollar would remain the world's strongest currency because of the inscription "In God We Trust."

He responded loudly, "No, it is not! It is in gold we trust. Americans love money!"

I calmly replied, "Its strength is the result of what it declares, whether one accepts it or not," but he continued insisting, "It is in gold we trust!"

On my second day in Gothenburg, I participated in the cultural event. It was enriching to meet women from many parts of the world.

Rigmore on the Right

I was about to discover that something I had never imagined awaited me in Gothenburg.

Two Ethiopian men knocked on my hosts' door asking for me. I stepped outside to meet them.

"Reverend Belina Sarka in Addis Ababa instructed us to ask you to preach at our Ethiopian and Eritrean fellowship this Sunday," one of them said.

"But I have never preached before," I replied.

"You have already been scheduled. We have been waiting eagerly," he said.

I returned to my room immediately and began praying for a message. As I prayed, the title *The Benefit of Tribulation* came to my mind. I argued silently with God: *These immigrants fled tribulation. There is no tribulation here.* I assumed that people in the West lived carefree lives.

Nevertheless, I began writing what came to my heart. I still have the outline from that sermon.

Sunday arrived, and I found myself standing at the pulpit. A young Ethiopian man stood directly in front, recording my message. When I finished, many people gathered around me saying, "God spoke to me. Thank you."

Then the man with the recorder approached.

"My name is Samson," he said. "I recorded you because the message was about me."

He continued:

"I am a nurse. Last Tuesday night, as I walked home from my evening shift, a white man followed me, cursing me because I am an immigrant and threatening to kill me. He forced me to open my apartment door, sat me down, ate my food, took my groceries and tape recorder, and left. I had no money to replace them. Yesterday, I found a check in my mailbox from an anonymous person and bought this new tape recorder. It is far better than the one that was stolen. From now on, I will pray, 'Tribulation, please come my way.'"

The following Monday, I took a train to Stockholm—my first time riding a train—and it was delightful. A former missionary friend, Mr. Karl Eric Lundgren, met me at the station, and we drove for more than an hour to his home in rural Stockholm. The long drive offered a slow, breathtaking view of dense forests stretching endlessly on both sides of the road. Mr. Lundgren explained that approximately 70 percent of Sweden's land area is covered with forest. As a result, Sweden is one of the world's leading exporters of pulp, paper, and sawn wood products. Out of the country's 40.8 million hectares of land, about 22.5 million hectares are productive forest.

While we were driving, Mr. Lundgren noticed a man speeding ahead of us and said, "Watch—we will catch up to him pulled over by the traffic police."

"How come?" I asked.

"There are cameras that record speed," he replied.

Just as he predicted, we soon passed the man pulled over by police. It felt like another world to me. In Ethiopia, traffic police stood on the roadside with ticket pads in hand. They judged speed by observation, stopped motorists, and either issued tickets or negotiated bribes to avoid penalties. I was happy to see Mrs. Lundgren and their two children after fifteen years. The next morning, Mr. Lundgren took me to visit his parents. What a small world! My parents had told me that I was among the last babies Karl Erik's father, Reverend Lundgren, baptized before he left Nedjo for good—and now I was meeting him and his wife in Sweden.

Reverend Lundgren & His Wife

The following day, Mr. Lundgren drove me into Stockholm to visit Ms. Birgit Andreasen, my former music teacher. I was saddened to learn that her husband, Reverend Andreasen, had passed away the previous year. She took me to her church and asked me to speak to the congregation. When I saw how small their congregation was, I said:

"You brought the Good News to my country and gave us Jesus. We tested His goodness, and it strengthened us to endure persecution under Communist rule. The church grew tremendously underground. But your people are losing the invaluable treasure they gave to us. I urge you to reclaim your treasure. This is what I owe you."

From Sweden I traveled to London. Heathrow Airport seemed enormous—larger than any airport I had seen until I later visited JFK in New York.

On my second day in London, a friend with whom I stayed at Kensington Temple showed me around.

"Don't stare at people—you don't do that in this country," he said when he noticed me watching passersby.

"In that case, they won't see me stare," I replied.

"It's not funny," he said. "Don't stare."

London differed in many ways. Motorists drove vehicles with steering wheels on the right-hand side. People appeared serious and rarely exchanged greetings. Everywhere—on the streets, at bus stops, on buses and trains—people were reading. The streets felt narrow, yet transportation was remarkably efficient. The underground trains were fast, and with a single pass you could transfer between trains and buses with ease.

After six weeks abroad, I returned to Addis Ababa. The timing proved remarkable. My study tour in Niger soon became instrumental in establishing the Ministry of Women's Affairs in Ethiopia. The Federal Democratic Republic of Ethiopia took power in May 1991, just four months after my visit to Niger. On September 6, 1991, I was rushed to the hospital with vomiting and severe pain in my right lower abdomen. As I arrived, I asked God in my heart why He allowed this to happen when I trusted in divine healing. I heard a soft inner voice say, "Because you cannot listen while rushing."

I responded silently, "Okay, I will take this sick leave and listen to You in the quiet time You have given me." The pain and vomiting stopped immediately, yet the doctor still granted me five days of sick leave.

The next morning, I sat quietly before the Lord. In that stillness, I sensed Him telling me that He had opened the door for my visit to the Ministry of Women's Affairs and Social Promotion in Niger so I could help establish a similar ministry in Ethiopia. I felt prompted to submit an application to Prime Minister Tamrat Layne proposing the creation of a Ministry of Women's Affairs. I did not understand how I could do such a thing. I had no political involvement. In fact, I had once been denied a state ID because I refused to join the Revolutionary Ethiopian Women's Association (REWA). I prayed for words and began to write.

On September 12, 1991, I submitted my petition and study-tour report to Prime Minister Tamrat Layne, recommending the establishment of a Ministry of Women's Affairs modeled after Niger's. In January 1992, I was officially notified that an Office of Women's Affairs had been established within the Prime Minister's Office, just as I had proposed. Soon afterward, I was invited to meet the new head of Women's Affairs—later the minister—Ms. Tadelech Hailemikael.

We met for three hours. She listened as I shared how God had given me the vision and guided me through the process. She told me my document had arrived at a critical moment, when officials did not know what to do with the Revolutionary Ethiopian Women's Association. I was deeply moved to learn that the same REWA that once denied me a state ID had now been replaced. Ms. Tadelech herself had spent twelve years and eight months imprisoned as a member of the EPRP antigovernment movement. Despite her past, she played a vital role in establishing the Ministry of Women's Affairs.

Women's groups from government institutions, NGOs, private businesses, and multiple sectors of Ethiopian society came together to draft the first national policy on Ethiopian women. I was privileged to be one of fifteen women who designed this policy in 1992. It was adopted and published in 1993.

God is Faithful — The Vision Takes Root on the Ground

Since the WSRA was starting from scratch, our needs were immense as we embarked on full-fledged production activities—but God supplied. Through divine guidance, I traveled to London at my own expense and secured eleven table-model sewing machines from Tools for Self-Reliance, a UK-based international development charity. It was my second time traveling to London, and everything felt easier. Even better, I met the executive director of an orphanage in Ethiopia, who shipped the machines to Addis Ababa in his forty-foot container filled with donations that was ready to depart London.

After conducting a site visit, the Self-Help Fund of the United States Embassy in Addis Ababa also found our project "excellent" and funded the purchase of two industrial sewing machines and additional hand tools. This support came at a critical time. Two industrial sewing machines and two flour mills that UNICEF had purchased for WSRA had vanished at Port Assab when the EPLF controlled the port in 1991. The U.S. Embassy's assistance sustained our work while we waited for UNICEF's reorder to arrive.

The Netherlands Embassy later provided a grant—twice. Then a grant from the Canadian International Development Agency (CIDA) followed. UNICEF's reordered donation eventually arrived as well. The Addis Ababa Region 14 administration allocated WSRA land at a prime location—just a mile from Bole International Airport—for the construction of a comprehensive center that would include an income-generating skills training workshop, a supermarket, and a day-care facility. A separate parcel from the kebele's holding was designated for a maternal and child health clinic.

We secured pre-project funds from UNFPA for the clinic, but the funding was never released because government policy did not allow direct UN funding to NGOs. Swedish Save the Children (Rädda Barnen) later approved a generous grant to begin the first phase of construction. With this level of success, the kebele offered to rent WSRA three rooms in their office building for 350 birr per month—but there was a hidden agenda behind the offer.

Success followed success. The organization gained recognition as a best-practices model and opened doors for international participation. One Friday morning in July 1993, I received a phone call from UNDP asking me to report to their office concerning a trip to Central America scheduled for Monday. It was hard to believe I would be traveling in two days.

At the UNDP office, the officer explained that I would travel with two government officials for a one-month study tour to visit PRODERE (the Development Program for Refugees and Returnees in Central America). PRODERE aimed to address the region's massive displacement crisis through negotiated peace and development assistance. He handed me my per diem check and travel package and instructed me to validate my passport and attend a U.S. consulate visa interview scheduled for 6:00 p.m. that same Friday. The timing was unusual: the consulate is normally closed Friday afternoons, and the interview time was after working hours.

On Monday, I boarded Ethiopian Airlines with the two government officials, flying to London Heathrow to catch our connecting flight to New York. We spent the night in London and returned to the airport the next morning. Because my ticket was issued at the last minute, I was placed on a different flight that departed one hour before theirs. We agreed that I would wait for them at JFK Airport since it was my first visit to the United States.

I arrived at JFK and waited for an hour. Then another. They did not come. Finally, I booked a hotel at the airport reservation desk and took a taxi for the night. My flight to El Salvador—our first destination—was scheduled for 6:00 a.m. At the American Airlines desk the next morning, I was told I could not board because I lacked a visa. I waited until the UNDP office opened at 9:00 a.m. and called them. A staff member instructed me to try another airline, but I refused to move until they secured the visa, believing immigration requirements would be the same everywhere.

They placed me on a three-way call with the airline to prove me wrong—but that airline also required a visa and advised them to have one faxed from El Salvador. Finally, a UNDP representative arrived at the airport with my faxed visa and escorted me directly to the plane's door—something still possible in those days. The two government officials missed their London connection and arrived two days later.

Central America Study Tour

Leaders of El Salvador, Guatemala, Nicaragua, Honduras, and Costa Rica signed the Esquipulas II Peace Agreement in 1987 to end military conflicts that had displaced millions. The United Nations launched a special plan of action to support the agreement, and the government of Italy contributed $115 million toward the initiative. Six Central American countries, the Italian government, and UNDP jointly implemented PRODERE (1989–1995), a regional peace-building and development program.

UNDP selected two government officials and one NGO leader from seven African countries and Madagascar facing similar displacement challenges. I represented NGOs in Ethiopia because WSRA was the only organization targeting internally displaced women.

I arrived in El Salvador on July 6, 1993. On the first day, we met representatives of both the government and former guerrilla forces. It was remarkable to witness former combatants negotiating peace at the same table. Before one session began, tension erupted when two participants from Somalia objected to the nameplate reading "Somalia." They insisted they represented Somaliland and left the room angrily.

It was winter in El Salvador, yet the tropical climate felt familiar and comfortable to me. Crossing an extremely narrow bridge—no wider than a footpath—was unforgettable. It felt like walking on a cord suspended in the air. During our second week, we traveled to Nicaragua. Conditions there were unstable; we were warned that the Sandinista forces remained hostile. Our program was interrupted, and we departed for Guatemala on the third day.

Before leaving, we visited Lake Nicaragua—the largest lake in Central America—and two active volcanoes. Trying to lighten the tension, we joked, "Goodbye if I don't make it," as we approached the volcano site.

Active Volcano (Cross on top of the mountain seems protective)

I was thrilled to sail across Lake Nicaragua and visit its islands. It was a prestigious tour; government ministers welcomed us at the sites we visited, and we traveled by helicopter to locations inaccessible by road. We arrived in Guatemala at the end of the second week. On our third day, we again boarded a helicopter to reach remote project sites.

By the Helicopter with Ethiopian Officials

Our first visit was to APECAFORM—the Maya-Mam Association of Smallholder Organic Coffee Farmers. As someone from the country where coffee originated, this visit fascinated me. Established in 1992 with assistance from the Catholic diocese and composed of two hundred members, APECAFORM was only one year old when we visited. APECAFORM members were organized as small-scale farmers who upheld their Mayan heritage, demonstrating deep respect for the land through holistic, organic farming practices while preserving their traditional culture and language.

With Rural Women in Guatemala

My visit to the Mayan ruins in Cancún, Mexico, fourteen years later reminded me how enduring and community-centered Mayan culture remains. While in Guatemala, I also witnessed something unimaginable in Ethiopian culture: a man carrying firewood on his back.

My group and I visited five community centers across the APECAFORM region. These centers provided training courses, hosted planning and feedback meetings, and served as collection points where coffee was gathered for transport and processing. As the third-largest country in Central America, Guatemala shared geographic similarities with El Salvador and Nicaragua.

A Trip That Redirected Me to God's Original Plan

After completing the tour, my return flight to Addis Ababa was routed through Minneapolis so I could visit my sister, Tsehai Wodajo, and her family. I began noticing the differences in America shortly after my arrival. Everything seemed big—highways, homes, and more—and strangers greeted me with a friendly "hi" as I passed by. Seeing people of many races and backgrounds made me think, *This is like heaven,* recalling Revelation 7:9: "a great multitude… from every nation, tribe, people and language."

My visit to Minneapolis introduced me to a future supporter, Ms. Kathleen Moore. She had served as a Peace Corps volunteer in Ethiopia and was preparing to return after twenty-six years. Let me share how that happened: Kathleen's friend Cheryl saw my sister looking at the photographs I had taken in Central America and asked if she could see them. My sister replied, "Sure. My sister, who is returning to Addis Ababa from Central America, asked me to pick up the prints for her from a photo shop," and handed them to her. Cheryl then told my sister that her friend Kathleen was planning to visit Ethiopia after many years and asked to be introduced to me so I could assist her in Addis Ababa.

Kathleen met me at my sister's house the following day and gave me her flight information. She arrived at Bole International Airport in Addis Ababa five days after I returned. I got to the airport early to pick her up. At the time, I was working for the Inter-African Committee (IAC) at the United Nations Economic Commission for Africa (ECA) and had a permit that allowed me to meet guests at immigration and customs, which enabled me to assist Kathleen.

Airport security was extremely tight under the socialist government; those receiving passengers were required to remain about five hundred feet away from the terminal. Kathleen was delighted to see her former student waiting for her, and I drove her to his beautiful home about five miles from the airport (mine was only a mile from the airport entrance). Three days later, Kathleen called and asked me to bring her to my house, and I hosted her for six weeks. She blended seamlessly with my family during her stay. My youngest son, Menase, loved her dearly and claimed her as his own: "She is my ferenji — she is mine." ("Ferenji" is the Ethiopian term commonly used for foreigners, especially white people.) In a sense, she truly became his a year later.

After returning home, I submitted my PRODERE tour report to Mr. Abadi Zemmu, commissioner of the Relief and Rehabilitation Commission (RRC), and to UNDP. I often wished Ethiopia had adopted the PRODERE model for addressing displacement and refugee crises—a need that remains urgent even today.

Another opportunity soon followed: a tour of Germany. German missionaries with whom I had worked in Ethiopia invited me and hosted me like royalty for three weeks. Remarkable details surrounded this trip. A young German man I had met at my church in Addis Ababa gave me one thousand dollars and invited me to visit him in Duisburg. Just before my departure, Ms. Regina Abelt—the wife of future Ethiopian president Dr. Neggaso Gidada—told me she would be on the same flight to visit her parents in Duisburg and offered to host me overnight in Frankfurt. We had grown close during her time in Addis Ababa, when she frequently visited my home.

Her parents welcomed me warmly before dropping me at Düsseldorf Hauptbahnhof to catch my train to Hermannsburg. The station was the busiest I had ever seen, crowds rushing in every direction. It reminded me of Daniel 12:4: "Many shall run to and fro, and knowledge shall be increased." Afraid of missing my stop, I moved to a seat near the door and watched carefully. When I stepped off the train, Reverend Tasgara Hirpo and Reverend Manfred Zach were waiting.

"All our guests miss their stop," Reverend Tasgara said with a smile. "You are the first to get off at the right station."

"I was afraid," I admitted. "So I stayed alert."

They placed me in their guesthouse and took turns hosting me for meals—my first true vacation and one of the most restful experiences of my life. Reverend Tasgara showed me Bremen, Lüneburg, and Hamburg. Visiting the Port of Hamburg, one of the world's most efficient ports, fascinated me. Sadly, I later lost all the film from the photographs I took during this journey. I also conducted business during this trip. Through an invitation facilitated by the Netherlands Embassy in Addis Ababa, I traveled to the Netherlands and secured a forty-foot container of supplies for WSRA—an act that would later attract an unforeseen and powerful adversary.

During my stay in Den Haag, I visited a Calvinist church and realized Christianity was declining; many churches stood nearly empty, some converted to secular uses. It was a sobering contrast to the vibrant underground faith I had witnessed in Ethiopia.

The container arrived in Addis Ababa five weeks later. WSRA was invited to participate in the October 1993 international trade fair, with the booth fee waived. Two representatives and I staffed the booth throughout the three-day event. The fair generated strong sales, and WSRA continued to succeed at international events and UN conferences. Five UN agencies—UNDP, UNESCO, UNFPA, UNHCR, and UNICEF—evaluated local NGOs and identified WSRA as one of the eleven best indigenous organizations in Ethiopia. Their report opened doors to international donors. Plan International funded the conversion of temporary shelters into permanent homes and the construction of neighborhood roads. Yet despite this progress, shifting political priorities redirected some opportunities elsewhere.

The remarkable doors that opened before us confirmed that obedience, perseverance, and faith were never wasted. Each step had been guided; each provision arrived in its time. What began as a burden to serve the displaced had grown into a movement restoring dignity and self-reliance.

Yet success does not end the journey. New seasons bring new tests. Under the new government, the future of WSRA—and my own path—was about to change once again.

Thorns Inside and Outside

I found myself surrounded by fire on every side — from external adversaries drawn by WSRA's success and from my husband, the companion of my life who had become an adversary within my own home. The pressure from outside forces surfaced openly in October 1993. Until then, encouraged by the remarkable progress we had achieved, I believed the future would bring cooperation and goodwill. Instead, I was about to learn that success can provoke resistance as easily as admiration. In the early days of the new administration, some local leaders began using their authority less for public service and more for personal advantage.

As members of the ruling party, the new Kebele 20 chairman and a Woreda 17 official (a kebele is similar to a city ward and a woreda to a county) exercised their influence in ways that caused serious harm to WSRA. When I moved into the kebele office space, I was unaware of their hidden agenda. I did not even realize the illegality of the rent we had agreed to pay. By law, a kebele in Addis Ababa could not charge more than 199 birr per month, yet WSRA signed a lease for 350 birr.

The first unexpected challenge arose from a container of donated used clothing from the Netherlands in 1993. After the shipment arrived and cleared Ethiopian customs, officials informed us that a newly enacted policy imposed taxes on used clothing and demanded forty thousand birr. We submitted a plea requesting exemption, explaining that we were a young NGO and that the policy had been enacted after the donation was shipped. We had not even been aware of the tax. Our request was denied. Forty thousand birr was an enormous sum for WSRA. I called a meeting with the women to seek their counsel. After reviewing the inventory, they concluded the items were valuable enough to justify borrowing money to secure the shipment. Based on their decision, we borrowed the funds, paid the customs fee, and retrieved the donated goods.

The second — and far more damaging — problem arose from my own misjudgment. In August 1993, Kebele 20 held a community meeting to evaluate local leadership. Unaware that honesty could be used against us, I offered constructive feedback on areas where improvement was needed. That moment became the turning point. Retaliation began almost immediately, targeting both me and WSRA. In hindsight, it was naïve to believe the meeting was meant to encourage accountability rather than reinforce authority.

Their intentions became public during a community gathering on Sunday, October 10, 1993, convened to discuss the government's land-lease policy. At that meeting, the Woreda 17 officer announced that the kebele would take over WSRA, claiming it had been found corrupt by an investigative committee. Members of the community asked for legal authorization to support such action. Their request was dismissed.

The following day, three men arrived at our workshop claiming they had been assigned by Kebele 20 leadership to investigate WSRA. They demanded that I hand over the organization's property. One of them was known locally for criminal activity and had escaped prison during the political transition in 1991. I refused. I told them they had no legal authority to interfere. WSRA was their tenant, and any concerns must be addressed through the Ministry of Labor and Social Affairs (MOLSA), the government body with which WSRA held a ten-year operational agreement.

We immediately reported the incident to MOLSA. In response, the ministry formed an inquiry committee composed of representatives from four government institutions and formally notified the kebele that an investigation was underway. Even so, peace did not return to my heart. I sensed that this confrontation was only the beginning. The pressure surrounding us was growing heavier, and I felt the familiar tightening that precedes a storm. Yet deep within, another voice whispered reassurance: when the battle is beyond human strength, it becomes the Lord's. I did not yet know how fierce the opposition would become — nor how deeply my faith, courage, and endurance would be tested in the days ahead.

Although they were instructed to await the findings of the inquiry committee, the kebele leadership continued a pattern of unlawful actions against our group. Melese Hagos, for example, was assigned a room facing our workshop so he could monitor and undermine our work full-time. The kebele locked the workshop's main entrance and ordered the women to use the building's front door instead, where security guards searched them upon entry and exit.

I received a summons signed by the Kebele 20 chairman ordering me to appear at the kebele office. They shut down our milling and food-processing unit, located on kebele premises adjacent to the plot allocated to WSRA. A technician we hired to repair sewing machines was forbidden from removing a machine that required off-site repair. We were formally notified that no WSRA property could be removed from kebele premises. The harassment escalated.

When surveyors from the Region 14 administration arrived to place boundary markers on the WSRA plot, the kebele dispatched armed guards to drive them away. Soon afterward, construction workers laying the foundation — funded by Rädda Barnen — were also stopped by armed guards. The Woreda 17 official rejected our construction permit in front of the team assembled against us. On October 22, 1993, we submitted a letter to the Region 14 administration's permit office requesting intervention.

A regional official scheduled a meeting at the Woreda 17 office. WSRA representatives, board members, and I attended. Although he represented a higher authority, he brought a large file from city council archives to prove the authenticity of our permits. He presented our land title, site inspection reports, correspondence, and legal documentation establishing our rights. (That plot of land remains registered under an NGO to this day.)

He urged the Woreda official to allow construction to resume immediately. She replied that she needed to consult "concerned persons," leaving us stalled indefinitely. The following month, two women attempted to take finished products to the international trade fair expo but were stopped by armed guards. We petitioned the Bole woreda police and secured release of the items in time for the exhibition. The illegal interference continued.

We followed the proper chain of command. First, we petitioned Woreda 17 administration, though we knew the official held significant influence there. Receiving no response, we submitted a petition to the president (mayor) of Region 14, detailing the illegal acts and requesting intervention. Again, we heard nothing. Later we learned the official was angered by our appeal and that our letter never reached the mayor. Finally, WSRA's board filed our complaint with the Zone 3 economic development sector. The zone authority concluded that the misuse of power warranted legal action and referred the matter to the regional prosecutor's office.

Upon review, the prosecutor ordered the Bole woreda police to investigate. We presented seven witnesses from Kebele 20. When summoned, the Woreda 17 official initially resisted investigation, asserting party membership as grounds for immunity. The police chief clarified that procedures only required notification prior to arrest of party members — not exemption from investigation. She was therefore questioned. After the investigation, I was summoned to review witness statements and the police report before submission to the prosecutor.

On December 21, 1993, the Kebele chairman and Melese Hagos were summoned to appear before the chief prosecutor. I attended as WSRA's representative. After hearing both sides, the chief stated he could order immediate arrest for crimes committed against WSRA and against me personally. Instead, he granted them one opportunity to correct their actions because they represented the community. Referring to me, he said, "You made her bow her head in humiliation among the community she serves."

He ordered them to dissolve the illegal investigative committee and to await the findings of the MOLSA inquiry committee. Rather than comply, they intensified their efforts.

The following day, in my absence, they gathered WSRA women, falsely accused me of stealing aid funds, and urged them to file a lawsuit against me with kebele backing.

Nine women stood up and refused.

Bekelech said, "You didn't know me when I was filthy from construction labor, carrying my baby on my back. Now you know me because of the dignity I gained through Agitu. I will not sign."

Alemitu Abera said, "I cannot bite the hand that fed me."

Taitu Gedamu said, "I would rather return to poverty."

Years later, during the COVID-19 pandemic, Taitu called from Addis Ababa, crying, "Mother of my life, may no evil come near you." Her words remain one of my greatest rewards.

Those who refused to sign were threatened with arrest. Fear divided the group. Memories of past brutality made resistance dangerous. Most women signed. Two who refused were arrested.

On January 27, 1994, we submitted another report to the prosecutor's office, documenting how the situation had worsened after the December hearing. Whether coincidence or consequence, within a month the chief prosecutor handling our case was no longer in office.

After two months of follow-up visits, the new chief informed us he was transferring the case to the supreme court due to the seriousness of the abuse-of-power charges. Meanwhile, we awaited the MOLSA inquiry report. Despite intimidation and uncertainty, we did not abandon our pursuit of justice. We sought no favor — only truth.

After months of investigation, the MOLSA committee issued its final six-page report. It documented the facts and sharply criticized the kebele for its damaging and demoralizing actions against WSRA. A few months later, the women who had signed the petition met with me and asked for forgiveness. I understood their guilt and fear. Holding resentment was contrary to my calling, so I released any bitterness. One group leader, Dinknesh Gelaneh, spoke words that pierced my heart:

"We treated you like a piece of meat thrown to hyenas." Though reconciliation occurred, the group maintained its relationship with the kebele administration. The wounds healed slowly, but the lessons endured.

As we awaited the court's decision, I remained committed to the original vision of empowering the women. Encouragingly, the WSRA's donors did not abandon us during this difficult period. Instead, their support continued. UNFPA and UNDP, in particular, sustained their confidence in my work by sponsoring my participation in trainings and workshops. In 1993, I was invited to attend a one-week leadership training at the Gorée Institute in Dakar, Senegal, organized specifically for African women NGO leaders.

The Gorée Institute, located on an island that stands as a historical symbol of suffering, resilience, and human dignity, provided a powerful setting for reflection and renewal. Surrounded by women leaders from across the continent, I gained not only technical skills but also renewed courage. We shared stories of struggle, injustice, and perseverance, and I realized that the opposition I was facing was not unique. Across Africa, women working for justice often encountered resistance, intimidation, and political interference.

The training strengthened my leadership skills, deepened my understanding of advocacy and community mobilization, and reaffirmed my conviction that empowerment must be rooted in dignity, self-reliance, and justice. More importantly, it renewed my strength at a time when the pressure against WSRA felt overwhelming.

With my Instructors at Gorée Institute

I returned to Ethiopia encouraged and spiritually fortified, ready to continue the struggle. While the legal battle and local opposition persisted, my vision remained clear: the work God had entrusted to me was larger than intimidation, and the future of these women was worth every trial we endured.

Riding the boat each day between Dakar and Gorée Island was both enjoyable and sobering. The round-trip journey across the Atlantic from our hotel in Dakar to the Gorée Institute brought moments of peace on the water. Yet the visit also exposed me to a painful chapter of human history that left an indelible mark on my heart.

Boat Ride to and From Gorée Institute

My visit to the House of Slaves became a lifelong memory of the crime against humanity that took place there. Built around 1776, the House of Slaves stands on Gorée Island, a forty-five-acre island located about four miles off the coast of Dakar, Senegal.

The building presents two starkly contrasting realities. Upstairs is a luxurious residence where slave traders lived comfortably. Downstairs, however, is a warehouse of narrow holding cells where enslaved men, women, and children were confined separately. Through an exit known as the "Door of No Return," captives were forced onto ships that carried them toward lives of bondage.

House of Slave

Captives were taken from their homes, sold, and held in cramped rooms with minimal light and air. They were chained neck to neck and shackled ankle to ankle, forced to sit for long periods without space to lie down. Illness spread easily in the suffocating conditions, and many never survived the waiting period before transport. Those who resisted were punished severely; the sick were sometimes cast into the ocean.

Standing in that place, I could almost feel the weight of despair and human suffering absorbed into its walls. Their temporary confinement was only the beginning of a life of forced labor and dehumanization. The visit deepened my awareness of humanity's capacity for cruelty—and the urgent need for justice, compassion, and dignity. Not long afterward, UNFPA sponsored my participation in the International Conference on Population and Development in Cairo (September 5–13, 1994), followed by an invitation from UNDP to attend the World Summit for Social Development in Copenhagen in March 1995.

Two months before leaving Ethiopia for the United States in August 1994, I secured funding from the Canadian International Development Agency (CIDA) and deposited funds into the WSRA women's cooperative account to cover one year of operating costs. We transferred ownership of the machines, tools, flour mills, and the leased workshop to the women so they could operate independently and sustain their progress.

While my public work advanced, my private life remained a battlefield. My husband's abuse—emotional, physical, psychological, sexual, and financial—continued alongside the external opposition I faced. Without the grace of God, his calculated cruelty might have destroyed my sanity. At one point, when my suffering felt unbearable, I thought, *Jesus suffered for one day, yet I have suffered for so long.* Immediately, the Holy Spirit confronted me with a question drawn from my medical training: "What is the concentration of iodine?" I answered, "One in one thousand." Then came the deeper question: "What was the concentration of the whole world's sin placed upon one man in one day?"

I was instantly convicted of self-pity and cried out, "Devil, nothing has happened to me!" From that moment, I learned to examine my heart instead of dwelling on my pain. I became less sensitive to harsh words and more anchored in spiritual resilience. Galatians 5:24 — *"Those who belong to Christ Jesus have crucified the flesh with its passions and desires"* — strengthened me.

I reflected on patients with leprosy who lose nerve sensation and unknowingly injure themselves. In a similar way, spiritual numbness can deepen wounds. God was teaching me to endure without hardening my heart, to suffer without surrendering my soul, and to grow stronger in faith rather than in bitterness. The fire did not consume me. It refined me. And though the thorns remained both within and without, I was being prepared for the next step of my journey — one that would carry me far beyond what I had imagined.

The Internal Thorn was Extending into My Work With Women's Group

My husband frequently called me *wusha*—"dog." Wives who make the "right" choices are called "honey," but perhaps he believed I deserved such a name for trusting him and continuing to defend him. I was so confused that I failed to recognize how my endurance had drifted beyond Scripture and God's counsel.

I had resolved to endure until what God had revealed about the end of my marriage came to pass—which it did five years later. During that long wait, I became emotionally numb. I often pretended not to notice his wrongdoing because whenever he suspected I knew something, he tried to convince me that I was the one at fault. I never raised my marital struggles as a prayer request in group settings. I believed doing so would be indirect gossip or self-righteousness. Looking back, I see how silence enabled injustice and violated both biblical truth and the law meant to protect victims.

The thorn inside my home did not stop at personal abuse; it opposed and threatened my work with WSRA. In the early days of WSRA, before we rented space from the kebele, we held meetings in my home. One day, while meeting with the women's leadership team, my husband burst in shouting, "Don't meet with these illiterate women in my house talking about 'projects!'" He struck my right foot with his shoe in front of the women and my three-year-old child. My foot bled from the assault.

The women fled in fear. I ran to the police station for the first time in our fourteen-year marriage. I told the police chief I did not want my husband charged; I only wanted him warned. He was arrested that afternoon but released the next day under his nephew's surety. In Ethiopia at the time, domestic violence rarely removed the abuser from the home. After weighing the consequences, I chose to endure.

The second incident was even more disturbing. On February 15, 1991, while I was finalizing a project proposal before my trip to Italy, my husband returned home unusually early and accused me of kidnapping my late brother-in-law's servant. Moments later, a police officer and two men entered with Wolela, who worked at the WSRA milling house.

"You are wanted. Let's go," the officer said.

"You will be wanted next for seeking my arrest without a court order," I replied.

They left, taking the poor girl into custody. I believed the incident had been orchestrated to obstruct my trip. The WSRA women urged me to file a complaint, and we did. The next morning I tried to bail her out, but I was not even allowed to see her. When I returned six weeks later, I learned she had been tortured in detention. The man who led the false accusation fled. I never learned her fate.

It would take an entire book to recount the suffering of eighteen years in an unendurable marriage. I have repented many times for my silence, yet the memory of the abuse inflicted on vulnerable servants still grieves me. Fear, confusion, and shame kept me from reporting what I should have reported.

While cultural stigma causes many women to hide abuse, I can no longer allow culture to excuse silence. Healing requires truth. To transform pain into purpose, I plan to dedicate the proceeds from this memoir to establishing holistic shelters for survivors of violence against women in Ethiopia, drawing on my experience in the United States. I pray that fulfilling this mission will deepen my healing. And I hope to continue this work through my next book:

How to Build Healthy Marriages and Families: Prevention and Cure. Through fire inside and outside, God preserved me — not merely to survive, but to stand, to speak, and to help others live free.

8

DELAYED BUT DIVINELY TIMED: GOD'S ANSWER

The answer I received from God concerning the end of my marriage came to pass ten years later. Four years had passed since I first heard from Moody Bible Institute (MBI) when I visited the United States in the summer of 1993 on my way home from my study tour in Central America. During that short stay, I stopped by the admissions office at Moody Bible Institute to find out why my application had been delayed for so long. They informed me that they had never received an application for my husband and gave me new applications for both of us to complete.

I was later told that my application was being processed for the fall semester of 1994 and that I was waiting for my I-20 when I received a surprising invitation from Minneapolis. One Tuesday in July 1994, I called Moody Bible Institute to check on the status of my application. The woman who answered said, "Oh my God! I have your application in front of me. I am sorry for our tardiness. You will be processed for the spring semester of 1995."

That Saturday, I heard unexpected news. My sister Rahel called from Minneapolis and asked me to pick up her wedding invitation from Reverend Yadasa Daba, who had returned from there. She said God had answered her prayer that my youngest children, Bethel and Menase, would participate in her wedding as flower girl and ring bearer. Rahel had come to the United States the previous year to study at Augsburg College in Minneapolis and was now preparing to marry. She had originally planned to start a small business with the money for her plane ticket, but I encouraged her to travel—unaware that she would soon make it possible for us to join her.

Before ending our phone conversation, Rahel asked me to promise that I would bring the two children to her wedding, scheduled for September 1994 in Minneapolis. When my three older children heard this, they asked, "What about us?" Not wanting to disappoint them, I obtained passports for all five children and applied for their visas. Because school was opening on September 18, I also registered them for the fall semester.

When I appeared at the United States consulate for our visa interview, the consular officer asked, "Which of the five children are participating in the wedding?"

I replied, "The youngest two."

"Can you tell me their names?"

"They are Bethel and Menase."

"How about the older three?" she asked.

"They aren't participating," I said. "They just want to go for fun." At the end of the interview, the consular officer instructed me to proceed to the next window and pay. I did not realize until I paid that visas had been issued for all five children.

Since I had not expected my older three children to receive visas and was not financially prepared for that possibility, I called my sister Tsehai in Minneapolis immediately after leaving the embassy. "The U.S. consulate issued visas to all five children. What shall I do?" I asked. She laughed loudly and said, "People go insane trying to get the opportunity to come to America. Even U.S. citizens have difficulty securing visas for their relatives." She encouraged me to thank God for the opportunity and attend the wedding with my children. Still, I was troubled and could not sleep that night. It was not what I had planned financially. I had hoped to secure provisions for our resettlement in the United States first, and my admission to Moody Bible School on a family scholarship was only four months away. I did not think it cost-effective to take the children for such a short trip.

The next morning, I took my parents to the U.S. consulate for their visa interviews, and they also received visas. Finally, I calmed myself and began preparing for our journey. While searching for a more affordable flight, I ended up booking Alitalia Airlines. Our flight to the United States was routed through Nairobi. I remembered a dream I had in 1983 and was amazed that our route matched exactly what I had seen ten years earlier.

I booked our round-trip flight for August 23, 1994, and the eight of us—my five children, my parents, and I—arrived at Bole International Airport on time for departure. Upon check-in, the Ethiopian Airlines agent informed us that our Alitalia connection flight had been rerouted through Cairo. We boarded Ethiopian Airlines and began our journey to Cairo. An intense heat unlike anything my children or parents had ever experienced greeted us at Cairo International Airport. As we stepped off the plane, it felt as though we were walking into an oven.

My Children and I Three months Before We left Ethiopia

Another unexpected situation followed at immigration. We were required to purchase entry visas on arrival—an expense I had not budgeted for—but I paid for all of us. At the immigration desk, the officer collected our passports and handed them to another officer, who escorted our group of eight to a separate room. A second officer joined him, and they began interviewing me immediately. I answered their questions and provided all the documents they requested. After the brief interview, we were cleared to proceed to baggage claim.

My mother, who had never seen an escalator before, became frightened and nearly lost her balance when she stepped onto it. My father, however, seemed surprisingly comfortable navigating it. When we arrived at baggage claim, my sister Tsehai Wodajo was waiting with a crowd of friends and family. They welcomed us with flowers, hugs, and joyful celebration. Among them was my new friend Kathleen Moore and her son, Michael. Tsehai then surprised me with unexpected news: my children and I would stay at Kathleen's home, and they would take us there after a welcome dinner at her house. I had not known that my worries about housing had already been taken care of before I left Addis Ababa.

As I mentioned earlier, As I mentioned earlier, I first met Kathleen in Minneapolis the previous year on my way back from Central America. Kathleen had temporarily moved in with a friend so my children and I could have her home and enough space. She worked as a systems analyst for Hennepin County Economic Assistance and even took a week off to help us settle in during our first days in America. Overwhelmed by her kindness, I told her I felt more comfortable giving than receiving and that it troubled me to see her go to such lengths for us. She gently replied, "It is time for you to learn to receive, because others also feel joy in giving."

We had hosted Kathleen in Addis Ababa in 1993, but she returned that kindness tenfold. We had given her our master bedroom with private bath; she gave us her entire home. When I first hosted her, I did not know her well, nor could I have imagined that I would one day move to Minnesota. Yet Hebrews 13:2 reminds us: "Do not forget to entertain strangers, for by so doing some have unwittingly entertained angels." Unaware of the hardships they would soon face, my children were excited to be in America. During our first week in the Twin Cities, we noticed many unfamiliar things. The weather was chilly, trees were shedding their leaves, and the leaves I saw were yellowish. I remembered thinking my Swedish handicraft teachers were wrong to use yellow leaves in their embroidery designs — now I understood.

The wedding day was approaching, and excitement filled the air. On Wednesday before the wedding, we shopped for groceries for the grand feast. The following day, my sister Tsehai, a group of women — friends and relatives — and I cooked in a church's commercial kitchen and stored the food in a deep freezer for Saturday's reception. Cooking together was joyful: chatting, singing, laughing, and sharing stories.

The wedding honored both our cultural heritage and Christian faith. The groom's party arrived at the bride's home singing Christian wedding songs and dancing. According to tradition, the bride's family blocked the entrance, playfully resisting the groom's entry. The groom's party sprayed perfume over the resisting group, gently pushing through until the groom entered.

The bride's parents and family blessed the couple in our traditional manner, after which the bride and groom departed with their attendants to a picnic site for photographs, followed by both families. The church ceremony began at 5:00 p.m., and Bethel and Menase were overjoyed to participate as flower girl and ring bearer.

Bethel & Menase at the Wedding

The reception was wonderful. Everyone in attendance enjoyed the food and the fellowship. After dinner, we sang Christian songs and danced with the bride and groom. The celebration concluded at 10:00 p.m. The first two weeks of our stay were stressful as we prepared for the wedding and wrestled with decisions about our future. As I mentioned earlier, I had not planned to travel with all my children on this trip. We made that life-altering move only because we believed it was God's will.

I had enjoyed a pleasant life in Ethiopia, and my children attended one of the best private schools in Addis Ababa. Despite the tribulations I had endured, I had never wished to live outside my country. Yet I took this step, trusting what God had spoken to me about the end of my marriage when I applied to Moody Bible Institute. I believed it was the right path to fulfill His will.

My parents did not like it here because of the cultural differences and returned home after the wedding. They were both sixty-seven years old and missed the social life and beautiful weather of Ethiopia. Like many older immigrants, they could not bear being indoors for long periods.

My Father During His Last Visit in 2001

While we were discussing our options, Kathleen shared her desire to support my women's NGO in Addis Ababa. That prompted me to reconsider my enrollment at Moody Bible Institute, which was only three months away. I remembered how the first application process had failed because of my husband and feared the same could happen again if I acted against what God had spoken regarding my immigration.

God had shown me that I would leave my husband behind and travel alone with my children. This journey had unfolded exactly as He revealed to me ten years earlier. I realized that trying to bring my husband into this new chapter would only prolong my journey, much like the Israelites who turned a forty-day journey into forty years through disobedience. After prayerful reflection, I told Kathleen that my children and I would remain. Kathleen then helped enroll my children — ages seven, eight, fourteen, sixteen, and seventeen — in public schools near her home. The older three joined Roosevelt High School. Watching the school bus arrive promptly each morning, gather my children along with others, and return them safely to our door increased my love for America. In Addis Ababa, I personally drove them to and from school every day.

On September 21, 1994, I visited Metropolitan State University in St. Paul to learn about its programs. I was excited about pursuing studies in human services and nonprofit administration to strengthen my ability to manage my women's NGO. On September 28, I submitted my application. Because I already had my TOEFL score from applying to Moody, I met the spring semester deadline. This felt like further confirmation that I was walking in God's will.

Not wanting to burden Kathleen, we stayed in her home for one month. In October, my children and I moved into Riverside Plaza Apartments. My second divine connection in South Minneapolis, Mr. Jerry Khan and his family, helped furnish our apartment and assisted us in adjusting to our new life. I met Jerry while waiting for my children's school bus during our stay with Kathleen. A member of Straight Gate Church, he brought us to his congregation. My children attended Sunday school there, and Pastor Dr. Roger Magnuson encouraged me to continue heeding my calling.

Riverside Plaza was home to immigrants from many parts of the world. Across the street, the Brian Coyle Community Center served this diverse population. I would soon discover that I was called to serve this immigrant community in a way similar to the displaced women and families I had served in Addis Ababa.

The following month, I left my children in the care of my niece, Sofiya Siyum, who also lived in Riverside Plaza, and returned to Ethiopia to attend the 1995 World Conference on Women. African Regional Preparatory Conference, November 94, Dakar, Senegal, which had been arranged before my move to the United States. I routed my trip through Ethiopia to attend to pending matters.

At African Regional Preparatory Conference

Before leaving for America, I had submitted a grant proposal to the United Nations Development Fund for Women (UNIFEM) in Nairobi to fund the salaries of the WSRA executive director and an administrative assistant. During this trip, I stopped in Nairobi to follow up. I received good news: the application had been approved. I relayed the news to the WSRA board in Addis Ababa — we had secured funding to cover salaries and benefits, including full medical insurance through the UN/ECA clinic.

Since I had never been paid by WSRA, securing this grant was significant. I left the organization in the capable hands of its seven-member board — including two members employed by the United Nations — and returned to Minneapolis.On my way back, I attended the African Preparatory Conference for the Fourth World Conference on Women NGO Forum (November 12–15), sponsored by UNFPA.

When I returned to the United States on November 27, 1994, I found my admission letter from Metropolitan State University waiting for me. Kathleen's friend Cheryl Bates had filed an Affidavit of Support on my behalf, enabling me to obtain my I-20. I remain deeply grateful for her confidence that I would support my family and not become a burden. (On one occasion, she voluntarily paid my $700 tuition — that was all.)

I enrolled for the spring semester and applied to the Immigration and Naturalization Service (INS) for F-1 student visas for myself and my dependent children. Three months later, INS sent a letter requesting additional documentation and answers to eleven questions. It stated that the documentation submitted was insufficient for favorable consideration. I promptly provided all requested materials, including return flight tickets should it not be God's will for us to remain. Less than a month later, our visas were approved.

Adjusting to life in America proved more challenging than adjusting our immigration status. After school, my children would sit in front of the television. In Addis Ababa, television viewing had been restricted, but here they were enjoying their new freedom. I warned them that excessive viewing could affect their academic performance. When they ignored my guidance, I removed the television from the apartment. My children did not argue; they respected and obeyed me. From then on, they completed their assignments immediately after school.

Our first major hardship was winter. The cold and snow were harsher than anything we had experienced. I had encountered winter in Europe, but my children had not. Thanks to Kathleen, who purchased winter coats and snow boots for them in October, they adjusted quickly. They enjoyed skating and playing in the snow like American children, while I remained resentful of winter — a sentiment that has not changed. Food was their only difficulty in adjusting. Ethiopian foods were organic and tasted different from what they encountered here. I had to pack lunches for Bethel because she became sick after eating school food.

Shortly after moving to Riverside Plaza, an incident confirmed that God had placed me there for a purpose. One day, a man called and told me about a woman in Riverside Plaza suffering domestic abuse. He gave me her name and apartment number. Amazingly, I had known this woman and her husband before coming to the United States. What a small world.

I went to her apartment that evening and knocked, but she would not open the door; her husband had threatened her. After several attempts, I called her name and announced my own loudly. She finally opened the door and shared her heartbreaking story.

Though I was new to the country and knew little about available resources, I searched the Yellow Pages and called First Call for Help. They provided referrals. The next morning, I contacted the International Institute of Minnesota — the exact right place. They immediately placed her in safe housing through Lutheran Social Service and began processing her green card under the Violence Against Women Act (VAWA), enacted in 1994. As one of the first beneficiaries, she received her green card quickly. VAWA allows immigrant victims of domestic violence to obtain legal status without relying on an abusive spouse's petition. God bless America abundantly.

Realizing I had been placed in that neighborhood for a purpose, I met with Mr. Mike Wayne at the Brian Coyle Community Center and shared my vision. He instructed me on how to establish a nonprofit and referred me to the Dorsey & Whitney law firm for pro bono assistance. I met with attorney John Somers for over two hours, sharing my WSRA experience and requesting help establishing a similar nonprofit for refugee and immigrant women. I provided WSRA bylaws and documents. He immediately agreed to help incorporate the organization and serve as its registered agent. We named it the International Self-Reliance Agency Women Inc. (ISAW).

I left his office deeply moved by the trust he placed in me, a stranger, and grateful that God was blessing me with Americans who demonstrated compassion through action. I arranged to use the nonprofit for my university internship. Because my F-1 visa allowed twenty hours of off-campus work, the internship provided valuable flexibility. I began my internship at the Brian Coyle Community Center by forming a core group of ten refugee women who met weekly. I conducted a needs assessment among immigrant families in the neighborhood. With Mr. Wayne's assistance, we wrote a grant proposal and secured our first grant — $10,000 from the Minneapolis Foundation. By then, Mr. Somers had completed incorporation. The mission of ISAW was to empower immigrant women in the Twin Cities to become self-sufficient and support their families. And the work had begun.

Looking back, I can see that every step — even those filled with uncertainty, pain, and sacrifice — was part of a divine design far greater than my own understanding. What began as a journey shaped by hardship, loss, and difficult obedience became the pathway through which God positioned me to serve beyond anything I could have imagined. Leaving Ethiopia was not an escape from suffering; it was an assignment. The same God who led me through fire in my homeland was now planting me in new soil, preparing me to serve immigrant families, empower women, and advocate for those whose voices were silenced by fear, poverty, and violence.

I did not arrive in America with wealth, security, or a carefully mapped future. I arrived with five children, untested faith in unfamiliar territory, and the quiet assurance that obedience to God never leads to loss — only to transformation. As I watched my children adjust to their new lives, as doors opened through divine connections, and as opportunities emerged to serve hurting women once again, I understood a profound truth: delay is not denial. God's answers come in His time, and His timing carries purpose beyond what we can see.

The wilderness seasons had refined me. The battles had strengthened me. The losses had loosened my grip on everything except God. And now, standing at the threshold of a new chapter, I sensed that the fire I had walked through was not meant to destroy me — it was meant to prepare me. The journey was not ending. It was beginning again.

9

MY SECOND HUMBLE BEGINNING

My children and I lived in Riverside Plaza Apartments for only five months before moving to a duplex in South Minneapolis, seven blocks from my friend Kathleen's house. This four-bedroom, two-bath duplex—with an extra living room—was owned by Project for Pride in Living, a nonprofit organization that helps low-income families with housing. By the grace of God, we qualified for subsidized housing. I was grateful to have enough space for my family of six, though I had yet to discover how rough the neighborhood was.

As we resettled there, I found myself in a new social class, having moved from a comfortable neighborhood in Addis Ababa. Theft, gang activity, burglary, and drugs were common on Fourth Avenue. I became a victim of theft myself when a brand-new printer was stolen from my car just minutes after I parked in front of our apartment. I tried to advise the neighborhood children to take advantage of the opportunities available to them—opportunities my own children had never had. Unfortunately, instead of accepting guidance, some began using our apartment as a safe haven when fleeing police officers.

The first year was extremely hard. I humbly picked up bread and cereal from Sabathani Community Center, five blocks away, for our breakfasts—our first experience with that kind of poverty. Our beautiful brick home, furniture, and car were no longer part of our lives. I had to ride a bus, something I had never done in Addis Ababa.

"Now it is our turn to be poor," my fourth child, Bethel, said. In truth, she did not even realize she came from a poor country.

One day she returned from school upset.

"My teacher lied, and I was outraged," she said.

"What did she lie about?" I asked.

"She said Ethiopia is poor. I raised my hand and said, 'Ethiopia is not poor,' and other students said it could be Somalia."

I replied gently, "Your teacher didn't lie. She is right. Actually, it is my fault that I didn't teach you about your native country."

Proverbs 14:20 says, "The poor are shunned even by their neighbors, but the rich have many friends." I saw this truth at work around us. Yet it did not discourage me, because the promise the Lord gave when He revealed His will to bring me to this land remained my strength.

Soon my children began helping themselves and building a ladder out of hardship. I expected adjustment to be difficult for them, since servants in Ethiopia had done everything—even making their beds—but they surprised me. Our landlord, Project for Pride in Living (PPL), provided them with paid summer jobs. Then God used Michael Moore, Kathleen's son, to create an even better source of income.

One weekend my daughters Jalale and Helen micro-braided Michael's hair. He was amazed by their speed and the quality of their work. Previously, two braiders had taken an entire day and charged him $150. Inspired, he opened a hair-braiding salon called Global Braids, and my two oldest daughters began working there after school. In a short time, they learned to drive and purchased their own car. They excelled academically—each receiving Presidential Awards—and enrolled in voluntary high-school courses such as sewing, photography, and postsecondary preparation.

I marveled at how God had arranged everything in advance. Kathleen cared for my children like a grandmother, while her son Michael acted as a big brother. Her home was only eight blocks away. She made sure they experienced the activities American children enjoy—skating, summer programs, and swimming. All my children loved swimming in Ethiopia, and they would have missed it if not for Kathleen. She also enrolled them in extracurricular programs suited to their talents. She registered Jalale for the Minnesota Institute for Talented Youth summer program to nurture her visual-art talent—a gift I did not fully recognize until I saw her on Ethiopian television receiving a painting award as a fifth-grade student.

Michael also supported my children as they adjusted to the new culture. Each morning he drove to our apartment and watched them board the school bus to ensure they were not bullied. If they missed the bus, he drove them to school. He treated my children as his siblings. As an only child in his twenties, he embraced the role of older brother. I will never forget seeing him step in to defend my youngest son when another child tried to bully him at the bus stop.

In my humble circumstances, I was also about to experience American generosity personally. In January 1997, I was offered the opportunity to participate in a one-month tour of China and Hong Kong through a course titled "Case Studies in International Business: Asia I," coordinated by the University of St. Thomas. Only two students from Metropolitan State University were selected. I did not know the cost until I received the travel packet. Unable to afford it, I asked to withdraw. I had initially registered only to maintain my immigration status while waiting for my credential evaluation. However, I was told I would still have to pay because my nonrefundable flight had already been booked. I prayed with my two youngest children, and during our prayer Menase said, "God will provide." So I traveled.

Our first stop was Beijing. On the first day we received a full-day briefing at a university. On the second day we visited China Daily, the national newspaper, and the Beijing Economic and Technological Development Zone, founded in 1991 and spanning nearly one hundred square kilometers designated for investment by Western companies, including Sino-American ventures. At that time, businesses from the United States, Germany, Britain, Italy, the Netherlands, and Australia were investing heavily in China to benefit from low labor costs. Hong Kong and Taiwan investors were also active there.

During the four-week tour, we visited development zones and programs in Beijing, Shanghai, Xi'an, Shantou, Kunming, and finally Hong Kong. Residential areas in these zones were designed to include apartments, villas, schools, and clinics, with plans to house between 400,000 and 500,000 residents by the year 2000.

Our Beijing tour also included visits to the Great Wall, Buddhist temples, the Marble Boat at the Summer Palace, and the mausoleum of Chairman Mao Zedong in Tiananmen Square. Visitors entering the mausoleum were required to follow strict rules: dress codes, no talking, no smoking, and no photography. We had to leave everything in our possession—including winter jackets—with the honor guards at the gate, even though it was bitterly cold. That January in Beijing was as cold as Minnesota, though without snow.

At The Great Wall of China

The total length of the Great Wall is 21196.18km (13170 miles), including the well-preserved Ming Dynasty (A.D. 1368-1644) Great Wall which is 8851km (5,500 miles) The average height of the walls is 7.8m

(25.6 feet) and the tallest being 14m (46 feet). The altitude of the highest point of the Great Wall is 1439.3 meters (4722.1 feet). The width of the top of the Great Wall is about 4-5m (13-16 feet) i, while the base is usually wider with and average width of about 6.5m (21 feet). (The width of different sections, this may differ from the average)

Chairman Mao Zedong's mausoleum.

Located in the center of Tiananmen Squire in Beijing, the Chairman Mao Memorial Hall, the Mausoleum of Mao Zedong, is the final resting place of Chairman Mao Zedchairman, chairman of Chinese Communist Party during the Chinese Civil War and until his death in 1976. All visitors entering Chairman Mao Zedong's mausoleum are required to follow strict rules, including dress codes, no talking, no smoking, and no photography. We had to leave everything in our possession. January in Beijing was as cold as in Minnesota, but it wasn't snowing.

The Marble Boat

Built in 1755 with a base made from a huge stone that supported a wooden pavilion in the traditional Chinese style, the Marble Boat was imitating the sailing boats of Emperor Qianlong (1711– 1799). Emperor Qianlong had this gigantic Marble Boat fastened in the water to indicate the steadfastness of the Qing Dynasty's rule (1644–1911). The wooden pavilion was burned in 1860 with only the hull of the boat remaining, and Empress Dowager Cixi had the boat rebuilt in 1893 in the Western design, the only Western-style structure found in the Summer Palace. Beijing felt overwhelmingly crowded. It seemed as if nearly everyone traveled by bicycle, streams of riders flowing through the streets in every direction. Pollution was impossible to ignore; a heavy haze hung over the city, giving it a constant foggy appearance.

In the second week, we traveled to Shanghai. There we visited the Waigaoqiao Free Trade Zone, which covers about 13.75 square kilometers and includes the Pudong development area as well as the Baoshan Iron and Steel Corporation. Located near the Port of Shanghai, the zone combines free-trade privileges with easy access to bonded warehousing and other trade services. Companies from around the world operate there; for example, 3M from Minnesota has a plant in the zone.

While visiting Yuyuan Garden, our group noticed a man wearing a Minnesota hat. Curious, we introduced ourselves and soon learned he was the manager of the 3M plant in Shanghai. That simple connection led to an unexpected opportunity: he arranged for us to tour the 3M facility.

At Bashan Iron and Steel Corporation in Shanghai

Two remarkable sites I visited during the third week of our tour left me with unforgettable memories: the Stone Forest in Kunming and the Terracotta Warriors in Xi'an. Walking through the tall, dense stone formations of the Stone Forest felt like entering a woodland of towering trees without leaves. The limestone pillars rose in every direction, creating narrow paths and shadowed passages that made the landscape feel both mysterious and awe-inspiring.

Stone Forest

The Terracotta Warriors in Xi'an, Shaanxi Province, were equally astonishing. Discovered in the 1970s, the site contains more than seven thousand life-sized clay soldiers, horses, and chariots arranged in battle formation. Each figure is uniquely detailed and once held real weapons, representing the imperial guard tasked with protecting the deceased emperor. These warriors were created to guard the soul of Emperor Qin Shi Huang, the powerful ruler of the second century BC (reigned 221–210 BC).

Terracotta warriors in battle formation

Replica of Terracotta warrior

They represent the actual imperial guard of those days. The Chinese people did all this to safeguard their tyrant king's soul, Emperor Qin Shi Huang in the second century BC (reign, 221–210 BC).

An Archer Kneeling to Shoot

Chariot

Charriot Driver

Infront of a Budha Temple in Shantou, With Fellow Metro State Student

My tour of China left me with an unforgettable memory of the Chinese people's talent and artwork. I was amazed to see their loyalty to their leaders and their dedication to promoting their country's economy. The Chinese government knew what it was doing when it welcomed the cheap-labor deal of the West, while Western companies were unaware of the effect of using their individual liberty to outsource so many services. China grabbed the outsourcing as an opportunity to advance its nation and promote its economic growth. Today, China is the main investor in and promoter of Africa in general and the major accelerator of Ethiopia's economic growth in particular. It plays a leading role in Ethiopia in the sectors of the state-run infrastructure investment.

I was expecting a bill from the University of St. Thomas for the travel expenses I owed, and the mail arrived a month after my return from this trip. What a wonderful surprise! The letter notified me that an anonymous donor paid for my case-study tour of China as Menase prophesized. I had no words to express my joy. I wished I knew my donor. I am sure God, who knows that person, has blessed him or her richly.

I graduated from Metropolitan State University in December 1997, and the best was yet to come a year later. I was about to experience God's miraculous provision through both divine favor and the kindness of compassionate Americans who became instruments of His blessing. It came to my mind to apply for the Bush Leadership Fellowship to pursue a master's degree. The Bush Foundation required applicants to have resided in Minnesota for at least six months and to be U.S. citizens or permanent residents. Although I had lived in Minnesota for only four and a half years and my green card was still in process, I prayed with Bethel and Menase. Menase assured me with childlike confidence that I would receive it, and I submitted my application along with the required essay in faith.

Because acceptance into a graduate program was required for the fellowship, I applied to the Humphrey School of Public Affairs at the University of Minnesota, located across the street from ISAW's office. Although the dean was on leave, he came into his office personally and issued my acceptance letter for their newly launched Executive Master of Public Affairs program. They considered me an excellent fit, and the acceptance letter itself became a powerful endorsement beyond its intended purpose.

By God's grace, I advanced through the competitive process and was selected as one of forty finalists. At the Bush Foundation's expense, we participated in a three-and-a-half-day final selection seminar held April 21–24, 1999, at the Oak Ridge Conference Center in Chaska, Minnesota. During the first two days, we were trained in interview presentation skills and prepared to deliver a two-minute speech on the final day. That speech was crucial. Although twenty-five awards were anticipated, only twenty finalists ultimately received the fellowship.

By God's favor, I was selected. Not only did I receive the fellowship for myself, but ISAW was also blessed. One of the judges who interviewed me was the director of a grant program; after my interview, she handed me an application packet, through which ISAW later secured funding. The Bush Leadership Fellowship provided a $3,600 monthly stipend throughout my studies, covered my tuition, and awarded an additional $6,000 for travel included in my proposal. This support enabled me to attend United Nations conferences at UN Headquarters in New York and maintain ISAW's Special Consultative Status with the UN Economic and Social Council.

At the UN Headquarters in New York

My visit to Cairo during this period was a striking experience. Although Egypt is part of Africa, its cultural expression reflects strong Arab and Islamic influences. The traffic felt chaotic and overwhelming compared to the order I was accustomed to. Streets were crowded with vehicles competing for space, pedestrians crossed fearlessly, and drivers relied more on instinct and persistence than formal right-of-way rules. It was both alarming and fascinating to witness.

In Cairo

One visit that deeply moved me was to the Association for the Protection of the Environment (APE) in Cairo. APE operates income-generating programs for marginalized garbage collectors, helping them improve their living conditions. The group I met consisted of poor Christian women who faced discrimination and were treated as second-class citizens because of their faith. Their resilience and dignity left a lasting impression on me.

The Bush Leadership Fellowship also became instrumental in another unexpected blessing: the purchase of my home in Brooklyn Center, Minnesota — a lasting financial blessing. Because I had devoted my life to serving others, I had no savings or retirement funds such as a 401(k). Yet God provided. Three months before receiving the fellowship, Habitat for

Humanity approved me for a newly constructed four-bedroom, two-bath home and showed me the site. However, I prayed for a different home design — one similar to the house I had lived in in Addis Ababa — and felt led to step aside so the Habitat home could go to someone with fewer options than I had.

In November 1999, I began searching for a home even though I had no money in my bank account. When the loan originator requested a bank statement for preapproval, the fellowship funds arrived at precisely the right time. I went to the bank in faith to print my statement, and there it was — two months of stipend totaling $7,200.

God honored my decision and answered my prayer swiftly. By January 2000, I was in my new home. Its design exceeded what I had asked for. The circumstances surrounding the purchase were themselves miraculous, and the interest rate I received was beyond anything I could have imagined. I have continued to benefit from the home's equity — a provision I recognize as God's faithful reward for obedience and sacrifice.

| From Metro State University | From Humprey School of Public Affairs |

Through this journey, I learned that God's timing is never delayed and His provision is never incomplete. What seemed impossible through human reasoning became reality through obedience and faith. When I released my fears and stepped forward with trust, God met every need — not only for my family, but for the mission He had entrusted to me. His blessings were never meant for comfort alone, but for service, stewardship, and the lifting of others. With my education advancing, ISAW growing, and my family stabilizing, a new chapter of responsibility and influence was about to unfold.

10

MAKING A DIFFERENCE IN AMERICA IS DIFFERENT

The differences I experienced in the United States compared to what I experienced in Ethiopia were remarkable. Countries like mine lose their gifted people, while America welcomes them — and that is part of what makes America great.

In Ethiopia, I was persecuted by a few selfish individuals for serving the poorest citizens. In the United States, however, I was recognized and encouraged for helping immigrant women and their families. I received awards and recognition from Metropolitan State University, the governor of Minnesota, the Department of Homeland Security, and KARE 11 for my commitment to bringing positive change to the immigrant community in the Twin Cities metro area. I was achieving success with my new women's nonprofit organization and in my academic life, while my children continued to thrive in every area of their lives — all because of the support and encouragement we received from wonderful Americans.

In early 1996, while I was still on a student visa at Metropolitan State University and working with my nonprofit organization through my internship, I wrote to First Lady Hillary Clinton. I shared my concerns about the need to review and revise the Illegal Immigration Reform and Immigrant Responsibility Act (IIRIRA) before it was signed into law. I was encouraged to do so by the eighth item in a summary of comments on the Beijing Platform for Action, which stated: "Before laws and policies are implemented, their effect on men and women must be studied." I received a kind reply from the First Lady informing me that my letter had been forwarded to the President's Interagency Council on Women. Then came an even bigger surprise: I received a response directly from the President of the United States.

You may laugh when you read this, but without even looking at the signature or the White House stationery, I sensed from the wording that the letter carried presidential authority. Because I never imagined receiving such a response, I took the letter to my instructor and asked, "Who is this man with this kind of authority?"

Pointing to the signature, she replied, "The President of the United States — good for you! Can't you read?"

What a cultural difference. Back in Ethiopia, a person like me could never expect to see the head of state passing by, let alone receive a direct response. Another difference I experienced was the compassion embedded within American leadership and civic systems. When President Clinton signed the Illegal Immigration Reform and Immigrant Responsibility Act, Section 245(i) provided a pathway for certain undocumented immigrants to adjust their status through family or employment petitions.

I did my best to spread the news to undocumented immigrants in the Twin Cities metro area. I organized a workshop to educate them about this one-time opportunity. Four volunteer immigration attorneys provided detailed explanations of the law and offered one-on-one consultations. Although we sent invitations and worked hard to reach immigrant communities, attendance was limited. Many Vietnamese immigrants came, but few others attended. Fear, isolation, and lack of information kept many away. ISAW petitioned successfully on behalf of one woman, and I witnessed how the law could transform lives for those who accessed it.

Many lost a golden opportunity because of fear and isolation, while those without a qualifying petitioner fell through the cracks. Yet Minnesotans continued advocating for immigrant rights. I joined an immigration task force formed by the Urban Coalition, where we participated in rallies and policy advocacy efforts to address the law's harsh impacts.

I continued to experience extraordinary generosity. During ISAW's first six months, Straitgate Church provided office space in its basement. Soon after, we secured grants from the McKnight Foundation and the Catholic Charites Christian Sharing Fund, both of which supported ISAW for three consecutive years. With this support, we leased a small office at the Cedar Riverside People's Center.

Soon after moving into our office, another opportunity arrived. A few days earlier, I had been one of three speakers at an International Women's Day event organized by Minnesota Advocates for Human Rights. The following Monday, a grant application packet from the Minnesota Center for Crime Victim Services arrived at our office. One of the attendees at the event had been Cindy Cook, the executive director of MCCVS. She sent the packet with a note that read: "I was moved by your speech."

I, too, was moved — by the compassion shown by the Americans God placed in my path. We had only two weeks before the deadline, but with God's help I completed the proposal. The application instructions advised contacting Aida Tosca for assistance. After reviewing my draft, she called and said, "This is the type of proposal we want to see on our table."

Two weeks later, I was invited to attend the grant review session. Ten nonprofit organizations were competing. When ISAW's proposal was reviewed, I heard the reviewers repeat the same words: "This is the type of proposal we want to see on our table."

Another reviewer remarked, "I grew up in this area, and even I couldn't describe the geographic distribution this clearly."

Our proposal was approved.

MCCVS continued funding ISAW for thirteen years.

With that first grant, ISAW established a culturally appropriate crime victim services model for vulnerable immigrant women and children, while building self-esteem and self-reliance. The program allowed isolated women and their children to attend summer camps and access life-changing services. The impact was profound. Many women described their experience with ISAW as "lifesaving" and "life-changing." All of this was possible because of the compassion of ordinary Americans and a constitutional system that values human dignity and human potential.

The story of every woman served by ISAW could fill a book of its own. Their experiences were vast and intertwined with so much pain and hardship that it would be impossible to describe them all here. Still, I would like to briefly share the stories of three women as examples

1. The Ugandan Woman

A Ugandan woman lost her husband in a car accident. Fifteen years after they had a child together, a Ugandan man who was a permanent resident of the United States visited her in Uganda. At the time, she was working as a bank manager. He persuaded her to return to Minnesota with their child.

About a year later, the man returned to Uganda and told her that their child was struggling emotionally because of being separated from her mother. He asked her to come to Minnesota on a visitor visa so she could spend time with her daughter. Trusting him and unaware of his true intentions, she agreed.

A few weeks after she arrived, he told her that he would help her obtain a student visa and enroll in a university so she could continue her education. He convinced her not to return to Uganda. Although their daughter later obtained a green card through her father's petition, this innocent mother never questioned why he had not done the same for her. She did not suspect that he had deceived her.

Soon, he began abusing her severely. Eventually, members of her church rented an apartment for her because she could no longer endure the abuse. She moved out, and her daughter joined her after revealing that her father had also sexually abused her without her mother's knowledge. They left with nothing because the man confiscated all of their belongings, including the daughter's green card.

That was when she called our office for help. Immediately after speaking with her, I contacted two Legal Aid organizations that partnered with us and asked whether they could assist her through the Violence

Against Women Act (VAWA). Both organizations declined because she could not provide proof of marriage and therefore did not meet the legal requirements.

VAWA allows immigrant women who came to the United States through marriage to U.S. citizens or permanent residents and became victims of domestic violence to seek legal protection. I could not accept giving up simply because lawyers had said "no". I took her case to court myself.

After explaining the VAWA requirements, I argued that she met every requirement except proof of marriage. I explained that many African couples marry through traditional ceremonies and do not always possess formal marriage certificates. Denying her protection simply because she could not produce such documentation was unjust.

God was gracious to me. She appeared before the judge with legal representation, and the man who had wronged her was ordered to bring their belongings to the court immediately. Though proof of marriage was still required later in the immigration process, God gave me wisdom, and eventually she was able to obtain her green card.

2. The Ethiopian Woman

An Ethiopian woman, whose name should remain confidential, came to Minneapolis with her three children on a visitor visa. With the help of her brother, she applied for asylum. Unfortunately, her application was denied, and she was ordered to leave the United States within one month.

That week I was away from Minnesota. When I returned home on Sunday, I saw her waiting for me anxiously and in great desperation. Three days earlier, I had dreamed that her asylum application had been denied. Immediately when I saw her, I said, "I saw in my dream that your asylum request had been denied," and I even described the appearance of the American officer who had interviewed her.

Surprised, she asked, "Why am I here then?" and began telling me everything that had happened. When I asked whether she had appealed, she explained that she had hired an immigration attorney for $2,000.

After an initial consultation fee of $200, the attorney told her that her case could not be won and declined to represent her.

The following Monday, she brought all of her asylum documents to my office as we had arranged. As I read through them, I realized that the attorney had been right—her application was absolutely impossible to win.

But God, who was helping her, gave me wisdom. I developed a new approach that would completely replace the previous application and create another opportunity for her case to be heard without requiring expensive legal fees. I contacted The Advocates for Human Rights, a nonprofit organization that provides free legal services to asylum seekers. When I explained my idea to the woman on the phone, she listened carefully and said, "Interesting." She immediately faxed me an application form and scheduled a prompt interview appointment.

The woman and I were excited. We completed the paperwork immediately and prepared for the interview. After giving her thorough guidance regarding the questions she would be asked, I accompanied her to the appointment and served as her interpreter. During the interview, I experienced a moment that deeply reminded me of God's protection. Thank God, she was saved from deportation along with her three children, and within three months her new asylum application was approved. I will never forget the words she later spoke to me with overwhelming joy: "Will whatever God does for you ever be too much for Him?"

3. A Nigerian Young Woman Jesufolakmi

The situation of the young Nigerian woman, Jesufolakmi, was even more heartbreaking.

While she was still in high school, a Nigerian man who was a United States citizen repeatedly traveled back and forth to Nigeria pursuing her. Immediately after she graduated from high school, he convinced her parents that he would provide her with a wonderful future in America. He promised that she would attend college while working at his own modeling company with a good salary. Instead, he smuggled her into the United States through Canada without a U.S. visa.

Soon after arriving, she discovered a shocking reality. Rather than taking her to a modeling agency, the man informed her that he had brought her to America to become his wife and that his two daughters would become her responsibility. Then came another painful discovery. He had deliberately brought her into the country illegally. He warned her, "You are an illegal immigrant. If you are caught, you will go to jail, so do not leave the house."

To make matters worse, after he disappeared for a week, she went to her neighbor's house hoping to find him. When she found him there having an affair with the neighbor, he beat her so severely that she was left devastated. Her story is long, but I will briefly explain how she came to me in what I believe was a miraculous way.

One day, determined not to remain trapped any longer, she went outside and happened to meet a Nigerian woman she had known back in Nigeria. After hearing her story, the woman took Jesufolakmi and her three-year-old daughter to Minnesota and began searching for organizations that could help her under VAWA. After many failed attempts and much frustration, Jesufolakmi eventually called me.

She said, "I had been desperately searching for help, and after almost giving up, a crisis center from New York gave me your number." As she explained her situation, I immediately contacted an organization that provided free legal services to women through our network. They instructed me to have her call and schedule an appointment with an attorney. I immediately called her back and gave her the information. However, despite repeatedly checking on her, her answer remained the same: "I will call."

Finally, I scheduled the appointment myself and told her when to go. After meeting with the attorney, she called and thanked me. She explained that she had not made the appointment herself because she had already been sent from one agency to another so many times that she had lost hope.

Thank God, her green card application was eventually approved. Three months later, I called to make sure she had received it. To my surprise, she explained that she was still trying to earn enough money to pay the

$1,000 immigration penalty related to her unlawful entry. As soon as I heard this, I gave her the money so she could complete the process and receive her green card. What she told me afterward touched me deeply:

"The first day I called you, you said, 'God loves you; do not be afraid.' I was so broken at that time that I had abandoned my faith. My faith returned immediately. My original name was Olufolakemi, a name rooted in ancestral beliefs. Now I have changed my name. Jesu means Jesus."

In addition to resettlement struggles, these women face language barriers, cultural isolation, social exclusion, and deep loneliness. Their needs were immense, and resources limited. I often worked day and night to help.

A Minnesota Women's Press journalist captured the reality in her opening line:

"Some help others by giving their money. Some give up their time. Agitu Wodajo has given up herself."

The experiences of the women ISAW served confirmed that God had answered the prayer I prayed when I first confirmed my calling — that He would reveal their needs and make me a solution.

One evening around 7:00 p.m., while I was in my office, I heard an inner prompting: "Jesufolakemi couldn't pay her rent."

I called her immediately.

"Do you have a problem paying your rent?" I asked.

"Yes," she replied.

"Did you receive an eviction notice?"

"Yes. I pawned my expensive jewelry to try to prevent it, but it didn't work."

I asked her to come to the office, and we were able to help cover her rent.

One day in 1999, Jesufolakemi came into our office and was silent for about five minutes. I paid no attention to her until she handed me a note she had written. When I read it, I was amazed at how well she expressed herself. Here is what the note said:

"It was one of the toughest and most sorrowful times in my life. God used a friend who got me ISAW's telephone number. Guess who answered the phone? It was my angel (Agitu). She instantly came to my rescue. She would call me from time to time with words of courage. Agitu has helped me in so many ways, even financially, just to put food on my table for me and my little girl. She just loves me. She loves people. She has helped me with my educational opportunity. I think of her as a mother because she treats me like a daughter. Sometimes I want to express my feelings about how much I appreciate all her effort and support, just to keep thanking her, but she would likely say, 'It is God who helps me.' She doesn't want to accept any credit for helping strangers (abused women) from different countries and cultures. Blessed is the day I spoke with Agitu. She has done wonderful things in my life, and my self-esteem is growing gradually. Thank God for our new Mother Teresa, Agitu Wodajo. Thank you, and may God bless you and your family. Amen. JV Jesuobadada"

Although I remained ISAW's sole grant writer, the organization continued securing funding that allowed us to expand services and move to a larger office near the University of Minnesota. This location enabled university students to serve as work-study interns. We established a computer training and resource bank to connect immigrant families with services matching their needs. Work-study students researched and compiled resource data, making services accessible to our community. Just two months after relocating, ISAW was granted special consultative status with the Economic and Social Council of the United Nations.

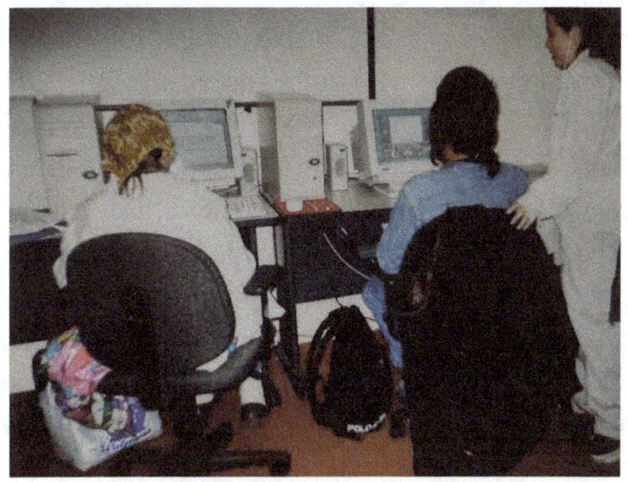

Computer Training

Resource Bank

At the time, African hair braiders in Minnesota were required to meet the Minnesota State Board of Cosmetologist Examiners' licensing requirements. This meant completing cosmetology training, fulfilling practical experience requirements, passing state board exams, and paying approximately fifteen thousand dollars in tuition for about ten months of schooling — excluding additional practical training.

For many African immigrant women, this requirement created an impossible barrier. Hair braiding is a traditional skill passed down through generations, and the licensing curriculum did not include instruction in natural hair braiding. It was unacceptable to me to see immigrant women prevented from supporting their families because of a policy that did not recognize their skills.

I picked up a cosmetology program brochure from St. Paul Community and Technical College and reviewed the course outline. When I confirmed that natural hair braiding was not included in the curriculum, I knew something had to change. I took the brochure and met with State Representative Lynda Wejesman, requesting her support in introducing legislation to exempt African hair braiders from cosmetology licensing requirements. She arranged a meeting at the State Capitol where I met with the executive director of the cosmetology association, a state senator, and a legislative assistant.

During that meeting, there was a brief but intense disagreement between me and the executive director, who insisted on enforcing the licensing policy. I expressed my position clearly: natural hair braiding is not fundamentally different from the daily hairstyling many women do at home without the need for a licensed salon. I further advocated for respecting African hair braiders' constitutional right to sustain the quality of life for themselves and their families by using the skills they have mastered.

A few months later, we received the Minnesota Commissioner of Commerce's decision that no lawsuit against hair braiders in Minnesota would be enforced. Then, on May 15, 2006, the Minnesota Board of Barber and Cosmetologist Examiners officially adopted a new rule exempting hair braiders from state licensing requirements. This change opened doors for many immigrant women to earn income with dignity and independence. I saw this victory as part of God's greater calling — not only to serve individuals in crisis, but to remove the barriers that kept them from living with dignity and self-reliance.

11

RAISING SUCCESSFUL CHILDREN AS A SINGLE MOM

I don't mean it literally when I call myself a *single mom*. I never felt that I was raising my children alone, because God—their heavenly Father was with me in every stage of their upbringing. Even while living with their father in Ethiopia, before we moved to the United States, God gave me the wisdom, strength, and resources to shoulder full responsibility for their physical, emotional, and spiritual growth.

As Proverbs 22:6 teaches, *"Train up a child in the way he should go, and when he is old he will not depart from it."*

Every evening we gathered for family worship and prayer. Each child had a turn leading from our family prayer book, which included topics and petitions written by every one of them. Their father never joined us, but I remained steadfast in ensuring they were raised with dignity and faith.

Matthew 6:33 says, *"But seek first the kingdom of God and His righteousness, and all these things shall be added to you."* President Theodore Roosevelt once remarked, *"To educate a man in mind but not in morals is to educate a menace to society."*

Parenting them with gate keeping, protection, prayer, and discipline, I raised my children to abide by biblical principles, think positively, maintain good character, and work diligently—and these values helped shape who they became in their adoptive country. I even made their school uniforms myself—using Western-style patterns I purchased from the former Elda Store—so they could take pride in their appearance and identity.

All of my children attended one of the best private Christian schools in Addis Ababa. Months before we moved to the United States, I enrolled my eldest son, Abdi, in keyboard music lessons and in one of the first computer training classes offered in the city. Behind closed doors, however, I carried burdens no child should ever bear witness to. I kept from them the immorality and abuse that darkened our home so they could grow up with pure hearts, unbroken spirits, and sound character. Let me share one example.

One evening, our maid came to me in tears and told me that my husband had been sexually assaulting her. She said she could not endure it any longer and felt she had no choice but to leave. My heart broke for her. I went to my husband and pleaded with him softly, asking him to leave her alone. Instead, he exploded in rage. He became violent and began beating both of us, screaming and cursing as he did. Then he ran to the maid's room and threw all of her school materials into our septic tank. She was only an eighth-grade student.

My children were in their bedrooms and had no idea what was happening. That night, the maid and I fled into the darkness, running for our lives. I walked nearly three miles to the home of the Secretary General of the Mekane Yesus Church. I spent the night there. Early the next morning, I asked him to drive me back home so that my children would not discover the terrible events that had taken place. My husband was a member of the Air Force, and he knew very well how to beat me. My body was bruised from my neck down to my ankle. I could not even go to work because of the pain.

Even then, my greatest concern was protecting my children from seeing the evil that had happened in our home. I chose silence for four reasons:

1. They might question God's justice and reject Christianity if they knew the truth and saw no justice served.
2. They might be emboldened to sin if wrongdoing appeared to go unpunished.

3. They should not grow up harboring hatred toward their father.
4. They might carry deep shame if they knew of the immorality within our home.

Planting Moral Roots in a New Land

When we arrived in Minneapolis, my five children were seventeen, fifteen, thirteen, eight, and seven. My plan was to sustain the moral foundation I had built for them in Ethiopia. The first year of our resettlement in South Minneapolis was very difficult. My children saw poverty they had never experienced—even in their poor native country. I had to pay my tuition while taking a minimum of twelve credits each semester to maintain my immigration status. At the same time, I had to be a vigilant gatekeeper, protecting my children from the dangers of unhealthy cultural influences.

By God's grace, they flourished in spirit and integrity, becoming living testimonies of His faithfulness. What I could not protect them from by my own strength, the Lord covered with His mercy, guarding their hearts and preserving their future. My strategy was simple but demanding: attend to details, correct them on the spot without judgment, keep them out of trouble, and defend them when they stumbled.

Soon after we moved into Riverside Plaza Apartments, my eldest son began spending time with the wrong crowd. He was seventeen and a senior in high school. The pattern continued after we moved to South Minneapolis five months later. He started coming home after midnight. I warned him that if it happened a third time, I would not open the door.

On the third night, he knocked just at midnight. Perhaps he thought he had made it in time—but I did not open.

Minutes later, two police officers knocked. I opened the door.

"Your son reported that you locked him out," one officer said.

"Yes, I did," I replied. "I have two reasons. First, I am a Christian raising my children with Christian principles."

The officer interrupted. "Me too."

"Praise God," I said. "Second, I come from a culture where children obey their parents. I warned my son. He chose to disobey." Then I asked, "Officer, what time does the law require minors to be home?"

"But there is democracy in this country," he replied.

"I understand democracy," I said. "It is the freedom to act without violating the rights of others. He chose to be locked out. If he prefers independence, he may find his own place. But please answer my question: what time must minors be home?"

"How many children do you have in this house?" he asked.

"Five."

"You did right," he said. "You may let him in if you wish. Close your door if you do not."

"I will let him in," I answered.

As they left, one officer added, "Send him back to his father if he won't stop."

When my son entered, he fell at my feet.

"Sorry, Mom. I didn't have a dime to go to Kathleen's house. The only thing free was a 911 call."

Poor child. He thought the police would scold me and let him in. He did not realize he could have endangered my immigration status and left his siblings without a parent. Two months later he turned eighteen and began college. I placed him with a small computer shop so he could build on the IBM training he had received in Addis Ababa and explore a career path. He bought a Honda Civic before I owned a car myself.

Though well-mannered and never given to drinking or smoking, he struggled with peer pressure. What troubled me most was that he stopped attending church and continued coming home late. One day Kathleen called to say she had received a citation for him. Because his car insurance was under her address, the notice went to her house. I contacted the detective handling the case and told him my son was a good young man and I did not want his future destroyed. The officer said "I will call you back in three days"

Three days passed. I called back.

"Your son is not guilty," he said.

Still, I hid his car at my sister's house during a harsh Minnesota winter. My sister was furious. My son, however, said, "Mom, you did the right thing."

Yet the late nights continued. I stayed awake with Scripture, counseling him each time he returned. One evening he said, "Mom, because we were raised glutted and glutted and glutted with the Word of God, we can't be like others however hard we try."

Still, I persisted in prayer.

One Thursday night I prayed intensely and waited. When he came home, he entered my room immediately.

"Mom, I know you are tired of my 'sorry.' Please trust me. Tonight is the last time. I will never be the same again. Let me go to church with you Sunday."

I did not tell him when I left for church. To my surprise, he went on his own. I saw him only when he responded to the altar call and rededicated his life to the Lord.

From that day forward, his life changed. He began serving in church, playing keyboard, and helping others with his technical skills.

Another struggle followed: he withdrew from college.

"My dad says I am worthless, leave me alone" he said.

"No one on earth is worthless, God never creates a life without purpose" I replied. "You must prove your father wrong instead of becoming proof for his words."

By God's grace, he returned to school, received Honeywell's Minority Scholarship and internship, and earned a degree in computer engineering. God blessed his mind and diligence, and he distinguished himself during his internship. Eventually, a position awaited him upon graduation, and he was hired by Honeywell Aerospace.

After the graduation ceremony, he embraced me with tears streaming down his face onto my shoulder and said, "Mom, you made me a man." In truth, it was his obedience, perseverance, and faith that shaped the man he became. He later earned a master's degree in software engineering.

Today, he serves as an aerospace engineer while remaining committed to serving his church.

My daughters also made me proud. Jalale and Helen received Presidential Academic Awards. Jalale earned a degree in architecture, building on her gift as a visual artist—a talent she has since passed on to her own multi-talented daughter.

Helen entered college with twenty post-secondary credits and earned a bachelor's degree in Management Information Systems, followed by master's degrees in Business Administration and Software Engineering.

My fourth child, Bethel, amazed me in many ways. She began receiving Presidential Academic Awards in sixth grade and continued through high school and university. She needed no help with schoolwork, except when she faced challenges adjusting to public high school. One day she asked permission to wear a head covering like Somali girls. I sensed serious issues that bothered her. Without asking her explanation, I enrolled her the next day at a private Christian school, Maranatha Christian Academy.

Bethel later earned multiple scholarships that also included a six-month exchange program at Bocconi University in Milan through the Carlson School of Management at the University of Minnesota. She won scholarships through essay contests and community service, teaching me what it truly means when we say America is a land of opportunity. Opportunity here is not a handout that breeds dependency. It is a "use it or lose it" chance — made possible because Americans are willing to teach, encourage, and help others rise.

Bethel later received $120,000 in merit scholarships for graduate study at Georgetown University and was hired by Johnson & Johnson immediately after graduation. She now serves as a Finance Director at one of the Fortune Five companies. Beyond her remarkable professional achievements, I praise God most for her humility, her reverence for Him, and her commitment to serving His purposes. When I congratulated her on her promotion, she gently redirected my praise:

"Thanks, Mom. Titles are meaningless. Work pays bills. What matters is whether I am a faithful servant to our Savior and whether I am raising human beings who are whole and well equipped to serve His Kingdom. You can congratulate me for those two achievements — not for titles in this world."

My youngest son, Menase, began working part-time at fourteen. By sixteen he purchased a Mazda and started driving. Responsible and caring, he too faced peer pressure. The ten-year age gap between him and his older brother contributed to this; my daughters had each other, but my sons had to seek friends elsewhere. One Saturday night, while giving a friend a ride, Menase began racing another friend's BMW, not realizing that a police officer was already pursuing the other car. When Menase exited the freeway, the officer followed him instead and arrested him on felony charges of fleeing a police officer. I was unable to secure his release until his court hearing on Tuesday. Determined to protect my son and ensure justice, I retained an attorney to represent Menase in court.

At the hearing, the officer testified truthfully. The director of the juvenile detention center also spoke on Menase's behalf, stating, "Menase presented himself very well before me. He is respectful and a well-disciplined young man. I recommend his immediate release."I could have blamed racism or reacted in anger, but instead I chose to trust due process and seek justice through the proper channels — and justice prevailed.

Menase later graduated from college and has remained a hardworking, dependable son. I call him "father" because he cares for me as though I were his child. He has helped maintain my home, supported me financially when needed, and even bought me a car—a gift I declined because I did not want to burden him. All my children lived at home until they were firmly established in life. Only Jalale moved closer to campus because of the intense demands of her architecture studies. After graduation, she returned home, and we enjoyed a beautiful season of life together.

I thank God that my children did not carry emotional wounds from their father's abuse. When Bethel and Menase once opened an abusive letter he had written to me, they responded with grace and maturity defending me with the truth. Through them, I learned they were not hurt at all. God, from whom all good gifts come, deserves the glory for the lives my children built and the citizens they became.

Looking back, I see that raising my children in a foreign land required more courage than crossing oceans. I stood as mother and father, guardian and guide, protector and provider. I corrected, defended, prayed, and persevered, trusting that God would complete what I could not. Though we walked through poverty, cultural shock, and hardship, the Lord shielded my children, preserved their character, and transformed struggle into strength. What the enemy intended to scatter, God gathered; what adversity threatened to break, God refined into resilience.

www.ingramcontent.com/pod-product-compliance
Lightning Source LLC
Chambersburg PA
CBHW050502160726

48003CB00001B/119